3036000

D0422974

E
185
.G453
1969
(1)

Gibson

Progress of a race

Date Due			
DEC 18 1974			

LIBRARY-ALLEGHENY CAMPUS
808 RIDGE AVENUE
PITTSBURGH, PA. 15212

PRINTED IN U.S.A.

THE AMERICAN NEGRO

HIS HISTORY AND LITERATURE

PROGRESS

OF

A RACE

THE COMMUNITY COLLEGE OF ALLEGHENY COUNTY

ALLEGHENY
CAMPUS
808 RIDGE AVENUE
PITTSBURGH, PA.
15212

LIBRARY

J. L. Nichols

William H. Crogman

Gibson, John William

ARNO PRESS and THE NEW YORK TIMES

NEW YORK 1969

Copyright © 1969 by Arno Press, Inc.
All rights reserved

*

Library of Congress Catalog Card No. 69–18552

*

Manufactured in the United States of America

General Editor
WILLIAM LOREN KATZ

E
185
.2453
1969
(1)

Progress of a Race

OUR HEROES OF DESTINY

Progress of a Race

=OR THE=

REMARKABLE ADVANCEMENT OF THE AMERICAN NEGRO

From the Bondage of Slavery, Ignorance, and Poverty to the Freedom of Citizenship, Intelligence, Affluence, Honor and Trust

REVISED AND ENLARGED BY

J. L. NICHOLS, A. B., AND WILLIAM H. CROGMAN, LL. D.

Author of "Talks for the Times"

With Special Articles by
Well Known Authorities

MRS. BOOKER T. WASHINGTON

CHARLES M. MELDEN, D. D.
President New Orleans University

M. W. DOGAN, D. D.
President Wiley University

ALBON L. HOLSEY
Editor "Tuskegee Student"

AND AN INTRODUCTION BY

ROBERT R. MOTON
Principal Tuskegee Institute

PUBLISHED BY

J. L. NICHOLS & COMPANY

NAPERVILLE, ILL.

Agents Wanted

Copyright 1920
By J. L. NICHOLS & COMPANY

*This book, including Illustrations, is protected by copyright.
Any infringement will be prosecuted to the
fullest extent of the law.*

DEDICATION

HOW many people know that there are Negroes who
are paying more than $100,000 a year income tax?
Or that a Negro is among the foremost American
critics of current verse? Or that a Colored man won the
first scholarship granted an American composer of music
by the French School of Musical Studies in Paris? Or that
Chicago's first settler was a Negro? Or that a regiment of
Colored soldiers in the late war won more decorations for
bravery than any other American unit?

America has failed to understand a loyal and dependable
group consisting of 12,000,000 of her own citizens.
Frederick Douglass, Paul Lawrence Dunbar and Coleridge-Taylor are names unknown to the millions of her
school children.

To them this book is dedicated, that they may read and
learn, and thus come to a wholesome understanding and
appreciation of what has been accomplished in spite of the
handicap.

ROBERT RUSSIA MOTON.
Successor to Booker T. Washington as Principal of Tuskegee
Institute.

(C) C. M. Battey.

INTRODUCTION

TO THE NEW EDITION

No race in such a limited period and under such trying circumstances has ever made more progress than has been made by the Negro in the United States of America. Instead of being discouraged over the conditions over which he had no control, the Negro has simply faced the situation, forged ahead, and written on the pages of history a record which has challenged the attention and respect of the entire civilized world.

It is significant that just at this time a great deal of attention is being given to the matter of not merely recording the stories of Negro progress, but also placing them before the public. I am certain that such printed records will serve to inspire the future generations of the Negro as well as to enlighten the children of other races as to the history of colored people, thereby giving them a larger and more sympathetic view of all human problems. It is for that reason that I believe that the revised edition of the "Progress of a Race," which the publishers are preparing, will fill a much needed want. Divided into three great major topics,—Education, Business and Religion, —this story of Negro progress should commend itself to the American reading public, and I bespeak for this volume a most cordial and favorable consideration.

ROBERT R. MOTON.

TUSKEGEE INSTITUTE,
ALABAMA.
March 30, 1920.

TABLE OF CONTENTS

LIST OF ILLUSTRATIONS

9

WE ARE RISING.

BY REV. GEORGE C. ROWE.

Among the sayings of our race,
  Suggestive and surprising,
That fill a most exalted place,
  Is, "Tell them we are rising!"

The question asked for right and truth,
  What to the North your greeting?
The answer from a Negro youth—
  "Tell them we are rising!"

Within Atlanta's classic halls,
  This youth, self-sacrificing,
Wrote high his name upon her walls,
  His motto: "We are rising!"

Out in the world he makes his mark,
  Danger and fear despising,
E'er soaring upward like the lark,
  My brethren: "We are rising!"

He meets the foe with voice and pen,
  With eloquence surprising!
Give us a chance, for we are men!
  Most surely we are rising!

Rising to take our place beside
  The noble, the aspiring;
With energy and conscious pride,
  To the best things, we're rising!

Within the class-room is his place,
  Greek, Latin, criticising,
To raise the youthful of his race,
  And show the world we're rising!

Go forth, my friend, upon your way,
  Each obstacle despising,
Prove by your efforts every day
  To all that we are arising!

In farming, trade and literature,
  A people enterprising!
Our churches, schools, and home life pure,
  Tell to the world we're rising!

NOTE.—About a score of years since, Gen. O. O. Howard, then connected with the Freedman's Bureau, on visiting one of the colored schools
in Georgia, asked the children: "What message shall I take from you to the
people of the North?" An intelligent boy answered promptly: "Tell them
we are rising!" The boy was Richard Wright, of Augusta, Ga , who has
since graduated from Atlanta University, ably filled the editorial chair,
and is now President of the State Normal School. of College, Georgia.

CHAPTER I.

Unity of the Race.—Attempts have been made in the past to prove that the Negro is not a human being. In this age of the world such a preposterous idea does not receive countenance. The remarkable progress of the Negro and the rapid disappearing of race malice and prejudice, have made this theory so absurd that to-day no one can be found to advocate it. It is, however, to be noted that as late as 1868 a minister of the South advocated this theory. Arguing from this standpoint he says, "Half an eye tells us the fate of the Negro on this continent is fixed, his doom is irrevocably sealed, he is out of his natural condition to which he aspires. If he is separated from *man* he sinks speedily to savage cannibalism. Men cannot refute the fixed decree of Omnipotence; nothing but the power of God can save the Negro from extinction. Four millions of blacks are doomed to extinction. The history of the Negro proves that he does not, never did possess, a self-directing, independent mind. The white man regards him as a natural, lawful slave, the Negro admits the fact and instinctively seeks the condition of slavery to man."

Of One Blood.—Why should we here refer to this theory so absurd and contradictory to all history? Not that we place any confidence in any of the arguments, nor that we will refute the arguments, they need no refutation; but that the young man of to-day, who is an American citizen, may know something of the tendency of the times when slavery existed.

13

To-day the universal belief is that God "Created of one blood all nations of man to dwell on the face of the earth." The unity of the race is demonstrated with emphasis in the possible and actual assimilation of all the races in the one man, and is distinctly shown in the personalities and careers of men like Benjamin Banneker, Frederick Douglass, and Alexander Dumas.

No Inferior Races.—God did not create an inferior race; there are races with inferior conditions, and these may be black or white, but, says Dr. Blyden, "There is no absolute or essential superiority on the one side, nor absolute or essential inferiority on the other. Man is a unity in the plan of salvation. No man is too inferior to be saved. In all the wondrous work of creation the making of man is God's crowning act, and whoever has His image has infallible credentials of his high origin and sonship. Man is our universal representative head and from him all peoples sprung. God never made a superior race nor an inferior one; and there is nothing in the heavens above, nor in the earth beneath, that can substantiate any such doctrine, "For God hath made of one blood all nations of men to dwell upon the face of the earth."

The Curse Theory.—Failing to establish the theory that the Negro is not a human being, we find an attempt on the part of those who would have held the Negro in perpetual slavery to show that he belongs to an inferior race. That against him an irrevocable curse has been pronounced. But the remarkable advancement of the race in all lines of activity has dispelled even the doubts of those who "hoped against hope" that this might be the case, and has scattered the mists of unbelief that rose above the horizon of a few of the Anglo-Saxon race.

Base of Arguments.—Such arguments are based upon passages of the scripture in which Noah cursed Canaan in these words: "Cursed be Canaan, a servant of servants shall he be unto his brethren. Blessed be the Lord God of Shem, and Canaan shall be his servant. God shall enlarge Japheth, and he shall dwell in the tents of Shem and Canaan shall be his servant." If this were a prophecy then the argument might have some weight, but it is considered a prophecy only by a very few writers, and these are those who would substantiate preconceived opinions thereby. The best evidence of a prophecy is its fulfillment. This statement was never fulfilled either in the case of Canaan, whose descendants have often conquered and been among the powerful nations of olden times, nor of Shem and Japheth, whose descendants were frequently enslaved. The Hebrews were in bondage in Egypt for centuries, they were the descendants of Shem; Egypt was peopled by the Children of Ham.

The Proper Interpretation.—We have neither inclination nor time to spend on extended argument against this theory so contradictory to all facts revealed by the light of true history and now no longer a question of debate, and yet a statement is necessary for the information of the youth who knows nothing of slavery, and the arguments and the attempts to hold in perpetual bondage a race destined to play an important part in the civilization and Christianization of the world. Noah was once a preacher of righteousness, but he afterward became drunk on the wine that he made. The exposure to which he was subjected by his drunken condition caused him in his irritable and self-defensive mood to utter these words, which cannot in any sense be prophetic. The best argument against this theory is the remarkable progress of the race and the moral and intellectual condition of the best of the race in these closing years of the nineteenth century.

Josephus says: "The children of Ham possessed the land from Syria to Amanus, and the mountains of Libanus, seizing upon all the maritime ports and keeping them as their own. Of the four sons of Ham, time has not at all hurt the name of Cush, for the Ethiopians over whom he reigned are even at this day, both by themselves and by all men in Asia, called Cushites."

Herodotus.—Herodotus states that Cambyses attempted to conquer Ethiopia but failed. He succeeded in conquering Egypt, but he found the Ethiopian equal to the Egyptian in refinement and intelligence and superior in military skill. Cambyses attempted, by means of spies and by means of various designs, to entrap and enslave the Ethiopian, but was forced to return to Egypt with but a remnant of his army.

The Case Stated.—Rev. Norman Wood puts it thus. "Whereas, Noah got drunk and cursed Canaan, an innocent party; and whereas, this curse was never fulfilled; therefore, all to whom these presents may come, greeting: Pagan, infidel, or pirate, are hereby empowered to kidnap and to enslave all the sable Africans who are descendants from Cush. We are here reminded of the statement of Liliuokalani, the recent dethroned queen of Hawaii, that the best blood of the English flowed in her veins, because her grandfather devoured Captain Cook."

The Color Theory.—Another argument in support of the curse of Noah is the color of the African. This argument also fails utterly when we take into account the climatic influence. Climate, and climate alone, is the sole cause. The predominant color of the inhabitants of the tropical regions of Asia and Africa is black, while the whites are found in the temperate and cold regions. We see and admit the change which a few years produce in the complexion of a Caucasian going from our northern latitude into the tropics. If a few years make such great changes why shall we hesitate to recognize the changes of centuries and ages?

Plants and Animals.—There is perhaps no better evidence of the influence of climate upon man than to witness its effects upon plants and animals. The flowers of the north are almost invariably white, while the arctic rabbit is spotless white, and the fox and polar bear are either white or pale yellow. The lack of color in the northern regions of animals which possess color in more temperate regions can be attributed only to change of climate. The common bear is differently colored in different regions. The dog loses its coat in Africa, and has a smooth skin.

Gradations of Color.—Let us survey the gradations of color on the continent of Africa itself. The inhabitants of the north are whitest; and, as we advance southwards towards the line, we find in those countries in which the sun's rays fall more perpendicularly, the complexion gradually assumes a darker shade. And the same men whose color has been rendered black by the powerful influence of the sun, if they remove to the north, gradually become white (I mean their posterity), and eventually lose their dark color.

Caucasians.—The Portuguese, who planted themselves on the coast of Africa a few centuries ago, have been succeeded by descendants blacker than many Africans. On the coast of Malabar there are two colonies of Jews, the old colony and the new, separated

by color and known as the "black Jews" and the
"white Jews."

The old colony are the black Jews, and have been
longer subjected to the influence of the climate. The
hair of the black Jews is curly, showing a resemblance
to the Negro. The white Jews are as dark as the
Gypsies, and each generation is growing darker.

Dr. Livingstone says: "I was struck with the
appearance of the people in Londa and the neighborhood; they seemed more slender in form and their
color a lighter olive than any we had hitherto met."

Lower down the Zambesi, the same writer says:
"Most of the men are muscular, and have large,
ploughman hands. Their color is the same admixture,
from very dark to light olive, that we saw in Londa."

Equator to Polar Circles.—Under the equator we
have the deep black of the Negro, then the copper or
olive of the Moors of northern Africa; then the Spaniards and Italian, swarthy compared with other Europeans; the French, still darker than the English, while
the fair and florid complexion of England and Germany
passes more northerly into the bleached Scandinavian
white.

From Inland to Coast.—As we go westward we observe the light color predominating over the dark; and
then, again, when we come within the influence of the
dampness from the sea air, we find the shade deepened
into the general blackness of the coast population."

If these opinions, given by the best authorities, mean
anything, and if we shall credit them as having any
value, then the color line can be drawn only where
there is deep-seated prejudice.

Black, a Mark of Reproach.—Prof. Johnson, in his
school history, justly says: "Black is no mark of re-

proach to people who do not worship white.   The West
Indians in the interior represent the devil as white.
The American Indians make fun of the 'pale face' and
so does the native African.   People in this country have
been educated to believe in white because all that is
good has been ascribed to the white race, both in pictures and words.   God, the angels and all the prophets
are pictured white, and the devil is represented as
black."

Ideals of Negro.—The ideals of the Negro are the
ideals of the white man.   The two races are both educated to one standard, that is, the white man's
standard.   While the white man would have the Negro
adopt his standard, at the same time there are those
who would repel him; somewhat like putting on steam
and throttling the valve.   True manhood knows no
color.   While the ideals are the same, the standards
the same, let all, black and white, aim to attain to a
virtuous manhood that would impress itself upon
mankind and make men more and more to see the
ideals shine out in the lives of all true leaders.

God Knows Best.—George Williams says: "It is
safe to say that when God dispersed the sons of Noah
he fixed the 'bounds of their habitation,' and that
from the earth and sky the various races have secured
their civilization.   He sent the different nations into
separate parts of the earth.   He gave to each its racial
peculiarities and adaptability for the climate into which
it went.   He gave color, language, and civilization;
and, when by wisdom we fail to interpret his
inscrutable ways, it is pleasant to know that 'he work-
eth all things after the counsel of his own mind.' "

Antiquity.—It is difficult to find a writer on ethnol-
ogy or Egyptology who doubts the antiquity of the

Negroes as a distinct people from the dawn of history down to the present time. They are known as distinctly as any of the other families of men. Negroes are represented in Egyptian paintings. They formed the strength of the army of the King of Egypt. They came against the King of Rehoboam as well as the armies of Sesostris and Xerxes.

John P. Jefferis, who is not friendly to the Negro, in his criticism nevertheless makes this statement: "Every rational mind must readily conclude that the African race has been in existence as a distinct people over four thousand two hundred years, and how long before that period is a matter of conjecture only there being no reliable data on which to predict a reliable opinion."

Further Evidence.—Further evidence in favor of the antiquity of the Negro is found in Japan and Eastern Asia. In these large, magnificent temples, hoary with age, are found idols that are exact representations of woolly-headed Negroes; other inhabitants of the country have straight hair. But why accumulate evidence, when monuments, temples and pyramids rise up to declare the antiquity of the Negro race?

The Word Negro.—The word Negro is a name given to a considerable branch of the human family possessing certain physical characteristics which distinguish it in a very marked degree from the other branches or varieties of mankind. "It is not wise," says George Williams, "for intelligent Negroes in America to seek to drop the word 'Negro.' It is a good, strong and healthy word, and ought to live. It should be covered with glory; let Negroes do it."

The Term Negro.—The term, Negro, is properly applied to the races inhabiting that part of Africa lying

Isaiah T. Montgomery. TWO VETERAN DELEGATES TO THE REPUBLICAN CONVENTION IN CHICAGO, JUNE, 1920. George W. Gale, former State Senator, Mississippi. The medal shows that Gale voted for General Ulysses S. Grant at Chicago in 1880. Montgomery, age 73, who worked for Jefferson Davis during the Civil War, and

between latitude 10 degrees north and 20 degrees
south and to their descendants in the old and new
world.   It does not include the Egyptians, Berbers,
Abyssinians, Hottentots, Nubians, etc., although in
some writings it comprises these and other dark-
skinned nations.   One characteristic, however, the
crisp hair, belongs only to the true Negro.

Africa for the Negroes.—Centuries of effort and
centuries of corresponding failure have fully demonstrated that the white man cannot colonize the largest
part of the great continent of Africa.   It seems that, in
the providence of God, this great and glorious continent is chiefly for the colored races, and especially for
the Negro.   Is it not possible that this great continent
with its millions of Negroes occupying the most fertile
portions, and in all more than one-half of the continent, is to be enlightened, civilized and Christianized
by the American Negro?

Deportation.—Let it not be understood that the preceding paragraph argues in favor of deportation of the
American Negro to Africa.   This is impossible, but
that the American Negro has a part in the elevation of
the black brother of the dark continent is as true as
that the Caucasian of America has a part in the Christianization of the white race in other parts of the
world.   The Negro is better adapted to the climate
and can endure the hardships of mission work in Africa
much better than the Caucasian.

Not Well Considered.—Booker T. Washington says:
"I recall that a few months ago, when, on the occasion
of six hundred deluded colored people sailing from
Savannah for Liberia, some of the newspapers and not
a few of the magazines gravely announced to an
expectant people that the race problem was in process

of solving itself. These newspapers and magazine writers did not take into consideration the important fact that perhaps before breakfast that same morning six hundred colored babies were born. I have a friend down in Georgia whose unfailing solution of the race problem is, that the Negro should be cooped up in some place, surrounded by a high fence, and kept separate from the whites. That would not even reach the dignity of touching the question, since it would be utterly impossible to keep the blacks inside the fence to say nothing of the impossible task of keeping the whites outside of it. If the Negroes were fenced in Africa the white men would break in at the first cry that gold existed in the inhabited territory. Besides, the Negro has never yet been able to exile himself to any place the white man would not follow him and break in.''

Separation would Not Relieve.—''Talks for the Times'' says: ''If such a separation were even possible, are we simple enough to believe that that would relieve us of the presence of the white man? He who is scouring the seas, dredging the oceans, tunneling the mountains, boring his way into the frozen regions of the North, parceling out the continent of Africa, and giving civilization and laws to its tribes—it is not likely, I say, that this restless, energetic white brother will respect the boundary line of a state or territory at home; he has not done so in reference to the Indian; he would never do so in reference to us. Were it possible for us to go off to-morrow to some territory by ourselves, within a week the Connecticut Yankee would be there peddling his wooden nutmegs. The patent medicine man would be there selling his nostrums. The Georgia Cracker and the Kentucky horse-trader would be there with their horses and mules. The Southern white man would especially be there, for he has been so accustomed to us from his childhood that he does not feel at home without us, although sometimes, in the heat of political excitement, he wishes we were in Africa or a warmer place.''

Not Possible.—Judge Gunby says: "The favorite remedy for the race problem with some has come to be the deportation of the Negroes. I am prepared to say with the utmost confidence that this remedy does not meet with general approval, although it is fair to concede that it has many able advocates. The Negroes do not desire to leave and the great majority of the whites do not want them to go. The enforced removal of the Negroes would be unnatural and unjust; cruel, bitter cruel, would be the task of tearing Negroes from their genial Southern homes, their Southern friends, their churches, their graveyards, and the haunts they love so well. Sadder than the melancholy processions that moved to the shore from Goldsmith's 'Deserted Village,' sadder than the doomed band of Acadian farmers that looked for the last time on their burning homes in Grand Pré, would be the final movement of the Negroes from the South. It would be worse than slavery; for the Negroes in a colony of their own would degenerate and speedily lose the civilization they have derived from contact with the whites. Such a crime would never be forgiven. It would raise a protest from whites and blacks alike and from an indignant world. The very stones would rise up and cry against it. Deportation is not conceivable; because, although a few might be transported to Africa or scattered elsewhere, yet reproduction will increase their number in spite of such trifling methods, and our only way to get rid of their presence in the country is to kill them—which would be difficult, for many of them already have guns.''

Points of Superiority.—A certain writer says that the Negro has less nervous sensibility than the white, and is not subject to nervous afflictions. He is comparatively insensible to pain, bearing severe surgical operations well; he seldom has a fetid breath, but transpires much excrementious matter by means of glands of the skin, whose odorous secretion is well known. His skin is soft, and his silky hair, though called wool, does not present the characteristics of wool, and differs but little from that of other races except in color and in its curly and twisted form. He flourishes under the fiercest heat and unhealthy dampness of the tropics where the white man soon dies.

Physical Characteristics.—The physical characteristics of the black, or Negro, race are: A large and strong skeleton, long and thick skull, projecting jaws, skin from dark brown to black, woolly hair, thick lips, flat nose and wide nostrils. The typical color of the race is not coal black but the dark brown of a horse-chestnut. Observation shows that the darkest specimens are found on the borders where Negroes have been in contact with lighter races, while in the population of the Congo basin, which has been almost completely free from mixture, the dark-brown type prevails. It should, however, be understood, that there is as great a difference among Negroes as among Caucasians.

Distinguishing Traits.—The Africans, as a race, are passionately fond of music and have many ingeniously contrived musical instruments. While some of their inventions may have been borrowed from other people,

it is a well established fact that they are the inventors
of an ingenious musical instrument.   They have a keen
sense of the ridiculous and are of a cheerful disposition.   They are naturally kind hearted and hospitable
to strangers and are generally ready to receive instruction and to profit by it.   They are quick to perceive
the beauty of goodness and hence they generally
appreciate the services of missionaries in their behalf,
and, but for the curse of intoxicating drinks brought
upon them by unscrupulous white traders, the dark
continent would shine more brightly with the light of
Him who is the light of the world.

Fidelity of the Negro.—During the Civil war the
fidelity of the negro was tested to a most remarkable
degree; and he stood the test.   Nearly all able-bodied
men of the South were in the Confederate army.   Only
helpless women and children, and old or disabled men
were left with the slaves to care for the plantation
houses.   While the white-faced "Copperhead" of the
North was aiding the South, the black-faced slave was
caring for the helpless ones in Southern houses.
Strange as it may seem, these same colored men knew
that victory for the Union meant freedom for themselves.   General Sherman, in describing his first day's
experience on his famous "March to the Sea," says:
"The negroes were simply frantic with joy.   Whenever they heard my name, they clustered about my
horse, shouting and praying in their peculiar style,
which had a natural eloquence that would move a
stone.   I have witnessed hundreds, if not thousands,
of such scenes.   *   *   *

"We made our bivouac, and I walked up to a plantation house close by, where were assembled many
negroes, among them an old, gray-haired man, of as

fine a head as I ever saw. I asked him if he understood about the war and its progress. He said he did; that he had been looking for the 'angel of the Lord' ever since he was knee-high, and, though we profess to be fighting for the Union, he supposed that slavery was the cause, and that our success was to be his freedom. I asked him if all the negro slaves comprehended this fact, and he said they surely did."

Every Union soldier escaping from Confederate prison-pen, knew that it was safe to make himself known to a colored man. No Union soldier **ever** asked in vain for help from his **dusky** brother.

Drink Traffic.—The drink traffic carried on by civilized nations in Africa is the curse of millions. The same ship that carries missionaries to its shores carries thousands of gallons of rum that does more to degrade the helpless and ignorant Negro than many missionaries through a lifetime can succeed in winning to a better life. Let it be known that the Christian (?) nations, Great Britain and the United States, are leaders in this degrading and soul destroying business. This can be permitted only where dollars and the greed of gain surpass in estimation the worth of true manhood and of immortal souls.

Ingenuity.—The African Negroes display considerable ingenuity in the manufacture of weapons, in the working of iron, in the weaving of mats, cloth and baskets from dyed grasses, in the dressing of the skins of animals, in the structure of their huts and household utensils and in the various implements and objects of use in a barbarous state of society.

In Other Continents.—In addition to Africa, Negroes are found in the United States, Brazil, West Indies, Peru, Arabia and the Cape Verd Islands. They are

rare in Europe and the islands of the Pacific. Africa
is, however, the native home of the Negro. Whenever
he is found outside of this great continent it is because
he has been carried away and subjected to slavery.

Unknown to Hebrews.—Negroes were almost unknown to Hebrews. They were unknown to the
Greeks until the seventh century B. C. About twenty-
three hundred years B. C. the Egyptians became
acquainted with the Negroes, who helped them on
their monuments as early as 1,600 years B. C.

Liberia.—Liberia is a Negro republic of western
Africa, on the upper coast of Upper Guinea. It was
founded by the American Colonization Company. The
first expedition of eighty-six emigrants was sent out in
February, 1820. It was organized as a home for the
Negro of the United States. The suffering that slavery
brought upon the Negro aroused his friends, and, following the plan of Wilberforce and other Englishmen,
Liberia was founded as a refuge for the colored men
who would avail themselves of its blessings.

The constitution of Liberia, like that of the United
States, establishes an entire separation of the church
from the state, but all citizens of the republic must
belong to the Negro race. The constitution has recently
been changed and this point has been modified. Its
present constitution was adopted in 1847 and is similar
to that of the Constitution of the United States. The
article on slavery reads thus: "There shall be no slavery within the republic, nor shall any citizen of this
republic, or any person residing therein, deal in slaves
either within or without the republic."

The first years witnessed the struggle of a noble band
of colored people who were seeking a new home on the
edge of a continent given over to idolatry. Immigra-

tion went forward slowly, but the republic continued establishing and extending itself until it now numbers more than two million inhabitants. Already in 1853 Bishop Scott, of the M. E. Church, stated that the government of Liberia was extremely well administered. In his visit of several months he saw no intoxicated colonists and did not hear a profane word, the Sabbath was kept in a singularly strict manner and the church crowded with worshipers.

Agriculture is carried on with increasing success. Sugar was formerly the principal article of produce and of manufacture, but through the efforts of Mr. Morris, coffee has become the principal article. Rice, arrowroot and cocoa are also cultivated; trade is rapidly extending. Although the circumstances that led to the founding of this republic passed away when the shackles were torn from the Negroes of the South, yet it had done a vast amount of good before the days of the great rebellion, and to-day stands as a beacon light penetrating the darkness and gloom of Africa. May we not hope that through the ages to come the light of this Christian republic will reach the dark, trackless regions of African Paganism and bring millions to the brightness of its shining?

DR. JAMES G. CARTER, UNITED STATES CONSUL TO MADAGASCAR.
(C) C. M. Battey.

EX-UNITED STATES SENATOR FROM MISSISSIPPI, HON. HIRAM
R. REVELS.
Born a slave, March, 1841, in Virginia. Died in Washington,
D. C., March 17, 1898.

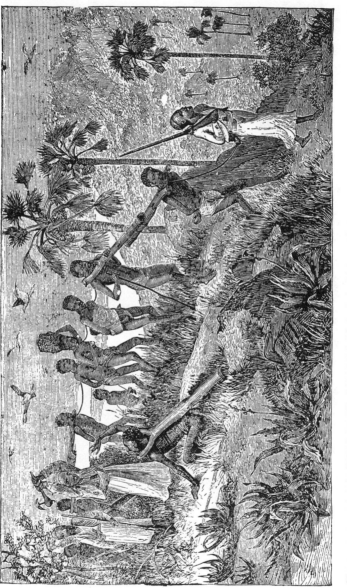

SLAVE TRADERS MARCHING THEIR CAPTIVES TO THE COAST, BUTCHERING DISABLED ONES ALONG THE WAY.

CHAPTER II.

Knowledge Worth Knowing.—Dr. Hamilton says: "The popular notions which have prevailed concerning African slavery have shaped imaginations and controlled opinions concerning the origin and destiny of the African race. Men have asserted boldly and arrogantly that the African people were designed in the very first cosmogony to be hewers of wood and drawers of water. Slavery was their natural relation. As the slaves in America within the recollection of the present generation have been Negroes, most persons have thought that all slaves have been Negroes. As Negroes have come from Africa, it has been commonly believed that all Africans were Negroes. As the sons of Ham in the dispersion went into Africa to live, it has been supposed that all Negroes were the sons of Ham And as Ham is said in the book of Genesis to have looked on the nakedness of his drunken father and so incurred his anger that he visited the sin of the father on the son of Ham, and in his anger cried out, 'Cursed be Canaan; a servant of servants shall be unto his brethren,' it has been claimed scriptural warrant is found for the enslavement of all Negroes. Of such knowledge and such argument it is pertinent to affirm, in the language of Mr. Josh Billings, 'that it would be better not to know so many things than to know so many things that are not so.' "

In Africa.—From time immemorial slavery has existed in Africa. The oldest records of the human race, the inscriptions of the Nile valley, shew us that

Negro slaves from the Soudan were then, as to-day, one of the principal articles of Egyptian trade.

Neither the institution of slavery nor the slave trade were introduced into Africa or forced upon the natives by Arabic, Moslems, or European Christians. At all times, so far as human knowledge goes, slavery has been a constituent element in the social order of Negro Africa. It is said of two or three African Negro tribes that they object to selling their own tribesmen, and oppose slave dealing in a general way. But these exceptions only confirm the rule that slavery is the universal practice of native Africa. There the trade in human beings is considered just as honest as trade in any other merchandise.

All those who want to work for the extinction of slavery in Africa should know from the start, that for one Arab or European slave-holder, slave-raider, or slave-dealer, there are hundreds of African slave-holders, slave-dealers and slave-raiders. Therefore, in their effort to conquer that monster they will have to face thousands of interested native opponents. This will be made clearer by a consideration of—

Sources of Slavery.—Chief among these is (1) the right of parents to sell their children. Every child born is the property of its maternal uncle; in a few tribes of its father. The uncle or the father has the right to dispose of his property as he pleases. He may even kill this human property and no one can prosecute him, claim damages, or demand his punishment. If he sells his children, separating child from mother, nobody seems to think he is doing wrong. The victim itself is expected not to protest against it more than a young girl of our land would protest against being sent to a boarding school for the first time.

(2.) **The Right of a Free Adult to Sell Himself.**—Runaway slaves, or liberated slaves, rather than be kidnaped, prefer to sell themselves to masters of their own choice. In times of famine hundreds are compelled to change their liberty for the food that will keep body and soul together. In war, cowards would rather live as slaves than die as freemen.

(3.) **Insolvent Debtors.**—Those who have lost all resources of material, animal and human property, sometimes give themselves for debt.

(4.) **Sale of Criminals by Legal Action.**—In Africa there are no prisons, hence punishment is always paid by death or the payment of a fine. If the fine cannot be paid the individual is sold to pay for it.

AN EX-SLAVE.

(5.) **Kidnaping.**—This is much more frequent than is generally supposed. The kidnaped generally resent the injustice committed, and frequently, with tears in their eyes, entertain a secret, though forlorn, hope of regaining their liberty and returning to their homes.

(6.) **Capture in War.**—Captives are often committed to slavery, many wars are often even made that captives may be taken and carried into slavery.

Siaves of Slaves.—It is not an unusual thing for slaves to own slaves, and in old Calabor plantation, slave-holding by slaves is so common that you often hear of slaves belonging to slaves of slaves. Any slave may by industry and thrift redeem himself, take his seat among the tribal headman, and aspire to the kingship.

Early History of Slavery.—The history of Negro slavery carried on by Europeans, beginning in Portugal over a period of 400 years, and involving the exportation by violence from their African homes of forty million of men, women and children, is one of exceeding and unimaginable bitterness. It is too late to criminate those who were responsible for beginning the slave trade and for perpetuating the system of bondage that grew out of it. Many of them were conscientious, Christian men, who worked without a thought of the wrong they were doing. Some of them really believed they were benefiting the Negro by buying him out of a condition of barbarism into the enlightening and purifying influences of Christianity.

AN EX-SLAVE.

Livingstone's Tomb.—On Livingstone's tomb-slab

ın Westminster Abbey are engraved these, among the
ıast words which he wrote: "All I can add, in my
solitude is: May Heaven's rich blessing come down on
everyone, Americans, English and Turk, who will
help to heal this open sore of the world, the slave
trade."

For What Purpose.—Slaves are hunted by Moslems,
Arabs, half-breeds, or Mohammedan Negroes, for the
three following purposes: 1, To supply labor for their
fields and plantations in the Soudan, in Zanzibar and
the adjoining coast belt; 2, to supply Negresses for the
harems of Turkey, especially Arabia, Egypt, Tripoli,
and Morocco; 3, to obtain carriers for the trading cara-
vans taking European goods to the interior and bringing down in exchange the tusks of ivory and the balls
of rubber so much coveted by Europeans and Americans.

European Plantation Slavery.—Under the pretense
of redeeming slaves from patriarchal native slavery
these poor creatures are taken into European plantation slavery, which means that the slave has no more
free time, no accumulation of property, no hope of
redeeming one's self by thrift, no home life, no possibility of flight, but unremitting toil from morning until
night in the broiling sun, under the lash of the driver,
without pay, and often with insufficient food. His only
prospect is that he is being worked slowly to death.

In Asia.—Slavery existed in Persia, China and
India. Parents sold their children to be slaves. There
was slavery among the Hebrews. All Africans are
not Negroes, many of them are entirely distinct from
the Negro—the idea that a slave is always black is
erroneous. It is not Noah, nor Ham, nor Canaan, nor
Africa, but sin and slavery that has cursed the Negro.

Portugal inaugurated the slave trade.   Antonio
Gonsalve brought home some gold dust and ten slaves
in 1443.   These were probably the first slaves taken
from western Africa by Europeans.   They were presented to Pope Martin V., and he conferred on Portugal the right of possession of all countries discovered

between Cape Bo-
jado and the Indies.
Portugal also had the
first of many chart-
ered companies to
trade in African gold
and slaves.

Columbus b e g a n
his intercourse with
the natives of Africa
by kidnapping and
he gave the word for
the opening of the
slave trade.

**S l a v e r y in the
New World.** — Afri-
can slavery was in-
troduced into the
New World by the

AN EX-SLAVE.

Spaniards.   Their cruelty to the inoffensive Indians in
the islands of the West Indies had greatly reduced their
numbers.   The poor Indian had been reduced to slavery,
and in order to prevent extermination the Spaniards resorted to importing slaves from Africa.   The first cargo
of Negro slaves was landed at San Domingo on the Island of Hayti in the year 1565.   These were at once put
to cultivating the plantations, and it was soon found
that, as Rev. Wood says, "These hearty sons of Africa

not only survived the oppressive cruelty of their heart-less taskmasters, but in time they rebelled against them, and under their invincible 'Black Prince,' Toussaint, killed them in battle and drove them from the island.''

First Slaves, First Liberty.—Bancroft aptly says: "Hayti, the first spot in America that received African slaves, was the first spot to set the example of African liberty.''

Slavery in the United States.—Slaves were brought by the Spaniards to Florida soon after the founding of St. Augustine, in 1565, but the first slaves brought to the colonies were landed at Jamestown, Va., in 1619, by a Dutch trading vessel. Twenty Negroes were exchanged for food and supplies. These had no personal rights, were doomed to service and ignorance by law, and could not leave the plantation to which they belonged without a written pass from their master. They received no religious instruction, and were sometimes given to white ministers as pay for their services. It was, however, nearly a half century from this time before the system of Negro slavery became well established in the English colonies.

Slavery Contended for.—The slave trade was the great industry contended for and carried on. In 1748 there were 97,000 slaves carried to America by all nations, and up to that time the total number was probably a million. During the eighteenth century six millions were carried to America, besides the horrible traffic which was kept up to the coasts of the Mediterranean, to Egypt and Asia, which has been carried on from time immemorial. It is estimated that the profits of the slave trade in the seventeenth and eighteenth centuries from the Dark Continent were equal to that on gold and all other products.

The Slave Trade.—We cannot in a few paragraphs, relate all the horrors and suffering entailed on the African race by means of the slave trade. While it is true that the revenue of the kings of the country sometimes depended on the sale of slaves, yet it remains as a blot on Christian England and America's record that they were the means of carrying out this cruel work. Some Americans, at least, went one step further, and, not content with selling slaves, sold their own sons and daughters.

The Slave Dealer.—Many chapters might be written upon the cruelties and inhuman treatment of the slave dealers, but as all who have engaged in this nefarious business have rendered their accounts to God, who is just, and have been justly dealt with, we will pen but a few items to show what the race has endured.

Kidnapping.—Probably the largest number of slaves were obtained by a system of kidnapping. In this case a village was often surrounded in the night and torches applied to the combustible huts; the able-bodied men and women were seized, bound, while children, the aged and infirm were cruelly murdered in the light of their burning homes. In journeying to the seashore, over rugged mountain sides and through fields of cacti, whose sharp thorns would lacerate and tear their flesh, they endured more than can be expressed. On reaching the coast the best of them were selected and placed on board ships, while those who had not endured the march, or were maimed were often murdered in cold blood.

It is said that King Loango, "rather than incur the expense of feeding slaves for whom he found no mar

ket, sent them to a side of a hill and cruelly butchered
them there.

Middle Passage.—The slave ships were frequently
crowded to such an extent that men were barely allowed
room enough to lie down.

Lord Palmerston says: "A Negro has not as much

CAPTURING SLAVES.

room in a sea ship as a corpse in a coffin." Bancroft
says: "The horrors of the middle passage correspond
to the infamy of the trade." Small vessels, of little
more than two hundred tons burden, were prepared
for the traffic, for these could most easily penetrate the
bays and rivers of the coast; and quickly obtaining

lading, could soonest hurry away from the deadly air
of Western Africa.   In such a bark, five hundred
Negroes and more were stored, exciting wonder that
men could have lived, within the tropics, cribbed in so
few inches of room.   The inequality in force between
the crew and the cargo, led to the use of manacles; the
hands of stronger men were made fast together, and
the right leg of one was chained to the left of another.
The avarice of the trader was a partial guarantee of
the security of life, as far as it depended upon him;
the Negroes, as they came from the higher level to the
seaside, poorly fed on the sad pilgrimage, sleeping at
night on the damp earth, without covering, and often
reaching the coast at unfavorable seasons, imbibed the
seeds of disease, which confinement on board ship
quickened into feverish activity.   There have been
examples where one-half of them—it has been said,
even two-thirds of them—perished on the passage.''

President Lincoln, who was always easily moved by
appeals for mercy, when appealed to by a slave trader,
promptly and sternly refused, although the appeal was
very pathetic, and the man had served a long time in
prison.   The President said: ''I could forgive the
foulest murder for such an appeal, but the man who
could go to Africa and rob her of her children and sell
them into endless bondage, with no other motive than
that of getting dollars and cents, is so much worse
than the most depraved murderer that he can never
receive a pardon at my hands.   No! he may rot in jail
before he shall have liberty by any act of mine.''

Profit.—Dr. Roy says: ''Before the annual meeting
of the American Missionary Association, in 1859, Rev.
Dr. George B. Cheever, from Harper's Encyclopedia
of Commerce, made the following statements as to the

slave trade: For it every year twelve vessels were fitted out by three cities each, Boston and Baltimore being of the number, and from other places enough to make forty slave ships, owned mostly by northern men. Each made two trips a year, at a total cost of three million dollars. The receipts being twenty million dollars, left for profit seventeen million dollars. One voyage of the fleet would bring in twenty-four thousand slaves, of whom four thousand were lost by death. The two trips a year would make the total importation forty thousand. These were mainly taken to Cuba, but fifteen thousand were for the United States the preceding year. A slave ship was landed after the war broke out, in a distant part of the South, and there the slaves were held till after the war. It has been estimated by Hon. John M. Langston and Col. Keating, of the Memphis Appeal, that up to 1825, forty million slaves had been imported to the West Indies and to the American continent.

Slavery a Curse.—Some writers will insist that American slavery has been a blessing to the race. Slavery is dead, and there is no one that would revive it. Ancient slavery may have been a step forward in evolution, because it ended in emancipation, and ultimately in the fusion of the races. But American slavery was a long step backward.

It was carried on by a desire of Europeans in a languid climate to have the work done for them instead of doing it themselves.

Fusion in the case of Negro slavery was fatally precluded by color; there could be no intermingling except that which arose from the abuse of the Negro woman by her white master. While household slavery may frequently have been mild, the plantation slave was overworked and tortured, and, with impunity, sometimes murdered. If certain writers are correct in attempting to show that the slave was contented in his bonds, why those fetters, those cruel slave laws, those bloodhounds? If he was fully content to live in slavery, why the laws that forbade the holding of meetings, the restraint from moving about freely, the liability to arrest when found alone, and the subjection to flogging when found away from the plantation Think of the revolting sights when, at public auction, husband and wife, parent and child, were sold apart, a sight of human cattle on the way to the auction and the advertisements of human flesh, especially of girls nearly white. Negro quarters on the plantation were hovels, his clothes rags, his food coarse, his life foul; it has been asserted that his life was happier than his African home, but it remains to be proven that this is the case.

Slavery Cannot Be Justified.—"Slavery cannot be justified," says Gov. Atkinson, "but may not God have intended that you, who are the descendants of those whom slavery has brought into the country, should pray and work for the redemption of your fatherland?"

Slavery Degrading.—Judge Stroud, in his "Sketch of the Laws Relating to Slavery," declares: "This maxim of civil law, the genuine and degrading principle of slavery, inasmuch as it places the slave on a level with brute animals, prevails universally in the slave-holding states." "It is plain that the dominion of the master is as unlimited as that which is tolerated by the laws of any civilized country in relation to brute animals to quadrupeds, to use the words of the civil law." To the unprincipled observer, at thirty-five years' distance, the whole system, as a system, was "the sum of all villianies," one universal harem, that, at the emancipation of the slave, had swept to the vortex of tyranny, degradation, fornication and diabolism of the most vicous character.

"In the case of Harris vs. Clarissa and others, in the March term, 1834, the chief justice, in delivering his opinion to the court, said: 'In Maryland, the issue (i. e., of female slaves) is considered not an accessory, but as a part of the use, like that of other female animals. Suppose a brood mare be hired for five years, the foals belong to him who has a part use of the dam. The slave in Maryland in this respect is placed on no higher or different ground.' "

The Slave Trade in the United States.—In 1774, the Articles of the Continental Association agreed that no more slaves should be imported and that the African slave trade should be wholly discontinued. These agreements were signed by the representatives of the colonies, but it was left to the next generation to carry out the agreement fully.

Abolishing African Slave Trade.—In his message to Congress at the commencement of the session in 1806, President Jefferson asked of that body the wisdom of abolishing African slave trade. The message was referred to a select committee, which reported a bill to prohibit the importation of slaves into the United States. This bill, of course, was fought by the Southern representatives. A long and fiery debate ensued and the act was finally passed, after several amendments, imposing a fine on persons engaged in the slave trade were added.

A Baltimore journal of this period says: "Dealing in slaves has become a large business. Establishments have been made in several places in Maryland and Virginia at which they are sold like cattle. These

places of deposit are strongly bolted and are supplied
with iron thumb- screws and gags ornamented with
cows' skins, ofttimes bloody.''

A Curious Advertisement in a religious paper of
Richmond, in March, 1850, is found the following:
''Who wants thirty-five thousand dollars in property.
I am desirous to spend the balance of my life as a
minister, if the Lord permits, and therefore offer for sale
my farm, the Vineyard, adjoining to Williams-
burg * * * and also about 40 servants, mostly young
and likely, and rapidly increasing in number and
value.''

Effect on Slave Owners.—While the slave owner
may have been hospitable, courteous, grave, the character of a true gentleman cannot be found where
reigns domestic despotism, amidst whips, manacles
and bloodhounds. The minds of young men were
tainted by familiarity with slaves. With slavery
always goes lust. If, as the advocates of slavery contended, the Negro was not a man, what were all these
half-breeds to be called. The tendency of slavery in
that which is not elevating in man. is clearly seen in
the inferiority of Southern to Northern life. Culture,
invention, literature, scientific research, were not found
South as long as slavery existed. It is only since slavery has been abolished that the South is beginning to
rise in all these lines.

Not Content in Slavery.—The argument against the
Negro is that he has never rebelled or resisted slavery,
that his docility and contentment in slavery suggested
that this was this normal condition. But we need
understand the true condition of the Negro, his helplessness and lack of leadership, to see the falsity of
such arguments. Negro insurrections, wherever the

opportunity presented itself, were not wanting in the
south land. We need but refer to what is called the
Nat Turner insurrection to show that the Negro was
struggling for freedom, and was not as docile as the
white slaver would make him.

The influence of this bloody insurrection in which
the lives of so many whites were taken spread throughout Virginia and the South. For years afterwards they
lived in a state of dread for fear another Nat Turner
might arise.

Serious Apprehensions.—"Talks from the Times"
says: "During the days of slavery there were continuous and serious apprehensions on the part of masters. The whole South was under patrol every night,
and the Negro, though regarded then, as many seem to
regard him now, as a harmless, spiritless being, a
'scrub race,' a 'race of timid rabbits,' was an object
of suspicion and distrust, and not infrequently was
consternation thrown into whole states by apprehensions of servile uprisings."

Uncle Tom's Cabin.—Dr. Edwards says: "The key
to 'Uncle Tom's Cabin' is one of the most abhorrent
and appalling commentaries ever written on African
slavery. It has made the cheek of many a slave-holder
tingle. But the legislation at that time in Virginia
was deemed a life and death question Nothing short
of it, for the time being, could allay the painful and
distressing excitement that prevailed everywhere
throughout the country. It almost makes one's blood
run cold, even at this remote period of time, to recall
the trepidation and alarm that pervaded the whole
community. The stoutest hearts were made to quail.

Negro Insurrection.—Rumors of Negro insurrection filled the air. Sleep ceased to be refreshing,

haunted as it was by hideous dreams of murder, blood
and arson. Mothers and maidens, and even little
children, for months, not to say years, following the
'Nat Turner Insurrection.' looked pale and ghastly as
the shadows of evening gathered around them, from
the horrifying apprehension that with bludgeon they
might be brained, or with torch might be burned to a
crisp before morning. I speak from experience. Nor
would I go through the agony of those years again for
all the gold that ever passed hands in the Negro traffic
from Colonial times till President Lincoln emancipated
them with a stroke of his pen. Pharaoh and his people, under the visit of the destroying angel, when the
first-born was convulsively quivering in the death
struggle in every household, did not more earnestly
desire the quick departure of the Hebrews out of the
land of Egypt than did the great majority of the slave
holders in the Carolinas and Virginias desire the
removal of the Negroes from among them immediately
after the Southampton Insurrection.''

Restriction of Slavery.—The African trade having
been abolished, the next question that agitated the
mind of the American abolitionist was that of restrict-
ing slavery; while the North would restrict it to its
present limits, the South insisted that slavery should
be permitted to be carried into the new territory and
states as they entered the Union. The Congressional
discussion of the slavery question aroused the anti-
slavery sentiment of the North, and thereby hastened
the day when it was possible to liberate the last slave.

Slavery in the Colonies.—Slavery was early introduced into all of the thirteen original colonies. But
climate and other considerations proved that it was
not so profitable to the Northern colonies as to those in

the South. After some years the Northern colonies liberated their slaves and adopted laws against slavery. While in the South, the large rice and cotton fields, where labor was in demand, the slave was held in cruel bondage, for no other reason than that of the profit that it might bring the owner.

The Southern Colonists.—The Southern colonists differed widely from the Northern in habits and style of living. In place of thickly settled towns and villages, they had large plantations, and were surrounded by a numerous household of servants. The Negro quarters formed a hamlet apart, with its gardens and poultry yards. An estate in those days was a little empire. The planter had among his slaves men of every trade, and they made most of the articles needed for common use upon the plantation. There were large sheds for cutting tobacco, and mills for grinding corn and wheat. The tobacco was put up and consigned directly to England. The flour of the Mount Vernon estate was packed under the eye of Washington himself, and we are told that barrels of flour bearing his brand passed in the West Indies market without inspection.

Maryland and Delaware.—While the North liberated the slave, the Quakers of Maryland and Delaware were rapidly emancipating theirs. Men felt that the best interests of white society demanded that the curse of slavery should be abolished. "The whole commerce between master and slave," says Mr. Jefferson, "is a perpetual exercising of the most boisterous passions, our children see this and learn to imitate it. If a parent could find no other motive for restraining the temper of passion against his slave it should always be a sufficient one that his child is present. The man

4

must be a prodigy that can retain his morals and manners undepraved by such circumstances, and what exe-
cration should come upon the statesman who permits
half the citizens thus to trample on the rights of others,
transform them into despots, and these into enemies,
destroy the morals of one, and the love of country of
the other.''

It was often difficult to tell whether the slave or the
master was injured the more, the ignorance of the
slave hid from him the great evils of his condition,
while the intelligence of the owner revealed the bane-
ful effects of slavery upon all who came within its area.
It made men sectional, licentious, profligate, cruel,
and selfishness paled the holy fire of patriotism.

Profitable in Maryland.—In Maryland the slave
trade became a profitable enterprise on account of its
rich soil and cultivation of tobacco. Labor was scarce,
and the Negro slave labor could be made as cheap as
his master's conscience and heart were small. Slavery
gained a foothold and at once became the bone and
sinew of the working force of the colony. While many
attempted to persuade themselves that slavery was an
institution indispensable to the success of the colony
here, as elsewhere, it was impossible to escape the bad
results of the trade which made men cruel and
avaricious.

Virginia.—There is no doubt that the colony of
Virginia purchased the first Negroes, and thus opened
the nefarious traffic in human flesh.

It may, however, be stated, that the first twenty
were forced upon the colony by the Dutch sailors who
were famishing and insisted upon the exchange of
Negroes for food.

It is to be noted that even after the institution of

slavery was founded, its growth was very slow in Virginia; according to the census of 1624, there were but twenty-two in the entire colony. The African slave trader was some time in learning that this colony was a ready market for his helpless victims. Whatever compunction of conscience the colonists had in reference to the sub-dealing in slaves, this was destroyed at the golden hopes of immense gains.

Slavery existed in this colony from 1619 until 1662, without any sanction of law, but in a later year slavery received the direct sanction of statutory law, and it was also made hereditary; with each returning year, this cruel inhuman institution flourished and magnified.

While in some colonies efforts were made to put down slavery from 1619 to 1775, there is nothing in history to show that Virginia ever sought to prohibit in any manner the importation of slaves. That she enriched herself by the slave trade cannot be doubted.

The slave had no personal rank; if he dared lift up a hand against any white man he was punished with lashes, or if he resisted his master he could be killed.

Virginia, the mother of Presidents, was also the mother of American slavery. In the absence of the slave trade which Great Britain had suffered, the demand for more Negroes in the cotton fields of the South was met by the conversion of Virginia, the old Dominion state, into a breeding state, a shameful, degrading end for the mother of Presidents.

New York.—An urgent and extraordinary demand for labor, rather than the cruel desire to traffic in human beings, led the Dutch to engage in Negro slave trade. The majority of them were employd on farms, and led quiet and sober lives. At first the Negro slave

LIBRARY - Allegheny Campus

was regarded as a cheap laborer, but after a time he became a coveted chattel. It is stated that Queen Elizabeth discouraged slavery and at one time attempted to rebuke a slave dealer, but soon after was found encouraging the slave trade. The condition of the slaves in the Christian colony of New York was no better than in many other colonies, they had no family relations, for a long time lived together by common consent, had no schools, neglected in life, and were abandoned to burial in a common ditch after death.

The Negro Plot.—In 1741, through a combination of circumstances, the Negroes of New York were accused of plotting against the whites, and in less than three months more than 150 Negroes were put into prison, some of them burned at the stake, others hanged, some transported, and the remainder pardoned. The hatred and mistrust of the Negro was the occasion of much of this supposed riot. Without evidence, and with the mere form of a trial, many Negroes were convicted and sentenced to death. The result of the supposed Negro plot in New York is a stain upon the fair name of that province. It is stated that the desperate valor of the Negro in the war with Great Britain gave her an opportunity to dispell injustice and wipe out with his blood the dark stains of 1841.

Rhode Island.—The institution of slavery was never established by statute in this colony, but in a few years after the establishment of the government it became so fully rooted that it was not possible to destroy it without explicit and positive prohibition of law.

Demand for Ignorance.—The education of the Negro in all colonies was considered to be a step against the best interests of their masters. The flourishing **of the**

slave trade demanded that the slave be kept in ignorance.

New Jersey.—It is not known when slavery was introduced into New Jersey, but early in its history the Dutch, Quakers and the English held slaves, but were more humane in their treatment of them than in the other colonies. Legislation on the subject was not undertaken until about the middle of the eighteenth century, and at no time did it reach the severity that exhibited itself in the other parts of the country. In this colony alone, of all the colonies north or south, was the American Negro given the right of trial by jury. In Virginia, Maryland, Massachusetts and in all other colonies, the Negro went into the court convicted, and went out convicted, he was executed on the flimsiest evidence imaginable, but be it said to the praise of New Jersey that justice was shown towards the Negro in this colony as in no other. The Negro slave was given the privilege of being tried by jury and permitted to be sworn in the courts.

South Carolina.—In South Carolina the inhumanities of the slave trade reached its height. The entire slave population of this province was regarded as a chattel. Rice fields of this state demanded labor and the increase of the slave was almost phenomenal. The laws were not surpassed in stringency by any other colony, and it was unlawful for any free person to inhabit or trade with Negroes. The cruelties of the code are without parallel.

Goldwin Smith says: "In the upshot she became the typical slave state, the heart of slavery and the focus of all the ideas and all the ambitions connected with the system; while Charleston, her social capital and seaport, became the paradise of planter society

with its luxury and pride. Her slave code transcended
even that of Virginia in cruelty and expressed still
more vividly the terrors of a dominant race. Every one
who found a slave abroad without a pass was to flog
him on the spot. All Negro houses were to be searched
once a fortnight for arms and for stolen goods. For
the fourth larceny a slave was to suffer death, and the
kind of death was left to the discretion of the judge.
For running away a fourth time a slave was to undergo
mutilation. For punishing a slave so that he died no
one was to suffer any penalty. For the wilful murder
of a slave the penalty was a fine of forty pounds.
It need not be supposed that the most revolting articles
of the code were often put in force, or that they represent the general relations between master and slave.''

North Carolina.—In this colony there was but little
improvement on the condition of the slave in South
Carolina. If any Negro showed the least independence
with white men he could be murdered in cold blood.
The free Negro population was small and were not
allowed any communion with the slaves; here, as elsewhere, the slave was left in a state of ignorance in
order to further the interests of his master.

New Hampshire.—Early in the history of New
Hampshire slavery was considered by the authorities
as a wicked, hateful institution. The colony never
passed any laws establishing slavery, but as early as
1714 passed several laws regarding the conduct and
service of the slaves. In New Hampshire there were
slaves up to the beginning of the war of the Revolution, but they were slaves in name only.

Massachusetts.—In Massachusetts, as well as in
some other colonies, slavery was first introduced into
individual families and afterwards into communities

where, without the sanction of the law, usage and custom made it legal. Finally, men desiring to enjoy the field of unrequiting labor gave it the sanction of statutory law.

Pennsylvania.—Since the habit of enslaving the Negro spread through the colonies north and south, Pennsylvania, even, tolerated slaves within her borders. It is said that William Penn himself once owned slaves. Efforts were made in early years to pass laws emancipating slaves, but the mother country would not permit such laws at that time.

Slave-Breeding States.—After the establishing of our republic, Maryland, Virginia, Kentucky and Missouri were the border states of slavery. North of these the slave was free, and even in these states slavery was found to be an unprofitable business as far as labor was concerned. We may well then ask, "Why was not slavery abolished in these states?" For the simple reason that it was found that since the African slave trade was abolished the South needed an increasing number of slaves for the great plantations. Here was found a profitable business, and these states became breeding states for the propagation of the race, increasing the number so as to flood the markets of the South. One of the largest exports of these states was slaves. It was estimated that in 1836 the number sold from the single state of Virginia was 40,000, yielding a return of twenty-four million dollars. This business, horrible as it seems in our day, was licensed and protected by law, advertised in papers, and recognized as one of the branches of legitimate production of trade.

Not Universally Countenanced.—It must not be supposed that this trade was countenanced by all in the South, even there, there were men who denounced in

GRANDCHILDREN OF SLAVES.

strong and vehement language the barbarous custom of separating man and wife, mother and child, scattering families never to meet again until at the great day they meet their inhuman masters as common accusers. The pathetic scenes that presented themselves to the better element in the South brought words of condem nation against the remorseless traffic that presented scenes along the streets and highways where crowds of suffering victims whose "Miserable condition was second only to the wretched borders of Hell," were made the victims of man's greed and gain.

Border States.—The states bordering on the slave states, while not permitting slavery within their borders, yet passed what were called "Black Laws," which left the free Negro but little better off in Ohio, Indiana and Illinois than in the Southern states. Black or mulatto persons were not allowed to reside in the state without having a certificate of freedom. Later, amended laws in Ohio required that a bond be given not to become a charge upon the county in which they settled. They were not permitted to give evidence in any court of record or elsewhere in the state against a white person. Severe penalties were inflicted on all who harbored such as had not given bonds. Thus, being denied the right of citizenship, ruled out of courts, compelled to produce a certificate of freedom, and in many other ways annoyed by laws limiting the rights they were suffered to enjoy, the free Negroes of these states were little better than slaves. That they endured patiently these restrictions which public sentiment threw across their social and political pathway is a matter of record.

Pensioning Old and Feeble Slaves.—This question has been discussed and urged upon our government

LEFT BY SLAVE TRADERS TO THEIR FATE.

repeatedly, but no definite action has been taken. While race prejudice is rapidly disappearing, it may be safe to say that before a sentiment can be obtained that will enact laws favorable to pensioning old and feeble slaves by congress or by any state legislature, every ex-slave will have passed into that life where he receives the recompense of reward for all his deeds, and where he is beyond the reach of the inhumanities of the slave master and needs no pension.

Added Items.—The emancipation of slaves in all the French colonies took place February 4, 1794.

The complete emancipation of slaves in the English colonies occurred in 1838 to 1839, when more than 800,000 men, besides women and children, were liberated.

Sweden emancipated her slaves in 1846, and this was soon followed (in 1848) by the Danish colonies proclaiming the freedom of her slaves.

Holland delivered her American colonies from slavery August 8, 1862.

The African slave trade was closed in this country on the first day of January, 1862.

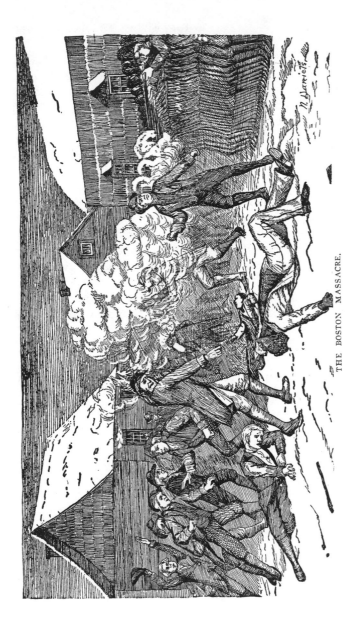

THE BOSTON MASSACRE.

CHAPTER III.

Slave Population.—In 1715 the slave population was about 60,000, but England's policy of crowding her American plantations with slaves increased the number rapidly, so that sixty years after, when the revolutionary war began, the slave population of the thirteen colonies was about 500,000; 50,000 of these were found in the North.

The desire to gain liberty with such a host of beings was not to be despised, and both sides contended for their services.

A Great Mistake.—If the colonists had at once willingly enlisted the Negro in the cause of liberty it can hardly be doubted that the struggle of eight years would have been shortened greatly, but in this case, as in many other instances, their enemy, the mother country, succeeded in using the slaves to a much greater extent than the colonists. Jefferson says: "That 30,-000 Negroes from Virginia alone went to the British army." Had the colonies permitted the Negro to enlist, and had the Negro been urged from the first to stand for the cause of liberty, much bloodshed might have been avoided. The selfishness of the colonists, especially in the South where the opposition to the arming of the Negro was much stronger than the love for independence, asserted itself to such a degree that any effort to enlist the Negro in that section seemed useless.

The First Blood for Liberty shed in the colonies was that of a real slave and Negro. On the 5th day of March, 1770, occurred the Boston massacre, which, although not opening the real struggle, yet was the bloody drama that opened the most eventful and thrilling chapter in American history.

Crispus Attucks, a runaway slave, at the head of a crowd of citizens resolved that the conduct of the British soldiers who marched through Boston as through a conquered city could no longer be endured, and led the charge against the British with the cry: "The way to get rid of these soldiers is to attack the main guard. Strike at the root, this is the nest." The troops were ordered to fire, the exposed and commanding person of the fearless Attucks went down first. Three others fell in the same attack, Caldwell, Gray and Maverick. This aroused the people of Boston. The burial of these four men from Faneuil Hall was attended by a large and respectable concourse of people.

"Long as in freedom's cause the wise contend,
Dear to your country shall your fame extend;
While to the world the lettered stone shall tell
Where Caldwell, Attucks, Gray and Maverick fell.'

The following notice appeared in the Boston Gazette twenty years before when Attucks ran away from his master:

"Ran away from his master, William Brown, of Framingham, on the 20th of Sept. last, a Mullato Fellow, about 27 years of age, named Crispus, 6 feet 2 inches high, short curl'd hair, his knees nearer together than common; had on a light colored Bearskin Coat, plain brown Fustian Jacket, or brown All Wool one, new Buckskin breeches, blue Yarn Stockings, and a checked woolen shirt. Whoever shall take up said runaway, and convey him to his abovesaid master, shall have ten pounds, old Tenor Reward, and all necessary charges paid. And all Masters of Vessels and others are hereby cautioned against concealing or carrying off said Servant on Penalty of the Law. Boston, October 2, 1750.''

Hero and Martyr.—Attucks cut the cord and knot that held us to Great Britain. "From that moment," says Webster, "we may date the severance of the British Empire." It touched the people of the colonies as they had never been touched before. Orators poured out upon this former slave, now a hero and martyr, their unstinted praise. At each succeeding anniversary of this eventful day Crispus Attucks and his noble companions were lauded until our National Independence was achieved, when the 4th of July was substituted.

Committee of Safety.—A committee of safety was early appointed after the beginning of the war, and according to its decision no slaves were to be admitted into the army under any consideration whatever. Some free men had already enlisted. Peter Salem was a slave who fought side by side in the ranks with white soldiers. It was he who, on that memorable occasion at Bunker Hill when Major Pitcairn, at the head of the British army made an attack upon the American forces, shouting, "The day is ours," poured the contents of his gun into that officer's body killing him instantly, and checking temporarily the advance of the British.

Of this occasion Mr. Aaron White, of the Massachusetts Historical Society, writes:

" With regard to the black hero of Bunker Hill, I never knew him personally nor did I ever hear from his lips the story of his achievements; but I have better authority. A soldier of the Revolution, who

was present at the Bunker Hill battle, related to my
father the story of the death of Major Pitcairn. At
the moment when the major appeared, startling the
men before him, a Negro stepped forward, and, aiming his musket at the major's bosom, blew him through.
I have frequently heard my father relate the story and
have no doubt of its truth. Salem was not the only
Negro at the battle of Bunker Hill. Others whose
bravery has not been recorded participated in the battle, showing valor and fidelity."

Major Lawrence, who fought through the war from
Concord to the peace of 1783, and who participated in
many of the severest battles, at one time commanded
a company of Negroes whose courage, military discipline and fidelity he spoke of with respect. On one
occasion, being out reconnoitering with his company,
he got so far in advance of his command that he was
surrounded and on the point of being made a prisoner
by the enemy. The colored men, soon discovering
his peril, rushed to his rescue and fought with the
most determined bravery till that rescue was effectually secured. He never forgot this circumstance,
and ever after took special pains to show kindness
and hospitality to any individual of the colored race
who came near his dwelling.

Freeing the Slave.—After the committee of safety
had excluded slaves from the army many of them
were freed by their masters on condition that they
join the army. But the prejudice against the Negro
asserted itself more and more until the legislative
bodies took action and entirely prevented Negroes
from enlisting.

Colonial Congress.—Edward Rutledge, of South
Carolina, moved that all Negroes be discharged that

were in the army. This proposition was strongly supported by the Southern delegates, but the Northern delegates succeeded in voting it down. The contest, however, continued until a conference committee was called at Cambridge, at which it was agreed that the Negro should be rejected altogether.

Reorganization.—In the reorganization of the army many officers who had served with Negroes in the militia, and who had been enlisted in the Colonial army, protested against the exclusion of their old comrades on account of color. Washington saw what might be the result if they were not permitted to enlist, and gave his consent to the enlistment with this proviso—"If this is disapproved by Congress I will put a stop to it." It could be clearly seen that if a Negro was not permitted in the army the British would gain the advantage over the Colonial forces, and no one could predict what the Negro might do. Congress reluctantly receded from its position and granted permission to enroll Negroes under certain conditions.

Lord Dunmore, who had charge of the British forces in the South, proclaimed freedom to all the slaves who would repair to his standard and bear arms to the king. The flocking of slaves to the British standard greatly alarmed the Colonial forces and caused them to utilize the Negro forces, but in this the British had already preceded them.

The Negro Prince.—It is impossible to recite all incidents and circumstances showing the heroism and bravery on the part of the Negro in this war, but a few stand out more prominently than others. Of these one is the Negro Prince, in Colonel Barton's command, who succeeded in capturing General Pres

5

cott in bed. The daring part that this negro took is shown in the following:

' The pleasing information is received here that Lieutenant-Colonel Barton, of the Rhode Island militia, planned a bold exploit for the purpose of surprising and taking Major-General Prescott, the commanding officer of the royal army, at Newport. Taking with him, in the night, about forty men, in two boats, with oars muffled, he had the address to elude the vigilance of the ships-of-war and guard boats, and, having arrived undiscovered at the quarters of General Prescott, they were taken for the sentinels; and the general was not alarmed till the captors were at the door of his lodging chamber, which was fast closed. A Negro man named Prince, instantly thrust his beetle head through the panel door and seized his victim while in bed. This event is extremely honorable to the enterprising spirit of Colonel Barton, and is considered an ample retaliation for the capture of General Lee by Colonel Harcourt. The event occasions great joy and exultation, as it puts in our possession an officer of equal rank with General Lee, by which means an exchange may be obtained. Congress resolved that an elegant sword should be presented to Colonel Barton for his brave exploit.''

Major Jeffrey.—Among the brave blacks who fought in the battles for American liberty was Major Jeffrey, a Tennesseean, who, during the campaign of Major-General Andrew Jackson, in Mobile, filled the place of '' regular '' among the soldiers. In the charge made by General Stump against the enemy the Americans were repulsed and thrown into disorder, Major Stump being forced to retire in a manner by no means desirable under the circumstances. Major Jeffrey, who was but a common soldier, seeing the condition of his comrades and comprehending the disastrous results about to befall them, rushed forward, mounted a horse, took command of the troops, and by an heroic effort rallied them to the charge, completely routing the enemy who left the Americans masters of the field. He at once received from the general the title of "major," though he could not, according to the American policy, so commission him. To the day of his death he was known by that title in Nashville, where he resided, and the circumstances which entitled him to it were constantly the subject of popular conversation.

Major Jeffrey was highly respected by the whites generally, and revered in his own neighborhood by all the colored people who knew him.

A few years ago, receiving an indignity from a common ruffian, he was forced to strike him in self defense, for which act, in accordance with the laws of slavery in that as well as many other of the slave states, he was compelled to receive on his naked person, nine and thirty lashes with a rawhide! This, at the age of seventy-odd, after the distinguished services rendered his country, probably when the white ruffian by whom he was tortured was unable to raise an arm in self defense, was more than he could bear; it broke his heart, and he sank to rise no more, till summoned by the blast of the last trumpet, to stand on the battlefield of the general resurrection.

Re-enslavement.—Many Negroes were induced to enlist in the Colonial army with the understanding that they were to have their freedom at the close of the war. But the re-enslaving of the Negro who fought for American independence by stay-at-homes was a flagrant outrage. In the legislatures of some states they passed acts rebuking the injustice of such treatment.

The Legislature of Virginia ordered that persons in the states who caused the slaves to enlist as free persons could not thereafter force them to return to a state of servitude, so contradictory to that principle of justice and their own solemn vows. Every slave who had enlisted in any regiment, and who had been received as a substitute for any free person whose duty it was to serve in a regiment, was held and deemed free in as full and ample a manner as if each one who came had been especially named in the act.

Simon Lee.—Simon Lee, grandfather of Wm. Wells Brown, was a slave in Virginia and served in the war of the Revolution. Although honorably discharged with the other troops at the close of the war he was sent back to his master where he spent the remainder of his life toiling on a tobacco plantation.

Massachusetts, although having abolished slavery in 1783, it seems was still subjected to slave hunts, and her Negro soldiers were insulted by attempts to re-enslave them.

The British Army.—Not only did the soldiers of the American army receive unjust treatment but the British, who had promised freedom to all who would join their ranks, after enduring the hardships of the war often committed them back to slavery.

Mr. Jefferson says: "From an estimate I made at that time, on the best information I could collect, I supposed the state of Virginia lost under Lord Cornwallis' hand that year, about thirty thousand slaves, and that of these twenty thousand died of the smallpox and camp fever. The rest were partly sent to the West Indies and exchanged for rum, sugar, coffee and fruit, and partly sent to New York, from whence they went, at the peace, either to Nova Scotia or to England. From this place I believe they have lately been sent to Africa. History will never relate the horrors committed by the British army in the Southern states of America.''

The Heroism of the Negro.—The heroism of the Negro has been eulogized by many of our American statesmen, notably Mr. Pinckney and Mr. Eustis.

Mr. Pinckney says: "It is a remarkable fact that notwithstanding, in the course of the Revolution, the Southern states were continually overrun by the British, and that all Negroes in them had an opportunity of leaving their owners, few did, proving thereby not only a most remarkable attachment to their owners, but the mildness of the treatment from whence their affections sprang. They then were, as they still are, as valuable a part of our population to the Union as any other equal number of inhabitants. They were in numerous instances the pioneers, and in all, the laborers of your armies. To their hands were owing the erection of the greatest part of the fortifications raised for the protection of our country; some of which, particularly Fort Moultrie, gave, at the earlier period of the inexperience and untried valor of our citizens, immortality to American arms. In the Northern states numerous bodies of them were enrolled into, and fought by the side of the whites, the battles of the Revolution.''

Mr. Eustis, of Massachusetts, said: "At the commencement of the Revolutionary war there were found in the Middle and Northern states many blacks and other people of color capable of bearing arms; a part

of them free, the greater part slaves.   The freemen
entered our ranks with the whites.   The time of those
who were slaves was purchased by the states, and they
were induced to enter the service in consequence of
a law by which, on condition of their serving in the
ranks during the war, they were made freemen.''

   '' The war over and peace restored, these men returned to their respective states, and who could have
said to them on their return to civil life after having
shed their blood in common with the whites in the
defense of the liberties of their country, You are not
to participate in the liberty for which you have been
fighting?   Certainly no white man in Massachussetts.''

   Rev. Dr. Hopkins, of Rhode Island, said:

   '' God is so ordering it in his providence that it
seems absolutely necessary something should speedily
be done with respect to the slaves among us, in order
to our safety and to prevent their turning against us
in our present struggle, in order to get their liberty.
Our oppressors have planned to get the blacks and in-
duce them to take up arms against us, by promising
them liberty on this condition, and this plan they are
prosecuting to the utmost of their power, by which
means they have persuaded numbers to join them.
And should we attempt to restrain them by force
and severity, keeping a strict guard over them, and
punishing those severely who shall be detected in attempting to join our oppressors, this will only be making bad worse, and serve to render our inconsistence,
oppression and cruelty more criminal, perspicuous and
shocking, and bring down the righteous vengeance
of Heaven on our heads.   The only way pointed out
to prevent this threatening evil is to set the blacks
at liberty ourselves by some public act and laws, and

then give them proper encouragement to labor, or take arms in the defense of the American cause, as they shall choose.   This would at once be doing them some degree of justice, and defeating our enemies in the scheme that they are prosecuting,''

Colonel Laurens.—No man stands out more prom-inently in the war of the Revolution than Colonel Laurens.   He labored earnestly for the South to over-come the prejudices and to raise colored regiments. Although supported by the general government the selfishness of the Southern slaveholder frustrated his plans.   In one of his letters to Washington he says: ''The approaching session of the Georgia legislature induces me to remain in these quarters for the purpose of taking new measures on the subject of our black levies.   I shall, with all the tenacity of a man, do everything that I can in regaining a last effort on so interesting an occasion.''   Washington's reply showed that he, too, had lost faith in the patriotism of the citizens of the South to a great degree.   He said:

''I must confess that I am not at all astonished at the failure of your plan.   That spirit of freedom which, at the commencement of this contest, would have gladly sacrificed everything to the attainment of its object has long since subsided, and every selfish pas-sion has taken its place.   It is not the public, but pri-vate interest which influences the generality of man-kind, nor can the Americans any longer boast an exception.   Under these circumstances it would rather have been surprising if you had succeeded; nor will you, I fear, have better success in Georgia.''

Negro Soldiers.—George Williams says as soldiers the Negroes went far beyond the most liberal expec-tations of their staunchest friends.   Associated with white men, many of whom were superior gentlemen and nearly all of whom were brave and enthusiastic, the Negro soldiers of the American army became worthy of the cause they fought to sustain. Colonel Alexander Hamilton had said: "Their natural faculties are as good as ours," and the assertion was supported by their splendid behavior on all the battlefields of the Revolution. Endowed by nature with a poetic element, faithful to trusts, abiding in friendship, bound by the golden threads of attachment to places and persons, enthusiastic in personal endeavor, sentimental and chivalric, they made hardy and intrepid soldiers. The daring, boisterous enthusiasm with which they sprang to arms disarmed racial prejudice of its sting and made friends of foes.

Their cheerfulness in camp, their celerity in the performance of fatigue-duty, their patient endurance of heat and cold, hunger and thirst, and their bold efficiency in battle, made them welcome companions wherever they went. The officers who frowned at their presence in the army at first, early learned from experience, that they were the equals of any troops in the army for severe service in camp and excellent fighting in the field.

CHAPTER IV.

Slavery Established in the South.—After the Revolution, when the new nation was recovering from the effects of the long continued war, it was found that slavery had established itself in the Southern States while in the North, slaves were being set free.

Responsibility.—The responsibility of fastening slavery upon the new republic was not the fault of the Declaration of Independence, which stated that all men are created equal and are endowed by the Creator with inalienable rights of life, liberty, and the pursuit of happiness. Southern statesmen proved themselves masters of the situation, and, seeing great gain in the traffic in slaves, labored to establish it more and more in the South. While they could not hide behind the walls of the constitution they took refuge, as they thought, behind the Bible, and urged that the divine origin of slavery was incontrovertible, that slavery was the normal condition of every Negro, and that the white man was God's agent to carry out the prophecy of Noah respecting the descendants of Ham.

Agitation.—While in the slave states there was a determined effort to establish slavery, yet throughout the whole nation, especially in the North, the anti-slavery sentiment was being agitated and increased. Some statesmen, notably Mr. Jefferson, prophesied a dissolution of the Union if the nation were to remain half slave and half free.

The whole commerce between master and slave was

denounced as the most unrelenting despotism on the one part and degrading submission on the other.

Property in Man.—Says George Williams: "When the doctrine of property in man was driven out of Europe as an exile and found a home in this New World in the West, the ancient and time honored anti-slavery sentiment combined all that was good in brain, heart and civilization, and hurled itself with righteous indignation against the institution of slavery the perfected curse of the ages.

The Quakers.—Foremost in the anti-slavery agitation were the good and kind-hearted Quakers, or Friends. In our poor Negro slaves they saw a brother, and very early in the history of the nation emancipated all their slaves and labored to increase the anti-slavery sentiment.

Benjamin Lundy.—One of the first agitators of the anti-slavery movement was Benjamin Lundy, who traveled through a number of states and labored incessantly for the freeing of the Negro. In 1830 he says: "I have within ten years sacrificed several thousands of dollars of my own earnings, I have traveled upwards of 5,000 miles on foot and more than 20,000 in other ways, have visited nineteen states of this Union and held more than two hundred public meetings, have performed two voyages to the West Indies, by which means the emancipation of a considerable number of slaves has been affected, and, I hope, the way paved for the enfranchisement of many more." Considering the extreme dangers to which any one agitating anti-slavery was subjected in these times this was a remarkable work. He was afterwards associated with William Lloyd Garrison. These men, together equally ardent in their efforts to abolish slavery, were, however, not agreed as to the method. Lundy favored gradual emancipation, Garrison immediate and unconditional emancipation.

William Lloyd Garrison.—This young man devoted his life to the cause of freeing the Negro. At an early period he edited an anti-slavery paper and afterwards

WILLIAM LLOYD GARRISON.

united with Mr. Lundy in publishing a paper at Baltimore. Seeing a load of slaves for the New Orleans market, the sundering of families, as well as the harrowing cruelties that attended these scenes, he denounced in his paper in no measured terms, the whole institution, and expressed his determination to cover with thick infamy all who were engaged in the transaction. The result was that his paper was destroyed, he was arrested, tried for libel, and convicted and imprisoned. The exorbitant fine imposed upon him was afterwards paid by the benevolent Arthur Tappan. Garrison went forth from the prison if possible a more inveterate foe to slavery than ever. It was not popular to denounce slavery and hence this young orator often encountered great dangers. When cautioned he replied: "I am aware that many object to the severity of my language, but is there not cause for severity. I am but as harsh as truth and as uncompromising as justice. Tell a man whose house is on fire to give a moderate alarm; tell him to moderately rescue his wife from the hands of the ravisher; tell the mother to gradually extricate her babe from the fire into which it has fallen; but urge me not to use moderation in a cause like the present. I am in earnest. I will not equivocate—I will not excuse—I will not retreat a single inch. And I will be heard." There never was a more intrepid leader against slavery than William Lloyd Garrison.

Anti-Slavery Societies.—In 1836 there were 250 auxiliary societies in thirteen states, and eighteen months later they had increased to 1,000.

Silence of the Pulpit.—It is true that many of the foremost ministers of the day maintained an unbroken silence on the slavery question, but all could not be kept silent. There were notable exceptions in many parts of the north, while in some parts anti-slavery men who had been hoping for aid from the church went out of the church temporarily, hoping that the scales would drop from the eyes of the preachers ere long. Dr. Albert Barnes stated: "That there was no power out of the church that would sustain slavery an hour if it were not sustained in it."

Leaders of the Anti-Slavery Party.—Among the leaders of the anti-slavery party we may mention Parker Pillsbury, Stephen Foster, James G. Birney and Samuel Brooke. Mr. Pillsbury said: "The anti-slavery movement has unmasked the character of the American church. Our religion has been found at war with the interests of humanity and the laws of God. And it is more than time the world was awakened to its unhallowed influence on the hopes and happiness of man while it makes itself the palladium of the foulest iniquity ever perpetrated in the sight of Heaven."

Theodore Parker was another of the strong men who lent his influence wholly against slavery.

Other Agitators.—Foremost among agitators were such men as E. P. Lovejoy, who afterwards gave his life for the cause, James G. Birney, Cassius M. Clay and John Brown. Of John Brown it may be said that it was given to him to write the lesson upon the hearts of the American people so that they were enabled, a few years later, to practice the doctrine of resistance and preserve the nation against the bloody aggressions of the Southern Confederacy.

Colonization Societies.—These were formed earlier than any other anti-slavery organizations. Their objects were to rescue the free colored people of the United States from the political and social disadvantages and to place them in a country where they might enjoy the benefits of free government with all the blessings which it brings in its train. The American Colonization Society was never able to secure the confidence and the support of the anti-slavery societies of the day nor the Negro in general. It did not oppose slavery in its stronghold, but simply sought to secure a place for freed Negroes. The press, in many cases, lent its aid to the colonization societies, but, notwithstanding the apparent favor which it received, it was readily seen that to send the Negro to Africa or some other favored spot was an impossibility. The society lost strength

WENDELL PHILLIPS.

yearly until all were convinced the race could not be colonized, but that the Negro must be emancipated here and remain here.

Wendell Phillips.—One of Mr. Garrison's most able and earnest supporters was Wendell Phillips. Although in many respects they strangely differed yet they stood united for the cause of freedom; one was a self-made man, the other a product of New England culture. One was the executive of the anti-slavery movement, the other the orator spreading the eloquence that melted the fetters from a race and transformed a nation. Mr. Phillips was a reformer and early espoused the cause of anti-slavery. One of his most remarkable addresses against slavery was made in Faneuil Hall, Boston, where a number had gathered after the murder of Lovejoy to discuss the subject of slavery. Faneuil Hall was secured by Dr. Channing. It was crowded at the time of the meeting, thronged with three factions, some being for free discussion, some to make mischief, and others, idle spectators, were swayed to and fro by each speaker in turn. Resolutions were offered denouncing the murder of Lovejoy. To defeat the adoption of these resolutions a popular politician, attorney-general of Massachusetts, made a captivating speech and almost succeeded in turning the audience against the cause for which they had met. The foes of freedom, through this astute attorney captured the hall and were ready to vote down the resolutions. It was at this important moment, under the very shadow of the pending catastrophe, that Wendell Phillips claimed the floor and with his marvelous voice captivated the ears of his audience. Mr. Phillips soon made himself master of the situation and hurled anathemas at the previous speaker, and so completely carried his audience with him that at the close, with a whirlwind of applause, the resolutions were carried by an overwhelming vote. Oliver Johnson says of this speech: "I had heard Phillips once before, and my expectations were high, but he transcended them and took the audience by storm."

It was a speech to which not even the ablest report could do justice, for such a report could not bring the scene and the speaker vividly before the people. Mr. Phillips, by espousing the cause of anti-slavery, was ostracised from social circles, for caste at that time in New England knew no recognition of true moral worth. It cost Wendell Phillips much when he became an abolitionist. This speech on Lovejoy's murder in Faneuil Hall, cut him from all social intercourse with previous friends. No one but those who have endured the persecutions of these days can understand what it cost these men to stand so earnestly for the freedom of the slaves. Their true moral worth cannot be too forcibly presented to the youth of to-day. Long live in the memory of the present and future generations men like Wendell Phillips who staked their all and were ready at any cost to stand for the suppression of the slave trade.

Convention of Colored People.—As early as 1831 the freed Negroes throughout the Northern states determined to do what they could for their brethren in bonds. Several conventions were held. A college was to be established and no doubt much good might have been done had they been permitted to continue in their work. Able leaders succeeded in making the convention a power, but the intense hatred of the slavery element succeeded in abolishing these societies composed of persons of color. These societies were disbanded and their members took their places in white societies.

The Proposed College.—A plan was proposed at one of these conventions that a college on the manual-labor system be established in New Haven. It seems, however, New Haven resented the idea of having a colored

CHARLES SUMNER.

A staunch anti-slavery man who did more in Congress for the
freedom of the slave than any other man. He was
Senator from Massachusetts.

college and another site was selected. The disband-
ing of the colored associations put a stop to this movement which might have brought so much good to the
whole of the colored race.

Anti-Slavery Women of America.—In 1837 the anti-
slavery women met in their first convention in New
York, and the question as to admitting colored women

6

was discussed and ably defended. It was finally decided that the society should admit colored members as well. The following lines by a colored member, Miss Sarah Forten, justified the hopes of her white sisters concerning the race:

> "We are thy sisters. God has truly said
> That of one blood the nations he has made.
> Oh, Christian woman, in a Christian land,
> Canst thou unblushing read this great command?
> Suffer the wrongs which wring our inmost heart,
> To draw one throb of pity on thy part.
> Our skins may differ, but from thee we claim
> A sister's privilege and a sister's name."

Anti-Slavery Orators.—The arguments of anti-slavery orators were often met by rotten eggs and many of them were abused. Mr. Garrison was dragged through the streets of Boston with a halter about his neck. Colored schools were broken up. Public meetings were disturbed by pro-slavery mobs. All this violent opposition added fuel to the flame and made the anti-slavery agitators all the bolder. While the foreign slave trade had been suppressed slave population was increasing at a wonderful ratio. Garrison's voice was not uncertain in those days. In July, 1860, he declared: "Our object is the abolition of slavery throughout the land. I am for meddling with slavery everywhere—attacking it by night and by day, in season and out of season—in order to effect its overthrow. Down with this slave-holding government! Let this covenant with death and agreement with hell' be annulled! Let there be a free, independent Northern republic and the speedy abolition of slavery will inevitably follow."

HARRIET BEECHER STOWE.

Author of "Uncle Tom's Cabin."

Literature.—Anti-slavery literature was scattered throughout the nation. Many pamphlets and books were written by eminent Negroes informing the public mind, stimulating the action and touching the heart of the civilized world of two continents. "Uncle Tom's Cabin," however, pleaded the cause of slavery more effectually than the millions of anti-slavery books and pamphlets, presenting the despairing cry of the enslaved, the struggle of fettered manhood, and touched the sympathies of the youth as well as the aged with a pity for the slave and a determination to abolish so hideous an institution.

Harriet Beecher Stowe.—Although Harriet Beecher Stowe was not permitted to take an active and direct part in freeing the slaves, yet her work, "Uncle Tom's Cabin," did more in bringing about the final liberation of the slave than any other agency. This volume has been translated into many languages. Everywhere read it is destined to create a sentiment against the traffic in man.

The Pro-Slavery Reaction.—The agitation of the anti-slavery question brought about a strong opposition to any effort made to free the slaves. Rewards of $10,000 and even $50,000 were offered for the heads of prominent abolitionists. Andrew Jackson in his message to Congress in 1835, suggested the propriety of a law that would prohibit, under severe penalties, the circulation in the Southern states through the mails of publications intended to incite the slaves to insurrection.

Attempts to Stifle Discussions.—The legislatures of the different states, as well as Congress, were next entreated to prohibit discussions of the slavery question. These efforts were generally defeated in the North, but in the South were successful.

Mob Riots.—In many places mob violence was resorted to in breaking up meetings called for the discussion of anti-slavery questions. Philadelphia had a riot, lasting three nights and the harmless and powerless blacks were mainly its victims. At Concord, N. H., the mob demolished an academy because colored boys were admitted as pupils. At Northfield, N. H., George Storrs attempted to deliver an anti-slavery lecture, but was dragged from his knees while at prayer. On trial he was acquitted, but soon after was again arrested and sentenced to three months' imprisonment. He appealed and that ended the matter.

At Boston, William Lloyd Garrison was dragged through the streets with a rope around his body, but was finally rescued by the mayor who protected him from further violence. In the same city a women's anti-slavery society was dispersed by a mob while its president was at prayer. In the South there was but one mode of dealing with the abolitionists. "Let your emissaries cross the Potomac and I promise you that your fate will be no less than Haman's," says a Southern writer.

Rifling the Mails.—Anti-slavery literature was not permitted to be sent through the mails in the South and a meeting in Charleston, S. C., unanimously resolved that all mail matter of this kind should be burned. The mails were searched and rifled for the purpose. Attempts were made to bring offenders to justice, but failure met them in every case.

Congress Suppressing Agitation.—Not only in the state legislatures, but in Congress, measures were adopted to suppress the discussion of the slavery question. In 1837 Congress adopted by a vote of 117 to 68 the following resolution: "That all petitions, memorials, resolutions, propositions, or papers relating in any way to the subject of slavery or the abolition of slavery shall, without being either first read or referred,

HENRY WILSON.

An anti-slavery agitator and Vice-President in 1872.   While in Congress in 1862 he introduced a bill for the employment of Negroes as Soldiers.

be laid on the table.'' Amazing as it may seem, this heroic treatment was not successful in arresting agitation and restoring tranquillity to the public mind, so that each succeeding Congress was necessitated to do the work over again.

John Brown.—One of the most prominent of the agitators of anti-slavery was John Brown of national fame. The story of this man's life is too well known to be repeated here. After laboring for many years and succeeding in aiding the cause of anti-slavery in many ways, he attacked Harper's Ferry in 1859 and, with a number of associates was made a prisoner It is vain to under-rate either the man or his work. With firmness of will and a purpose unconquerable, he labored for the cause so dear to him and to which he had given most of his years. After the fight at Harper's Ferry he said: "I never intended plunder or treason or the destruction of property, or to excite the slaves to rebellion; I labored only to free the slaves." South Carolina, Missouri and Kentucky each sent a rope to hang him, but Kentucky's, proving the strongest, was selected and used. His last letter, written before his death to Mrs. George L. Stearns, Boston, Mass., follows:

"CHARLESTON, JEFFERSON Co., 29th Nov., 1859.
"MRS. GEORGE L. STEARNS, Boston, Mass.

"My Dear Friend: No letter I have received since my imprisonment here has given me more satisfaction or comfort than yours of the 8th inst. I am quite cheerful and never more happy. Have only time to write you a word. May God forever reward you and all yours.

"My love to ALL who love their neighbors. I have asked to be spared from having any mock or hypocritical prayers made over me when I am publicly murdered; and that my only religious attendants be poor little, dirty, ragged, bare-headed and bare-footed slave boys and girls led by some old gray-headed slave mother. Farewell. Farewell,

"Your friend,

"JOHN BROWN."

John Brown gave slavery its death wound and his immortal name will be pronounced with blessings in all lands and by all people till the end of time.

JOHN BROWN, THE ABOLITIONIST.

CHAPTER V.

THE FUGITIVE SLAVE LAWS.

Fugitive Slave Laws.—Very severe and stringent laws were passed to prevent anyone from aiding the slaves in attempting to escape to the North. These laws permitted owners to follow slaves and legally claim them in other states. Any one suspected of showing even an act of kindness to a fugitive slave was liable to be flogged, fined or imprisoned. The greater the agitation of the question the more severe were these laws.

Calvin Fairbanks.—Many respected citizens were imprisoned and fined for aiding slaves. Calvin Fairbanks spent nearly eighteen years in a Kentucky penitentiary for the crime of aiding poor slaves in gaining freedom. It is said that during this time he received 35,000 stripes on his bare body. Early in life he had heard of the sufferings and miseries endured by slaves and had resolved then to do all in his power to right the wrongs suffered by the race. He was one of the first in the Underground Railway work along the Ohio. A number of times he was arrested in the act of giving assistance to slaves and committed to prison, where he suffered untold cruelties from the hands of his keeper. "I was flogged sometimes bowed over a chair or some other object, often receiving seventy lashes four times a day, and at one time received 107 blows at one time, particles of flesh being thrown upon the wall several feet away." All this was endured by a white man in order to free the Negro.

Rev. John Rankin, of Ohio, was fined $1,000, besides serving a term in prison.

W. L. Chaplin aided two young slaves of Georgia to escape. Caught in the act, he was imprisoned for five months and released on a bail of $25,000. His friends, knowing that he would be convicted and sent to the penitentiary for a number of years, and perhaps for life, resolved to pay his bail. All his property was sacrificed, and through the liberality of that princely man, Garrett Smith, the sum was raised.

Thomas Garrett, a Quaker of Delaware, one of the most successful agents of the Underground Railway, assisted nearly 3,000 slaves to escape from bondage; he was at last convicted and fined so heavily that he lost all his property When the auctioneer had knocked off his last piece of property to pay the fine he said: "I hope you will never be guilty of doing the like again." Garrett, although penniless at the age of sixty, replied: "Friend, I have not a dollar in the world, but if thee knows a fugitive slave who needs a breakfast send him to me." It is with pleasure we learn Mr. Garrett lived to see the day when the slaves obtained their freedom.

Levi Coffin.—This man of high social position, a Quaker of Cincinnati, was frequently called the president of the Underground Railway. He succeeded in aiding about 25,000 slaves in gaining their freedom.

Captain Jonathan Walker.—Mr. Walker took a contract to build a railroad in Florida and for this purpose employed a number of Negroes. By kind treatment he gained the confidence of these slaves who afterwards persuaded him to aid them in gaining their liberty. They attempted to escape in a boat to an island not far away. Captain Walker was taken violently sick, and the Negroes, not understanding how to manage the boat, were taken up by another vessel and taken to Key West. Captain Walker was tried in the United States Court and was sentenced to be branded on the right hand with the capital letters "S. S." (slave stealer), and to pay as many fines as there were slaves; to suffer

THOMAS GARRETT.

From " Underground Railroad," by permission of Author.

as many terms imprisonment; and to pay the costs and stand committed until the fines were paid. The initials of the words " slave stealer " were branded upon his hand and he was imprisoned, but his friends succeeded in raising money to pay his fines and he was released in 1845. The following lines by Whittier gave quite another meaning to the brand "S. S.," making it a badge of honor, signifying the heroism and self-sacrifice in spirit of these forerunners of liberty.

"Then lift that manly right hand, bold plowman of the wave,
Its branded palm shall prophesy Salvation to the Slave;
Hold up its fire-wrought language, that whoso reads may feel
His heart swell strong within him, his sinews change to steel;
Hold it up before our sunshine, up against our Northern air.
Ho! men of Massachusetts, for the love of God, look there!
Take it henceforth for your standard, like the Bruce's heart of
    yore;
In the dark strife closing round ye let that hand be seen
    before."

Underground Railroad.—By this term we designate the many methods and systems by which fugitive slaves from the Southern States were aided in escaping to the North or Canada.

After slavery was abolished in the North slaves frequently ran away from their masters and attempted to reach the free states of the North, or better still, Canada, where they were beyond the reach of their former masters.

These so-called railroads were most useful auxiliaries in giving aid to the Negro. Fugitive slave laws gave masters the right to pursue the slaves into another state and bring them back. The men interested in these railways were men who felt they should fear God rather than man, that the fugitive slave laws were unjust and that they should not be obeyed. They were composed of a chain of good men who stretched themselves across the land from the borders of the slave states all the way to Canada. Many fugitive slaves were thus permitted to escape. They were carried by night to a place of safety and then turned over to another conductor who very often

would load up and convey the fugitives in a covered
wagon to the next station. Thus they were carried
on from one place to another. As soon as leaders
rose among the slaves who refused to endure hard-
ship, the fugitive then came north. George Williams
says: "Had they remained, the direful scenes of St.
Domingo would have been re-enacted, and the hot
vengeful breath of massacre would have swept the
South as a tornado and blanched the cheek of the
civilized world."

Different Branches.—It would be very difficult to
name all the branches of the "Underground Railroad."
They extended all the way from New Jersey to Illinois. Probably those on which the greatest number
was rescued extended through Pennsylvania and Ohio.
Many local branches existed in different parts of the
country.

William Still.—One of the most active workers in
freeing slaves was William Still. He was chairman and
secretary of the eastern branch of the road. It is wonderful what work such men as Mr. Still did in those
days when opposition was so great. A part of the
work that he has done is recorded in " Underground
Railroad." In the preface of this work Mr. Still
says: "In these records will be found interesting narratives of the escapes of men, women and children
from the present House of Bondage; from cities and
plantations; from rice swamps and cotton fields; from
kitchens and mechanic shops; from border states and
gulf states; from cruel masters and mild masters;
some guided by the north star alone, penniless, brav-
ing the perils of land and sea, eluding the keen scent
of the bloodhound as well as the more dangerous pursuit of the savage slave-hunter; some from secluded

DESPERATE CONFLICT IN A BARN.

From "Underground Railroad," by permission of Author.

dens and caves of the earth, where for months and
years they had been hidden away awaiting the chance
to escape; from mountains and swamps, where indescribable sufferings and other privations had patiently
been endured.   Occasionally fugitives came in boxes
and chests, and not infrequently some were secreted
in steamers and vessels, and in some instances jour-
neyed hundreds of miles in skiffs.   Men disguised in
female attire and women dressed in the garb of men
have under very trying circumstances triumphed in
thus making their way to freedom.   And here and
there, when all other modes of escape seemed cut off,
some, whose fair complexions have rendered them
indistinguishable from their Anglo-Saxon brethren,
feeling that they could endure the yoke no longer,
with assumed airs of importance, such as they had
been accustomed to see their masters show when traveling, have taken the usual modes of conveyance and
have even braved the most scrutinizing inspection of
slave-holders, slave-catchers, and car conductors, who
were ever on the alert to catch those who were considered base and white enough to practice such decep-
tion.'' Mr. Still says that the passengers on the Underground Railroad were generally above the average
order of slaves.

Agents.—As the branches of the railroad were numerous it would be impossible to name any considerable number of the agents of the road.   Some of these
nobly periled their all for the freedom of the oppressed.   Seth Concklin lost his life while endeavoring
to rescue from Alabama slavery the wife and children
of Peter Still.   Samuel D. Burris, whose faithful and
heroic service in connection with the underground
railway cost him imprisonment and inhuman treat-

ment, at last lost his freedom by being sold from the auction block.

WILLIAM STILL.

Indeed, prudence often dictated that the recipients of favors should not know the names of their helpers and vice versa, they did not desire to know others. The slave and his friends could only meet in private to transact the business of the road. All others were outsiders. The right hand was not to know what the left hand was doing. The safety of all concerned called for still tongues. For a long time no narratives were written. Probably the best and most authentic of these thrilling accounts of the struggle for liberty are found in "Underground Railroad."

Methods Pursued.—Different methods were pursued to aid fugitive slaves; some availed themselves of steamboats, railroads, stage coaches, but more frequently a more private method was resorted to, so as to escape detection. A number of cases are reported where colored men were boxed up and shipped by express across the line.

William Jones, from Baltimore, succeeded in having his friends box him up and ship him by express to Philadelphia; for seventeen hours he was enclosed in the box, but friends at the Philadelphia underground station succeeded in getting the box safely, and after a time in sending the slave to Canada.

Mr. Pratt, in his sketches of the underground railway, gives a number of interesting accounts of escapes, among which are a mother and daughter who escaped in a box from Washington to Warsaw, New York. With the aid of a friend they secured a box, put in it straw, quilts, plenty of provisions and water, and their friend carried the box in a spring wagon to the North. This friend, in order to succeed in his efforts, passed himself off as a Yankee clock peddler, and as he drove a wagon and good team, no questions were asked.

7

When out of sight of settlements he would open the box and give the inmates an opportunity to walk in the night for exercise.   The master heard of their whereabouts and sent slave-hunters to recapture them,

A BOLD STROKE FOR FREEDOM.
From "Underground Railroad," by permission of Author."

but the sentiment against slavery was so strong that they were not permitted to take them back.

Henry Box Brown.—The marvelous escape of Henry Box Brown was published widely in papers when the anti-slavery agitation was being carried on.   In point of interest his case is no more remarkable than any other; indeed, he did not suffer near as much as many. He was a piece of property in the city of Richmond. He seemed to be a man of inventive mind, and knew that it was no small task to escape the vigilance of Virginia slave hunters, or the wrath of an enraged master, for attempting to escape to a land of liberty.

The ordinary modes of travel, he concluded, might prove disastrous to his hopes, he therefore hit upon a new invention, which was to have himself boxed up and forwarded to Philadelphia by express. Size of box was 2 feet wide, 2 feet 8 inches deep and 3 feet long. His food consisted of a few small biscuits. He had a large gimlet which he intended to use for fresh air if necessary. Satisfied that this would be far better than to remain in slavery, he entered the box. It was

RESURRECTION OF HENRY BOX BROWN.
From "Underground Railroad," by permission of Author.

safely nailed up and hooped with five hickory hoops, and addressed by his friend, James A. Smith, a shoe dealer, to Wm. Johnson, Arch street, Philadelphia, marked "This side up, with care." It was twenty-six hours from the time he left Richmond until he arrived in Philadelphia. The notice, "This side up," did not avail, for the box was often roughly handled. For a while the box was upside down and he was on his head for miles. The members of the vigilance com mittee of Philadelphia had been informed that he would be started. One of the committee went to the depot at half past two o'clock in the morning to look after the box, but did not find it. The same afternoon he received a telegram from Richmond, ''Your case of goods is shipped and will arrive to-morrow morning.''

Mr. McKim, who had been engineering this undertaking, found it necessary to change the program, for it would not be safe to have the express bring it directly to the anti-slavery office. He went to a friend who was extensively engaged in mercantile business who was ready to aid him. This friend, Mr. Davis, knew all the Adams Express drivers, and it was left to him to pay a trusty man $5 in gold to go next morning and bring the box directly to the anti-slavery office.

Those present to behold the resurrection were J. M. McKim, Professor C. D. Cleveland, Lewis Thompson, and Wm. Still. The box was taken into the office. When the door had been safely locked, Mr. McKim rapped quietly on the lid of the box and called out ''All right.'' Instantly came the answer from within, ''All right, sir.'' Saw and hatchet soon removed the five hickory hoops and raised the lid of the box. Rising up in his box, Brown reached out his hand, saying, ''How do you do, gentlemen.'' He was about as wet as if he had come up out of the Delaware. He first sang the psalm beginning with these words: ''I waited patiently for the Lord, and he heard my prayer.'' At the home of Lucretia Mott he received a cordial reception, and was entertained for some time, when he went to Boston.

The success of this undertaking encouraged Smith, who had nailed him up in the box, to render similar service to two other young bondmen. But, unfortunately, in this attempt the undertaking proved a failure.

The young men, after being duly expressed and some distance on the road, were, through the agency of the telegraph, betrayed, and the heroic young fugitives were taken from the box and dragged back to helpless bondage. Smith was arrested and imprisoned for seven years in a Richmond penitentiary. He lost all

CHARITY STILL,
Who Twice Escaped from Slavery.

his property, was refused witnesses on his trial, and for five long months, in hot weather, he was kept heavily chained in a cell 4x8 feet in dimensions. Mr. Smith had, by his efforts, aided many to gain their liberty. He received five stabs aimed at his heart by a bribed assassin. But all these things did not move him from his purpose. After his release he went North and was united in marriage at Philadelphia to a lady who had remained faithful to him through all his sufferings.

Amanda Smith, in her autobiography, tells how her

father assisted runaway slaves. "Our house," she says, "was one of the main stations of the underground railway. My father took the Baltimore Weekly Sun newspaper, that always had advertisements of runaway slaves. These would be directed by their friends to our house and we would assist them on their way to liberty. Excitement ran very high, and we had to be very discreet in order not to attract suspicion. My father was watched closely, as he was suspected of aiding slaves. After working all day in the harvest field he would come home at night, sleep about two hours, then start at midnight and walk fifteen or twenty miles and carry a poor slave to a place of security, sometimes a mother and child, sometimes a man and wife, then get home just before day. Thus he many times baffled suspicion, and never but once was there a poor slave taken from my father's hands, and if that man had told the truth he would have been saved.

"One week the papers were full of notices of a slave who had run away. A heavy reward was offered, a number of men in our neighborhood deterimned to get the reward if possible. They suspected our home as a place of safety for the poor slave. We had concealed the poor fellow for about two weeks, as there was no possible chance for father or anyone else to get him away, so closely were we watched. One day four men came on horseback. As father saw them he called to mother that four men were coming. He met them and they demanded of him to know whether he had a nigger there. Father said, 'If I tell you I have not you won't believe me, if I tell you I have it will not satisfy you, so search for yourself.' Mother had in the meantime concealed him between the cords and the straw tick. The men searched the house, looked under the bed, and satisfied themselves that he was not there; thus we succeeded in saving him from slavery."

William and Ellen Craft were slaves in the state of Georgia. The desire to become free became so strong that they commenced planning to escape. Ellen, being fair, would pass for a white man, and was to act the part of master, while William was to be the servant. She dressed in a fashionable suit of male attire, and was to pass as a young planter. But Ellen was *beardless*. After mature reflection her face was muffled up as though the young planter was suffering from a face or toothache. In order to prevent the method of registering at hotels, Ellen put her right arm in a sling, put on green spectacles, and pretended to be very hard of hearing and dependent upon the faithful servant.

Ellen, disguised as a young planter, was to have nothing to do but to hold herself subject to her ailments and put on the air of superiority. The servant was always ready to explain in case of inquiry. They stopped at first-class hotels in Charleston, Richmond and Baltimore, and arrived safely in Philadelphia, where the rheumatism disappeared, her right arm was unslung, her toothache was gone, the beardless face was unmuffled, the deaf heard and spoke, the blind saw. The strain on Ellen's nerves, however, had tried her severely, and she was physically prostrated for some time. Her husband, William, was thoroughly colored, and was a man of marked ability and good manners, and full of pluck. They were sent to Boston, where they lived happily until the fugitive slave law was passed. Then slave hunters from Macon, Georgia, were soon on their track, but the sympathy of friends in Boston would not permit their being returned to Georgia. It was, however, considered best for them

to seek a country where they would not be in daily
fear of slave capturers, backed by the United States
Government. They were therefore sent by their
friends to Great Britain.

In England the Crafts were highly respected. After
the emancipation they returned to the United States
with two children, and, after visiting Boston and
neighboring places, William purchased a plantation
near Savannah, and is living there with his family.

Emancipators Tried.—Those who aided slaves in
their struggle for liberty were often tried and imprisoned. Many of them lost all of their property and
suffered much from the hands of slave dealers

Seth Concklin's noble and daring spirit induced him
to put forth the most strenuous efforts to redeem a
family of slaves. He learned to know Peter Still and
found that his wife and children were still in Alabama
in bondage. After considering the hazardous undertaking, he decided to make an attempt to bring the
wife and children of Peter Still to the North. He went
South, laid his plans well, and succeeded in carrying
the family for seven days and seven nights in his skiff,
then traveled hundreds of miles on foot. They at last
reached Vincennes, Indiana. By this time the advertisements of the runaway slaves had spread all over the
country, and at Vincennes they were arrested and
taken South to their former owner.

Imagine the state of mind of these enslaved ones,
who, after having endured so many hardships and pain,
so near to freedom's territory, were caught and returned
to slavery. Seth Concklin was brutally murdered on
the way south.

Thus we might give numerous cases where slaves
were secreted for months and endured the greatest

hardships and were willing rather to meet death than to remain in slavery. Several girls made their escape in male attire, some secreted themselves in woods, traveling at night. Others succeeded in having friends hide them in steamers, but the underground railroad, with all its stations and well-planned schemes, succeeded often in defeating the plans of the slave hunters. As soon as a slave ran away papers were filled with advertisements and rewards were offered for their return. In this way many were looking for slaves so as to secure the rewards, making the escape of some more difficult. One cannot read such books as "The Underground Railroad, by Wm. Still," or the story of Peter Still, the kidnapped and the ransomed, without sincere thankfulness that slavery is ended, and that a man is a man without respect to the color of his skin.

Slave Population.—In 1800 the slave population was over 900,000; in 1830 it had reached about 2,000,000; in 1840 it was estimated to be about 2,500,000; and in 1850 it was about 3,000,000. In 1860 the aggregate Negro population in the United States was about 4,500,000, of which about 4,000,000 were slaves. Nearly 3,000,000 of the slaves were in the rural districts of the South. Southern prosperity depended upon the product of slave labor, which amounted to about $140,000,-000 per year. It can be readily seen that the Civil War, which commenced in 1861, was destined to shake the very foundation of Southern civilization. While both North and South attempted to keep the real cause of the war in the background the maxim, "No question is settled until it is settled right," asserted itself here, and no real progress was made in the war until the Northern leaders acknowledged slavery as the issue, and met the question direct by freeing all slaves.

ABRAHAM LINCOLN.

CHAPTER VI.

THE NEGRO IN THE CIVIL WAR.

The part enacted by Negro troops in the War of the Rebellion is the romance of North American history.

Number Enrolled.—The records of the war department show that there were 178,595 colored men regularly enlisted as soldiers in the Union army during the rebellion who by their good conduct established a commendable record and did efficient service in camp, fortress and field. The first enlistment of Negroes was by Gen. Hunter in the Department of the South in June, 1862. It was made without the authority of the War Department and was due to an emergency. Gen. Hunter needed men.

Ready for Enlistment.—At the sound of the tocsin at the North the Negro waiter, barber, cook, groom, porter, boot-black, and laborer, stood ready at the enlisting office; although the recruiting officer refused to take his name he waited patiently for the prejudice to be removed, waited two long years before the door was opened, but even then he did not hesitate but walked in, and with what effect the world knows.

Opposition to Enlistment.—From the beginning there was great opposition to enlisting the Negro in the army. The Northerners even went so far as to return runaway Negroes to their owners, while the South kept the Negro on the plantation. The Confederates, however, found it no easy task to watch the Negro and the Yankee too; their attention could be given to but one at a time; as a slave expressed it.

"When Marsa watch the Yankee, nigger go—when Marsa watch the nigger, Yankee come."

Objections.—The "New York Times," of February 16, 1863, in an editorial summed up the objections to enlisting the Negroes as follows: "First, that the Negroes will not fight. Second, it is said that the whites will not fight with them. Third, that the prejudice against them is so strong that our citizens will not enlist or will quit the service if compelled to fight by their side, and thus we shall lose two white soldiers for one black one that we gain. Fourth, it is said that we shall get no Negroes—or not enough to be of any service. In the free states very few will volunteer, and in the slave states we can get but few because the rebels will push them southward as fast as we advance upon them. Fifth, the use of the Negroes will exasperate the South. We presume it will—but so will any other scheme we may adopt which is warlike and effective in its character and results. We are not ready with Mr. Vallandinham, to advocate immediate and unconditional peace! The best thing we can do is to possess ourselves in patience while the experiment is being tried."

The President and Secretary of War and a large majority of the generals in the army acted on the theory, "This is a white man's war, and the Negro has no lot or part in it."

They seemed to be ignorant of the fact that slavery was the real cause of the war, and hence held to the principal that all runaway slaves must be returned to their owners by the Union army.

General Hunter.—To General David Hunter, commanding the army in the South, is given the honor of organizing the first southern colored regiment. He could not get white recruits and was surrounded by a multitude of able-bodied Negroes who were idle, but anxious to serve as soldiers. In advance of public opinion he organized a regiment and was called to account for it by the Secretary of War. He replied that he had instructions to employ all loyal persons in defense of the Union and the suppression of the rebellion, and hence was not limited as to color. He informed the secretary that loyal slaves everywhere remained on their plantations to welcome them, aid them, supply the army with food and information, and since they were the only men who were loyal, he had organized them into a regiment and appointed officers to drill them. He closed with these words: "The experiment of arming the blacks, so far as I have made, has been a complete and even marvelous success. They are sober, docile, attentive and enthusiastic; displaying great natural capacities for acquiring the duties of the soldier. They are eager, beyond all things, to take the field and be led into action; and it is the unanimous opinion of the officers who have charge of them that in the peculiarities of this climate and country they will prove invaluable auxiliaries."

Mr. Wyckliff created a scene in the house by denouncing General Hunter and declaring that the enlistments of Negroes was an insult to every white soldier in the army. Nevertheless Congress authorized the President to enlist "persons of African descent," but provided that they should be used as laborers in the camps and forts, and were not to be allowed to bear arms.

After a Year.—Towards the close of 1862 the war clouds were still growing thicker. The Union army had won few victories; the Northern troops had to fight in a tropical climate, the forces of nature and an arrogant, jubilant and victorious enemy, but in the face of

all these discouraging features the President still held
to his views of managing the war without bringing the
subject of slavery to the front. In reply to a deputa-
tion of gentlemen from Chicago, who urged a more
vigorous policy of emancipation, the President denied
the request and stated: "The subject is difficult and
good men do not agree. For instance: The other day,
four gentlemen of standing and intelligence from New
York called as a delgation on business connected with
the war; but before leaving two of them earnestly be-
sought me to proclaim general emancipation, upon
which the other two at once attacked them. You know
also that the last session of Congress had a decided majority of anti-slavery men, yet they could not unite upon
this policy. And the same is true of the religious people.
Why, the rebel soliders are praying with a great deal
more earnestness, I fear, than our own troops, and
expecting God to favor their side; for one of our
soldiers, who had been taken prisoner, told Senator
Wilson a few days since that he met nothing so discouraging as the evident sincerity of the prayers of those
he was among."

He admitted that slavery was at the root of the
rebellion, but was not willing to act, but just nine days
from that time when he thought a proclamation not
warranted and impracticable, he issued his first Emancipation Proclamation.

Public Opinion Changes.—When the Union men
began to see the worth of the Negro to the Confederate
army in throwing up breastworks that were often
almost impregnable, they began to complain that the
Negro with his pick and spade was a greater hindrance
to their progress than the cannon ball of the enemy;
slowly but surely public opinion changed. Congress

GENERAL GRANT AND A COLORED GUARD.

The guard, being under instructions, would not permit even General Grant to pass before he had thrown away his cigar.

111

prohibited the surrender of the Negroes to the rebels, the President issued his Emancipation Proclamation and the Negroes were rapidly enlisted.

In the Union Ranks.—Charles Sumner says: "Those who have declaimed loudest against the employment of Negro troops have shown a lamentable amount of ignorance, and an equally lamentable lack of common sense. They know as little of the military history and martial qualities of the African race as they do of their own duties as commanders. All distinguished generals of modern times who have had opportunity to use Negro soldiers have uniformly applauded their subordination, bravery, and power of endurance. Washington solicited the military services of Negroes in the Revolution, and rewarded them. Jackson did the same in the War of 1812. Under both these great captains the Negro troops fought so well that they received unstinted praise."

Confederate Measures.—The enlistment of Negroes in the Northern army changed the policy of the South, and public opinion, now so strongly endorsed in the North, affected the rebels, who soon passed a measure for arming 200,000 Negroes themselves.

In the Navy.—In the navy a different course was pursued from the first. Negroes were readily accepted all along the coasts on board the war vessels, this being no departure from the regular and established practice in the service.

Official Authority.—General Rufus Saxon was the first officer to receive official authority to enlist Negroes as soldiers. On the 26th of August, 1862, the Secretary of War ordered him to proceed to the Department of the South and organize 5,000 troops of "African descent," which were to be designated for service in garrisons not in danger of attack by the enemy, to relieve white regiments whose terms of enlistment had expired. But one of General Saxon's first acts after recruiting a regiment was to send it on a foraging expedition into the enemy's country. The result was entirely satisfactory. The colored men proved to be remarkably good foragers, and brought in more supplies than three times the number of white men could have secured.

Recruiting Offices.—Recruiting stations were established throughout the South, and officers were sent out to enlist slaves. In these journeys through the country officers often met with strange experiences. Recruits were taken wherever found, and as their earthly possessions usually consisted of but what they wore upon their backs, they required no time to settle their affairs. The laborer in the field would lay down his hoe, or leave his plow, and march away with the guard. On one occasion a large plantation was visited and the proprietor asked to call in his slaves; he complied, and when they were asked if they wished to enlist replied that they did, and fell into the ranks with the guard. As they started away the old man turned and, with tears in his eyes, said: "Will you take them all? Here I am an old man; I cannot work; my crops are ungathered, my Negroes have all enlisted or run away, and what am I to do?" Several recruiting officers were tarred and feathered and others were shot. Several officers were dismissed from the army for refusing to command Negro troops; others resigned in preference to doing so.

Indignation.—Although the Confederates anticipated the Federal government in the employment of Negroes as military forces, they exhibited a good deal of indig-

8

nation when their example was followed, and the Records of the Confederate Congress show some sensational measures of retaliation threatened against the government of the United States on this account. It was proposed, among other things, to raise the black flag against Negro soldiers and white officers who commanded them, and in some cases this retaliation was enforced, as at Port Pillow, but finally the Confederate Congress formally recognized the usefulness of the Negro as a soldier as well as a laborer, and authorized President Davis to enlist an unlimited number of colored troops.

Governor Yates.—This fact was commented upon by Governor Yates, of Illinois, in a message he sent to the legislature of that state, as a most extraordinary phenomenon in history. He said the leaders of the insurrection had called upon the cause of the insurrection to save it, and had recognized the intelligence and manhood of the despised race by lifting it to a level with themselves. A wise providence, he said, was directing the destiny of the Confederates, so that they will terminate the very evil they are fighting to maintain. Slavery was to be the corner stone of their new Confederacy, but, says Governor Yates, a man who has been a soldier will never be a slave.

Discrimination.—In the matter of pay there was for a long time discrimination against the Negro troops. While the troops of the regular army were paid $13.00 per month, the Negroes received but $10.00, three of which was deducted on account of clothing. Some regiments refused to receive $10.00 per month and others were paid in full. The injustice done the Negro soldier in this discrimination was often a violation of a solemn and written pledge of the govern-

ON PICKET DUTY.

ment that declared that they should receive the same
pay and allowances as the white men.   In definite
terms, Congress and the War Department was denounced as the enemy of the Negro in this discrimination.   All honor to the Fifty-fourth colored regiment
of Massachusetts that refused to receive the $7.00 per
month until the authorities were driven to give equal
pay to Negroes and whites.

General Butler.—Nearly all the generals of the army
opposed the enlistment of the Negro.   General Phelps,
stationed at Louisiana, made a bold fight for the
Negro, and attempted to enlist them in and around
New Orleans, but being so strongly opposed by General
Butler, he was forced to resign and return to his home.

The sentiment of the North seemed to admit the
right of the South to hold slaves.   That General Butler
afterwards entirely changed his opinion is seen by his
speech on the floor of Congress, when he said: "It
became my painful duty, sir, to follow in the track of
the charging column, and there, in a space not wider
than the clerk's desk, and three hundred yards long,
lay the dead bodies of three hundred and fifty-three of
my colored comrades, slain in the defense of their
country, who laid down their lives to uphold its flag
and its honor as a willing sacrifice; and as I rode along
among them, guiding my horse this way and that way
lest he should profane with his hoofs what seemed to
me the sacred dead, and as I looked on their bronzed
faces upturned in the shining sun as if in mute appeal
against the wrongs of the country for which they had
given their lives, and whose flag had only been to them
a flag of stripes on which no star of glory had ever shone
for them—feeling I had wronged them in the past, and
believing what was the future of my country to them

—among my dead comrades there I swore myself a solemn oath: 'May my right hand forget its cunning, and my tongue cleave to the roof of my mouth, if I ever fail to defend the rights of those men who have given their blood for me and my country this day, and for their race forever;' and, God helping me, I will keep this oath."

President Lincoln, when urged by Dr. Patton, of Chicago, to press the Negro into service said: "If we were to arm them, I fear that within a few weeks, the arms would be in the hands of the rebels."

In Congress.—In Congress a bill was passed to raise and equip 150,000 soldiers of African descent. Colonel T. Higginson now watched the acts of Congress and ascended the St. John's river in Florida and captured Jacksonville, which had been abandoned by white Union troops.

The New York Tribune said: "Drunkenness, the bane of our army, does not exist among our black troops." "Nor have I yet discovered the slightest ground of inferiority to white troops."

Prejudice Broken Down.—The bravery and excellence of the Negro in the battlefield soon broke down prejudices against the Negro on the part of the white officers, and it was not long before 100,000 Negroes were found in the Union ranks.

Colonel Shaw.—Colonel Shaw commanded the first colored regiment organized in the free states, the Fifty-fourth Massachusetts, and it was this regiment that played such an important part in the attempt to take Fort Wagner. After making a forced effort and march for a day and a night, through swamps and drenching rains, without food or rest, hungry and fatigued they reached General Strong's headquarters on that memorable morning, just as they were forming into line of battle. Colonel Shaw made a thrilling patriotic speech to his men, and, after a most desperate and gallant fight, succeeded in planting the regimental flag on the works. The Negro color bearer, John Wall, was killed. But. Wm. H. Carney seized it, and, after receiving several wounds, one of which mangled his arm, brought the flag to the standard with his own blood on it and shouted, "Boys, the old flag never touched the ground."

Fort Wagner.—M. S. Littlefield, in writing of Fort Wagner says: "Sergeant W. H. Carney, Company C writes he was with the first battalion, which was in the advance of the storming column. He received the regimental colors, pressed forward to the front rank, near the colonel, who was leading the men over the ditch. He says, as they ascended the wall of the fort, the ranks were full, but as soon as they reached the top 'they melted away' before the enemy's fire 'almost instantly.' He received a severe wound in the thigh. but fell upon his knees. He planted the flag upon the parapet, lay down on the outer slope, that he might get as much shelter as possible; there he remained for over an hour, till the second brigade came up. He kept the colors flying until the second conflict was ended. When our forces retired he followed, creeping upon one knee, still holding up the flag. It was thus that Sergeant Carney came from the field, having held the emblem of liberty over the walls of Fort Wagner during the sanguinary conflict of the two brigades, and having received two very severe wounds, one in the thigh and one in the head. Still he refused to give up his sacred trust until he found an officer of his regiment.

SERGEANT WM. H. CARNEY.

119

"When he entered the field hospital, where **his** wounded comrades were being brought in, they cheered him and the colors. Though nearly exhausted with the loss of blood, he said: 'Boys, the old flag never touched the ground.' Of him as a man and soldier I ean speak in the highest terms of praise."

Milliken Bend.—"Tauntingly it has been said that Negroes won't fight. Who say it, and who but a dastard and brute will dare to say it, when the battle of Milliken's Bend finds its place among the heroic deeds of this war? This battle has significance. It demonstrated the fact that the freed slaves will fight."

General Grant says of Milliken Bend: "This was the first important engagement of the war in which colored troops were under fire. These men were very raw, perhaps all had been enlisted since the beginning of the siege, but they behaved well."

First Colored Regiment.—The first colored regiment raised in New Orleans under General Butler, after remaining in camp for about six months, were quite efficient in the use of arms. It was then ordered to report to General Dwight. Its commanding officer, Colonel Stafford, was disabled, and was not permitted to go with the regiment. Before the regiment left the officers assembled at the quarters of Colonel Stafford. The colored guared marched up to receive the regimental flags. Colonel Stafford made a speech full of patriotism and feeling, and concluded by saying: "Colored guard, protect, defend, die for it, but do not surrender these flags." The reply of the sergeant was, "Colonel, I will bring back these colors to you in honor, or report to God the reason why."

Port Hudson.—At Port Hudson, "the deeds of heroism performed by these colored men were such as the proudest white men might emulate. Their colors were torn to pieces by shot, and literally bespattered by blood and brains. The color-sergeant of the First Louisiana, on being mortally wounded, hugged the colors to his breast, when a struggle ensued between the two color-corporals on each side of him as to who should have the honor of bearing the sacred standard, and during this generous contention one was seriously wounded. One black lieutenant actually mounted the enemy's works three or four times, and in one charge the assaulting party came within fifty paces of them. Indeed, if only ordinarily supported by artillery and reserve, no one can convince us that they would not have opened a passage through the enemy's works.

"Captain Callioux, of the First Louisiana, a man so black that he actually prided himself on his blackness, died the death of a hero, leading on his men in the thickest of the fight. One poor wounded fellow came along with his arm shattered by a shell, and jauntily swinging it with the other, as he said to a friend of mine: 'Massa, guess I can fight no more.' I was with one of the captains, looking after the wounded going to the rear of the hospital, when we met one limping towards the front. On being asked where he was going, he said: 'I have been shot bad in the leg, captain, and dey want me to go to the hospital, but I guess I can gib 'em some more yet.' I could go on filling your columns with startling facts of this kind, but I hope I have told enough to prove that we can hereafter rely upon black arms as well as white in crushing this infernal rebellion. I long ago told you there was an army of 250,000 men ready to leap forward in defense of freedom at the first call. You know where to find them and what they are worth."

"Although repulsed in an attempt which, situated as things were, was all but impossible, these regiments, though badly cut up, are still on hand, and burning with a passion ten times hotter from their fierce baptism of blood. Who knows but that it is a black hand which shall first plant the standard of the republic upon the doomed ramparts of Port Hudson."

In the Mississippi Valley.—In many engagements of the Mississippi valley the colored soldiers won for themselves lasting glory and golden opinions from the officers and men of white organizations.

The Battle of Wilson's Wharf.—The following account is given: "At first the fight raged fiercely on the left. The woods were riddled with bullets; the dead and wounded of the rebels were taken away from this part of the field, but I am informed by one accustomed to judge, and who went over the fields today, that from the pools of blood and other evidences, the loss must have been severe. Finding that the left could not be broken, Fitz-Hugh Lee hurled his cavalry—dismounted of course—upon the right. Steadily they came on, through obstruction, through slashing, past abattis without wavering. Here one of the advantages of the colored troops was made apparent. They obeyed orders, and bided their time. When well tangled in the abattis the death warrant, "Fire," went forth. Southern chivalry quailed before Northern balls, though fired by Negro hands. Volley after volley was rained upon the superior by the inferior race, and the chivalry broke and tried to run."

Petersburg.—This was a stronghold of the Confederacy. To dislodge them tons of powder were buried near their lines. It was to be exploded and in the consequent confusion in the Confederate ranks a charge

FIERCE ENCOUNTER WITH BLOODHOUNDS.

In October, 1862, the Confederates attacked the 1st South Carolina Regiment with bloodhounds. The hounds, so long a terror to the Negro, rushed fiercely upon the troops. The troops, equal to the occasion, quickly shot or bayonetted them, and triumphantly held up the beasts speared with their bayonets.

was to be made and capture their forces.   Four thousand four hundred Negro braves were on hand to do
this work.   The refusal to allow them to do so, many
believe, lost the day to the Union army.   Ah! but the
black braves that day proved that they were willing to
fight, bleed and die for their kindred in chains so
cruelly forged.   Black men fell on the very parapet of
the enemy's works, in a hand-to-hand fight with their
white antagonists.   The soil was saturated in the
blood of the colored valiants.   When Petersburg did
fall into Federal hands, and Richmond followed later,
Negro soldiers were among the first to enter the field
and claim these cities in the name of the Federal government.   Close on the fall of these Confederate cities
Lee surrendered at Appomatox under the shade of the
old apple tree.   Thus ended the war, leaving our brave
black heroes covered with glory crowned with imper-
ishable laurels.   When, therefore, the last drum shall
beat, the last bugle note shall sound, and the roll call
of nations shall be heard, and the names of Phillips,
Leonidas, Alexander, Hannibal, Caesar, Napoleon and
Wellington are sounded on the lips of the worshipers
of heroes, with equal praise shall be heard the name
of Attucks, Peter Salem, Captain Cailloux, Colonel
Shaw the talented, and Toussaint L'Overture.   A race
with such indomitable courage, under such discourage-
ments, must have under God a future inspiring and
glorious.

General Smith on Petersburg.—"The hardest fighting was done by the black troops.   The forts they
stormed were the worst of all.   After the affair was over
General Smith went to thank them, and tell them he was
proud of their courage and dash.   He said: 'They cannot be exceeded as soldiers, and that hereafter he

will enter them in a difficult place as readily as the best.' ''

"The charge on the advanced works was made in splendid style, and as the 'dusky warriors' stood shouting upon the parapet, General Smith decided that 'they would do,' and sent word to storm the first redoubt. Steadily these troops moved on, led by officers whose unostentatious bravery is worthy of emulation. With a shout and rousing cheers they dashed at the redoubt. Grape and canister were hurled at them by the infuriated rebels. They grinned and pushed on, and with a yell that told the Southern chivalry their doom, rolled irresistibly over into the work. The guns were speedily turned upon those of our 'misguided brethren,' who forgot that discretion was the better part of valor. Another redoubt was carried in the same splendid style, and the Negroes have established a reputation that they will surely maintain.

"Officers on General Hancock's staff, as they rode by the redoubt surrounded by a moat with water in it, over which these Negroes charged, admitted that its capture was a most gallant affair. The Negroes bear their wounds quite as pluckily as the white soldiers."

Adjutant General L. Thomas pays the following tribute to the Negro soldiers: "On several occasions when on the Mississippi river, I contemplated writing to you respecting the colored troops, and to suggest that, as they have been fully tested as soldiers, their pay should be raised to that of white troops, and I desire now to give my testimony in their behalf. You are aware that I have been engaged in the organization of freedmen for over a year, and have necessarily been thrown in contact with their orders.

Strict Obedience.—"The Negro, in a state of slavery, is brought up by the master from early childhood to strict obedience and to obey implicitly the dictates of the white man, and they are thus led to believe that they are an inferior race. Now, when organized into troops, they carry their habits of obedience with them, and their officers, being entirely white men, the Negroes promptly obey them.

Important Addition.—"A regiment is thus rapidly brought into a state of discipline. They are a religious people—another high quality for making good soldiers. They are a musical people, and thus readily learn to march and accurately perform their maneuvers. They take pride in being elevated as soldiers, and keep themselves, as their camp grounds, neat and clean. This I know from special inspection, two of my staff officers being constantly on inspecting duty. They have proved a most important addition to our forces, enabling the Generals in active operations to take a large force of white troops into the field; and now brigades of blacks are placed with the whites. The forts erected at the important points on the river are nearly all garrisoned by blacks—artillery regiments raised for the purpose, say at Paducah and Columbus, Kentucky; Memphis, Tennessee; Vicksburg and Natchez, Mississippi, and most of the works around New Orleans.

Heavy Guns.—"Experience proves that they manage the heavy guns very well. Their fighting qualities have also been fully tested a number of times, and I have yet to hear of the first case where they did not fully stand up to their work. I passed over the ground where the First Louisiana made the gallant charge at Port Hudson, by far the stronger part of the rebel works. The wonder is that so many have made their

GENERAL EDWARD JOHNSON AND G. H. STEWART AS PRISONERS
IN CHARGE OF A FORMER SLAVE.

127

escape. At Milliken's Bend, where I had three incom-
plete regiments—one without arms until the day previous to the attack—greatly superior numbers of the
rebels charged furiously up to the very breastwork.
The Negroes met the enemy on the ramparts, and both
sides freely used the bayonet, a most rare occurrence
in warfare, as one or the other party gives way before
coming in contact with the steel. The rebels were
defeated with heavy loss. The bridge at Moscow, on
the line of railroad from Memphis to Corinth, was
defended by one small regiment of blacks. A cavalry
attack of three times their number was made, the
blacks defeating them in three charges made by the
rebels.''

General S. C. Armstrong, who for years was at the
head of Hampton Institute, says: "Two and one-half
years' service with Negro soldiers (half a year as
captain and major in the One Hundred and Twentieth
New York Volunteers) as lieutenant-colonel and
colonel of the Ninth and Eighth regiments of the
United States colored troops, convinced me of the excellent qualities and capacities of the freedmen. Their
quick response to good treatment, and to discipline,
was a constant surprise. Their tidiness, devotion to
their duty and their leaders, their dash and daring in
battle, and ambition to improve, even studying their
spelling books under fire, showed that slavery was a
false, though doubtless for the time being an educative,
condition, and that they deserve as good a chance as
any people.

A Cavalry Force.—"A cavalry force of three hundred and fifty attacked three hundred rebel cavalry
near the Big Black with signal success, a number of
prisoners being taken and marched to Vicksburg.

Forrest attacked Paducah with 7,500 men. The garrison was between 500 and 600, nearly 400 being colored troops recently raised. What troops could have done better? So, too, they fought well at Fort Pillow till overpowered by greatly superior numbers. The above enumerated cases seem to be sufficient to demonstrate the value of the colored troops."

Few of Many Tributes.—These are but few of the many tributes that generals and white leaders have cheerfully given to the loyalty, valor and bravery of the colored troops during the war. George Williams truly says: "No officer, whose privilege it was to command or observe the conduct of these troops, has ever hesitated to give a full and cheerful endorsement of their worth as men, their loyalty as Americans, and their eminent qualifications for the duties and dangers of military life. No history of the war has ever been written without mentioning the patience, endurance, fortitude, and heroism of the Negro soldiers who prayed, wept, fought, bled and died for the preservation of the Union of the United States of America."

Items of Interest.—History records the fact that during the late rebellion the Negro soldiers participated in more than four hundred engagements.

There were between four and five hundred Negro soldiers who were engaged in the battle of New Orleans.

About 6,000 Negroes were connected in different ways with the Confederate army.

The first colored regiment to enter the services of the rebellion was the Fifty-fourth Massachusetts Volunteers.

ROBERT S. ABBOTT, EDITOR OF THE CHICAGO DEFENDER, LEADING RACE JOURNAL IN ILLINOIS, SHOWN ON ACTIVE DUTY WITH CHICAGO LIBERTY LOAN COMMITTEE.

(C) U. & U.

CHAPTER VII.

Written expressly for this book by Prof. W. H. Crogman, A. M.

The persistent efforts of Spain to retain under her
cruel, corrupt, and inefficient government the fertile
island of Cuba have again, in these closing years of the
nineteenth century, brought to light the splendid qualities of the Negro soldier. Of limited education, poorly
armed, poorly clad, and poorly fed, he has shared the
toils, the perils, the privations of his white compatriots,
and has exhibited such fortitude and loyalty, such
unswerving devotion to the cause of Cuban liberty
as to win unstinted praise even from those cherishing
strong prejudice against his race. Whatever may be
the future of Cuba, impartial history will ascribe to the
Negro no small part of the sacrifice made for her deliverance. Both as a slave and as a freedman his sympathies were with the insurgents. In the first revolution, beginning October 10, 1868, and lasting ten years,
there were thousands of blacks under the insurgent
standard. It is reasonable to believe, that in this first
uprising they imbibed the martial spirit, and acquired
that training and discipline which made them so efficient in the last struggle to throw off the Spanish yoke.
It has been officially stated that of the thirty thousand
Cubans recently under arms two-fifths were Negroes,
commonly so called.

Leadership.—Not only soldiers, however, but Negro leaders of conspicuous ability were brought to light by the recent Cuban insurrection. Prominent among these may be mentioned Flor Crombet, a dashing leader, a stubborn fighter, unflinching in his loyalty to Cuba as he was unrelenting in his hostility to Spain.

Equally brave, and more of a military genius, perhaps, was Quintin Bandera, a Negro of unmixed blood. Indeed, there is much of romance in the life of this man. Hon. Amos J. Cummings, one of the five congressmen invited by the New York Journal to visit Cuba, and report the state of things there, had this to say about Quintin Bandera, in his speech before Congress, Friday, April, 29, 1898:

"Quintin Bandera means 'fifteen flags.' The appellation was given to Bandera because he had captured fifteen Spanish ensigns. He is a coal-black Negro, of remarkable military ability. He was a slave of Quesada. With others of Maceo's staff, he was sent to prison at Ceuta. While in prison the daughter of a Spanish officer fell in love with him. Through her aid, he escaped in a boat to Gibraltar, where he became a British subject and married his preserver. She is of Spanish and Moorish blood, and is said to be a lady of education and refinement. She taught her husband to read and write, and takes great pride in his achievements."

Antonio Maceo.—Of all the leaders produced by the Cuban war the most colossal and imposing figure is Antonio Maceo. Says Mr. Cummings of him:

"He was as swift on the march as either Sheridan or Stonewall Jackson, and equally as prudent and wary. He had flashes of military genius when a crisis arose. It was to his sudden inspiration that Martinez Campos owed his final defeat at Coliseo, giving the patriots the opportunity to overrun the richest of the western provinces and to carry the war to the very gates of Havana."

GEN. ANTONIO MACEO.

Speaking of his attachment to the cause of Cuban liberty, the same author says:

" No one has ever questioned his patriotism. Money could not buy him; promises could not deceive him.

His devotion to Cuban freedom was like the devotion
of a father to his family.   All his energies, physical
and intellectual, were given freely to his country."

It is well known that of all the men arrayed against
them the Spaniards dreaded Maceo most.   Through
emissaries they made repeated efforts to have him
poisoned; but without success.   When finally the news
reached them of his fall by Spanish bullets, their joy
was indescribable and their hope of success corre-
spondingly raised.

The greatness of this man as a leader, however, apparent as it was in his life, became even more so in his
death.   His fall sent a shock throughout the civilized
world.   Men felt instinctively that the Cuban cause
had lost its mightiest chieftain, its loftiest source of
inspiration.   It is doubtful, indeed, whether the death
of any man within the century produced a sorrow more
general and profound.   So sincere was the regret that
for weeks, nay, almost months, people would not believe that the daring leader was gone.   They said it
was only a ruse he was practicing on the Spaniards,
and at some moment when they least expected him he
would strike like a thunderbolt.   Alas! that moment
was never to come.   His death, however, won universal sympathy for the Cuban cause.   So far, then, as
he was personally concerned, it was as well for him to
die when he did as to die later.   He had shown to the
world what was in his heart and brain; he had written
his name high upon the scroll of the world's heroes;
he had done this, too, not for vain-glory, not for self
aggrandizement, not for the purpose of crushing and
humiliating his fellow-men; but for the purpose of
rescuing a suffering people from a hideous and oppressive tyranny.

The Negro Soldier in the Spanish-American War.
—It is an historic fact that reflects no little credit on the Negro, that on the very verge of hostilities with Spain the first regiment ordered to the front was the Twenty-fourth United States regulars. This colored regiment, like all the regiments of its kind, had, in time of peace, maintained in the West a splendid record, not only for soldierly efficiency, but for manly and respectful conduct. Wherever quartered in that section of country the Negro regiments were liked, and in more than one instance did the citizens petition for their retention when they were about to be moved, preferring their presence to that of white troops. It is safe to say, perhaps, that the best behaved men in times of peace are the best and most reliable men in times of war. Character always tells. The ruffian and the rowdy are brave under favorable conditions, when the odds are on their side. It requires courageous men to face coolly all sorts of dangers and difficulties. The short war with Spain has shown Negroes to be just such men. From no service have the black soldiers shrunk. At no time did they show the white feather. With far less to inspire them they have shown themselves on every occasion not one whit inferior to their white comrades in arms. Nay, some are inclined to give them the palm for bravery displayed in the recent war around Santiago and at other stubbornly-disputed points. A correspondent of the New York Sun—a paper quick, by the way, to recognize the merits of the black troops—describing the scenes on that fatal Friday at Santiago, said:

"While the proportion of colored men wounded has been large, by their courage and supreme cheerfulness they have really carried off the palm for heroism."

"THE NEGROES SAVED THE FIGHT."

Heroic charge of colored troops in the battle of La Quasina, seven miles from Santiago.

Here is what one of the wounded Rough Riders, Kenneth Robinson, has to say about the black soldiers. Robinson is lying in one of the tents here suffering from a shot through his chest. A pair of underdraws and one sock, the costume in which he arrived from the front, is all that he has to his name at present. On the next cot to him lies an immense Negro, who has been simply riddled with bullets, but is still able to crack a smile and even to hum a tune occasionally. Between him and the Calumet man there has sprung up a friendship. 'I'll tell you what it is,' said Robinson this morning, 'Without any disregard to my own regiment I want to say that the whitest men in this fight have been the black ones. At all events they have been the best friends that the Rough Riders have had, and every one of us, from Colonel Roosevelt down, appreciates it. When our men were being mown down to right and left in that charge up the hill it was the black cavalry men who were the first to carry our wounded away, and during that awful day and night that I lay in the field hospital, waiting for a chance to get down here, it was two big colored men, badly wounded themselves, who kept my spirits up. Why, in camp every night before the fight the colored soldiers used to come over and serenade Colonels Wood and Roosevelt; and weren't they just tickled to death about it! The last night before I was wounded a whole lot of them came over, and when Colonel Roosevelt made a little speech thanking them for their songs, one big sergeant got up and said: 'It's all right, colonel, we'se all rough riders now.' "

From another source we take the following:

"I was standing near Captain Capron and Hamilton Fish." said the corporal to the Associated Press correspondent tonight, "and saw them shot down. They were with the Rough Riders and ran into an ambush, though they had been warned of the danger. Captain Capron and Fish were shot while leading a charge. If it had not been for the Negro cavalry, the Rough Riders would have been exterminated. I am not a Negro lover. My father fought with Mosby's rangers, and I was born in the South, but the Negroes saved that fight, and the day will come when General Shafter will give them credit for their bravery."

A correspondent of the Atlanta Evening Journal, July 30, 1898, has this to say:

"I have been asked repeatedly since my return about what kind of soldiers the Negroes make. The Negroes make fine soldiers. Physically the colored troops are the best men in the army, especially the men in the Ninth and Tenth cavalry. Every man of them is a giant. The Negroes in the Twenty-fourth and Twenty-fifth infantry, too, are all big fellows. These colored regiments fought as well, according to General Sumner, in whose command they were, as the white regiments. What I saw of them in battle confirmed what General Sumner said. The Negroes seemed to be absolutely without fear, and certainly no troops advanced more promptly when the order was given than they."

In the course of the war, however, there came to the colored troops a severer test than that of facing Mauser bullets. A yellow fever hospital was to be cleansed and yellow fever sufferers were to be nursed. An order went forth from General Miles that a regiment be detailed for such service. "In response to this order," said Mr. Robert B. Cramer in the Atlanta Constitution, Tuesday, August 16, 1898, "the Twenty-fourth infantry, made up entirely of colored men, left

their trenches at night, and at dawn the next morning
they had reported to Dr. LaGarde. An hour later they
were put at work, and before sunset again the lines of
their tents were straightened out, the debris of the
burned buildings was cleared away, the waterworks
were put in operation, and the entire camp became a
place in which a sick man stood at least a fighting
chance of getting well.''

"It was peculiarly appropriate," continues Mr.
Cramer, "that the Twenty-fourth should be selected
for that place, because it was one of unquestionable
honor, and at that time there was nothing that could
be done for the colored troops in paying tribute to their
work as soldiers that ought not to have been done.   In
all the disputes that historians will indulge in as to who
did and who did not do their duty at the siege of Santiago no one will ever question the service of the dark-
skinned regulars, who from the time the Tenth fought
with the Rough Riders in the first day's fight, until
the Twenty-fifth infantry participated in the actual
surrender, did their whole duty as soldiers.   All that
can be said in praise of any regiment that participated
in the campaign can be said of those regiments which
were made up of colored troops, and I am glad to
quote General Wheeler as saying:

'The only thing necessary in handling a colored
regiment is to have officers over them who are equally
courageous.   Give them the moral influence of good
leadership and they are as fine soldiers as exist anywhere in the world.   Put them where you want them,
point out what you want them to shoot at and they will
keep on shooting until either their officers tell them to
stop or they are stopped by the enemy.' ''

Such testimony from a hard-fighting ex-Confederate

general ought to be sufficient to establish the merits of the Negro as a soldier; but it may be well, as there is evidence varied and abundant, and from high authority to hear from others.   Mr. George Kennan of Siberian prison fame, special correspondent for the Outlook, wrote in the issue of August 13:

"I have not, as yet, the information necessary to do anything like justice to the regiments that particularly distinguished themselves in Friday's battle; but upon the basis of the information I already have, I do not hesitate to call especial attention to the splendid behavior of the colored troops.   It is the testimony of all who saw them under fire, that they fought with the utmost courage, coolness, and determination, and Colonel Roosevelt said to a squad of them in the trenches, in my presence, that he never expected to have, and could not ask to have better men beside him in a hard fight.   If soldiers come up to Colonel Roosevelt's standard of courage, their friends have no reason to feel ashamed of them.   His commendation is equivalent to a medal of honor for conspicuous gallantry, because, in the slang of the camp, he himself is 'a fighter from 'way back.'   I can testify, furthermore, from my own personal observation in the field hospital of the Fifth army corps Saturday and Sunday night that the colored regulars who were brought in there displayed extraordinary fortitude and self control. There were a great many of them, but I can not remember to have heard a groan or a complaint from a single man."

His Patriotism.—At the outbreak of the war with Spain, there were not wanting those who questioned the patriotism of the Negro.   To all such skeptics we commend the following extract from the organ of the American Missionary Association:

A VALIANT NEGRO SOLDIER

Dislodging a Spanish Sharpshooter on the eight-mile march toward San Juan Hill.

141

"Never can the students of Talladega college forget the commencement of 1898, when so many brave men left their cherished plans to engage in the war with Spain. Those laughter-loving boys, earnest in study, but full of fun and careless sometimes, as boys will be —one hardly knew them when the war spirit rose and they stood in line with the new, steady light of resolution shining in their dark eyes. In 1860 young men of Anglo-Saxon blood left that same building to fight against the Union. One of those young men, now governor of the state, thirty-eight years later, telegraphs to the same school asking Negroes to defend the same government, and they cheerfully respond. Is not this a revolution of the wheel of time?

The governor's telegram came Wednesday, almost two weeks before commencement. All volunteers were prompt, having completed satisfactorily the work of the year with the exception of the closing exercises.

Thirty in all volunteered, three or four of whom were not students, a third of this number being unable to pass the severe physical test. A farewell meeting was held in the chapel, and the young soldiers told in stirring words the motives that led them to offer their lives to their country; their resolve to fight for the freedom of bleeding Cuba, their love of the Stars and Stripes in spite of the wrongs they themselves had suffered, their strong desire to show that Negroes could not only live and work, but die, like men. Many earnest appeals were made for prayers, that they might never turn their backs to their enemies, nor yield to the temptations of camp life. At last a quiet little woman with an earnest face arose and told in trembling tones her determination to go as nurse, if she could find an opportunity. She was called to the platform and it was beautiful to see the reverence with which the tall, young fellows gathered about her.

Talladega college had reason to be proud of her sons as they marched to the station with a flag and a band, and went off with a ringing cheer. Nor were her daughters wanting; their hearts were aching, but their faces dressed in smiles as they sent their brothers away as patriotically as those of fairer hue.

The Talladega students have not been permitted to meet any Spaniards in battle, but their record in camp at Mobile has been true to their promises. They have shown to every one the advantage of education. Their officers prize them highly, and the rough, ignorant men who are their comrades, have felt their influence, so that the governor has publicly commended their behavior.''

Commenting on the above, the writer says:

''Probably no institution in the East sent as large a percentage of student soldiers to bear the flag of our common country to victory as did our missionary schools. Our students have not been taught that war is glory. It was conscience with them. They went as deliverers from oppression and saw their opportunity to prove their devotion and gratitude to the country for their own deliverance. They have made their record.''

Surely this is very refreshing, especially just now when a certain class of persons are endeavoring to deprecate Negro education, or at least to confine it to manual training, as best suited to the sphere in which he is to move, a proposition, we may add, as absurd as any that could be propounded by enlightened men living under a republican form of government. Von Moltke attributed his success at Sadowa to the influence of the Prussian schoolmaster, and Wellington thought that the battle of Waterloo was first won on the cricket field at Rugby.   Evidently a machine is a good thing, but a thinking machine is better.   What the Negro needs is thought power, and that kind of education which will develop this power in him will fit him not only for the best mechanic, but for the best soldier and most efficient citizen.

In closing this chapter we would add that we have by no means exhausted the evidence in favor of the Negro soldier; but have presented enough to show that he has won universal admiration and respect, and is entitled to the generous consideration and gratitude of the whole country.

TRUCK TRAIN OF THE 365TH INFANTRY UNLOADING TROOPS AT
BRUYERES, VOSGES, FRANCE.

DELEGATES TO THE REPUBLICAN NATIONAL CONVENTION, JUNE, 1920.
Left to Right—Dr. W. J. Higgins, Providence, R. I.; M. H. Davis, Lewiston, Idaho; Walter L. Cohen, New Orleans, La. Mr. Cohen was chairman of the Louisiana delegates.

(C) U. & U.

10

DR. V. CONRAD VINCENT-SURGEON, WHO HAS RECENTLY MADE VALUABLE
CONTRIBUTIONS IN HIS CHOSEN FIELD.

(C) C. M. Battey.

CHAPTER VIII.

No history of the Negro could be complete without some word regarding his record in the European War.

A Wonderful Heritage.—Starting with the Boston Massacre, there is Lake Erie, Lexington, Fort Wagner, Milliken Bend, Port Hudson, Santiago, Carrizil and countless others all through the list. With such a record to fall back on, is it any wonder that the world waited confidently for the race to meet the supreme test? Has a Negro ever been convicted of disloyalty, sedition, or conspiracy with the enemy?

The Slate Is Clean.—Prejudice, discrimination, unfairness, even brutality there has been in dealing with the Negro both in peace and in war. But in spite of the handicap, the American Negro has as much right to be proud of his showing on the battlefields of the world as any other nation or people on earth.

A Brief Outline.—It is not our purpose or desire to render a detailed account of Negroes' war work. We will try merely to present some of the most important facts and figures in their relationship to the entire conflict.

In the Same Way we shall endeavor to pass over the unalterable fact that our boys gave their all to make the world safe for democracy, even when the fundamental rights of democracy were denied them in their own land.

We Can Never Forget the organized propaganda of prejudice against us, the unfair segregation of both officers and men, the dirty, underhanded methods of dis-

147

THE FAMOUS FIGHTING TENTH CAVALRY IN MARCHING ORDER. A PART
OF THE AMERICAN EXPEDITIONARY FORCES IN MEXICO.

325TH FIELD SIGNAL BATTALION STRINGING WIRE ON THE MARNE.

17TH PROVISIONAL RESERVE OFFICERS TRAINING REGIMENT, FORT DES MOINES, IOWA. JULY 28, 1917, COL. C. C. BALLOU COMMANDING.

crimination, or the lies about us. We do not forget, but we would far rather remember that France welcomed us as men and equals, that we did our plain duty as we saw it, and that the whole world honors us for it.

The Black Colonials.—Germany was whipped at the first battle of the Marne—and beaten by Negroes. Two hundred and eighty thousand black Senegalese *volunteers* blocked the passing of the Marne and the Ourcq. Then there were over 30,000 blacks from the Congo in the Belgian army, and at least 20,000 West Indians with the British. German Africa was taken by thousands of black warriors.

But We Are More interested in the American Negro. Two hundred thousand of them went overseas with the American Expeditionary Forces.

Stevedores.—Of this number about 150,000 were stevedores or laborers, carrying on in the S. O. S. under unbelievable circumstances. They were Jim Crowed as to food, clothing and housing; worked like dogs, insulted, even beaten; they built roads, hewed logs, worked as section hands, moved freight, often twelve to fifteen hours per day.

Think of a body of men working honestly and faithfully under these trying conditions and you will know what manner of men they were. Even the Y. M. C. A.'s were subject to Jim Crow regulations to avoid fraternizing between black and white.

NEGRO OFFICERS.

The 17th Provisional R. O. T. C. was organized at Fort Des Moines, Iowa, in June, 1917, with 1,200 educated Negroes drawn from every section of the country. Of this number 639 were given commissions and assigned to train the colored men in the draft. There were 106

LEFT—BERT WILLIAMS, WORLD FAMOUS COMEDIAN.
RIGHT—COL. WILLIAM HAYWARD.

MOMENTS WHICH LIVE FOREVER IN THE MEMORY
OF MAN.

LIBRARY - Allegheny Campus

UNITED STATES FLAG AND 369TH REGIMENTAL COLORS AFTER DECORATION WITH THE CROIX DE GUERRE, DECEMBER 11, 1918.

captains, 329 first lieutenants and 204 second lieutenants. The rank of captain was the highest given.

The Color Question.—Naturally the status of colored officers came up, but in most cases they were received on a basis of complete equality commensurate with their rank.

White or Colored Officers.—There seems to be little doubt but that the colored troops fought best under the leadership of Negro officers. We cite the case of the 370th Inf. under Negro officers, the 371st under white officers, and the 372d and 369th under both black and white. The record of the 370th Inf. stands out more conspicuously than any of the others.

Colonel Charles Young.—Here was a Negro officer worthy of leading an entire division of his own troops. One of the three colored graduates of West Point, he was denied the opportunity of participating in the World War for democracy. At the beginning of the war he was put on the inactive list, despite the fact that he rode over five hundred miles on horseback from Ohio to Washington in an effort to convince the War Department of his fitness for military duty.

NEGRO COMBAT TROOPS.

The 92d.—In the spring of 1918 when the German drive menaced Paris and the whole world waited in an agony of suspense for America to prepare, the call came from Pershing for the 92d Division. No one could doubt its readiness. They went through embarkation, debarkation, training areas, quiet sectors, and never had a real chance until the end of the war. In spite of every conceivable difficulty in France, no other American division has a better record.

COL. WILLIAM HAYWARD COMMANDING 369TH INFANTRY. SENDING
A MESSAGE BY CARRRIER PIGEON.

THE OLD 15TH NEW YORK, ONLY COLORED REGIMENT ON THE
SKIRMISH LINE.

NEGRO RED CROSS NURSES MARCHING DOWN FIFTH AVENUE, NEW YORK, IN GREAT RED CROSS PARADE.
(C) U. & U.

The 93d Division.—This division never functioned as a complete unit, but was for the most part brigaded with the French. The men fought splendidly in the Champagne and Argonne, and were highly praised by the French. For instance, the 370th Regiment received more citations for bravery than any other American regiment on the field of battle; this, mind you, under leadership of colored officers.

SUPPLEMENTARY WAR WORKS.

Negro Women in the War.—An entire book could be written about the Negro woman's enthusiastic service in the emergency of war, how she overcame the race problem by sheer patriotism, how the colored hostess houses and rest rooms were established. Statistics show that she did far more than her share in Red Cross and Y. M. C. A. work, Liberty Loan Drives and important work in war industries. She shut her eyes to past wrongs and present discomforts, and did her best to make the world a better place to live in.

The Y. M. C. A.—It was not until a colored man was put in charge of Negro Y. M. C. A. work that this organization ever did anything for the Negro troops. Even then sufficient secretaries and materials were not furnished to make the work effective. The color line was strongly drawn by all white secretaries, and colored troops were refused the privileges of the huts.

The Knights of Columbus.—Take, on the other hand, the Knights of Columbus, while they did maintain separate huts in various camps, never raised the color question. This organization was highly spoken of for its work, both at home and abroad, by members of Negro units.

COLORED SOLDIERS WHO HAVE BEEN WOUNDED AND ARE NOW CON-
VALESCING AT BASE HOSPITAL NO. 3, NEW YORK CITY.

THE LATE LIEUT. "JIMMIE" EUROPE AND HIS FAMOUS "15TH" JAZZ
BAND SNAPPED ON THEIR TRIUMPHANT RETURN TO NEW YORK.

Here is the Record in Black and White:

Number of Negroes registered.........2,290,527
Number of Negroes examined......... 458,838
Number of Negroes inducted.......... 367,710
Number of Negroes accepted for full
military service 342,277
Number of Negro soldiers mobilized in-
cluding regular army units.......... 380,000
Number of combat troops overseas..... 42,000
Number of divisions sent to France.... 2

The following number of Negro organizations other than combat troops served across the seas:

Engineer Service Battalions................ 46
Labor Battalions 44
Labor Companies 24
Pioneer Infantry Regiments............... 15
Stevedore Regiments 3
Stevedore Battalions 2
Butchery Companies 2

Decorations, Citations and Awards for Bravery.— Four complete Negro infantry regiments and one whole battalion were awarded the Croix de Guerre by the French government as a reward for gallantry in action. They are the 369th, 370th, 371st, 372d, and the 1st Battalion of the 367th Regiment.

Privates Roberts and Johnson.— Two Negro warriors, Privates Henry Johnson and Needham Roberts, were the first American soldiers to be awarded the Croix de Guerre in France.

Our Colored Heroes Cited for Bravery in Battle.— The following members of the colored officers and men were decorated individually for bravery in action while members of the American Expeditionary Forces:

WATCHING A GERMAN AIRPLANE AT MESS TIME.

COLORED SOLDIERS IN THE TRENCHES UNDER BATTLE CONDITIONS.

325th Field Signal Battalion.............   2
349th Field Artillery...................   5
350th M. G. Battalion..................   1
351st M. G. Battalion.................   1
365th Infantry   26
366th Infantry   40
367th Infantry...........Entire 1st Battalion
368th Infantry   14
369th Infantry   120
370th Infantry   83
371st Infantry   85
372d Infantry   102

Other Officers.—In addition to the 639 officers who were commissioned at Fort Des Moines, in 1917, we find a record of the following other Negro officers:

Chaplains   60
Commissioned later, infantry............   107
Commissioned later, artillery............   33
Medical officers   125

SOME TRIBUTES TO THE HEROIC PATRIOTISM OF THE NEGRO.

President Woodrow Wilson issued a special memorandum in which he paid tribute to the loyalty and fidelity of the colored Americans.

Honorable Newton D. Baker, Secretary of War, said: "The Negro soldiers in the service of their country proved faithful and efficient, and will uphold the traditions of their race."

General John J. Pershing, Commander in Chief of the American Expeditionary Forces, is quoted as follows: "I cannot commend too highly the spirit shown among the colored combat troops, who exhibit fine

GENERAL HOFFMAN AND STAFF OUTSIDE OF 93D DIVISION HEAD-
QUARTERS IN FRANCE.

BAPTIZING NEGRO SOLDIERS AT CAMP GORDON.

capacity for quick training and eagerness for the most dangerous work."

The Late Theodore Roosevelt said in his last public appearance: "Had I been permitted to raise troops to go on the other side, I should have asked permission to raise two colored regiments. I had intended to offer Colonel Charles Young the leadership of one regiment, telling him I expected him to choose only colored officers."

Colonel C. E. Goodwyn, in charge of the largest colored stevedore camp in France, said on relinquishing his command: "I will always cherish a loving memory of the men of this wonderful organization which I have had the honor and privilege to command."

"**The Negro Race** in the United States is loyal to the core. There is a Negro loyalty which is one of the finest traits of the race."—*St. Louis Globe Democrat.*

"The black man stood pat and fought the good fight." —*Houston Post.*

"The loyalty of the colored citizens has never been in doubt."—*Secretary of State Daniels.*

From Congress.—"It gives me pleasure to place upon the enduring records of the Government this brief but true and deserved tribute to the loyalty, fidelity and patriotism of the colored citizen of America."—*Hon. R. W. Austin of Tennessee on the floor of the House of Representatives.*

The Mayor of Pittsburgh, Pa., issued a proclamation on the return of the 351st F. A., from which we quote in part: "When President Wilson issued his appeal calling on the people of the United States to rally to the support of Old Glory, none was more spontaneous than the response from the colored people of the nation. By their deeds they have written their names in golden letters in history."

THE 368TH INFANTRY ADVANCING ON A CAMOUFLAGED ROAD NEAR BINARVILLE, FRANCE.

ONE OF THE FIRST AMERICAN PRISONERS IN A GERMAN PRISON CAMP. NOTE THE CHARACTERISTIC GOOD HUMOR IN A DESPERATE SITUATION.

The Chief Engineer.—The following letter was sent to the 805th Pioneer Regiment: "The chief engineer desires to express the highest appreciation to you and to your regiment for the services rendered to the first army in the offensive between the Meuse and the Argonne, starting September 26th, and the continuation of that offensive on November 1st, and concluding with the armistice on November 11th. The success of the operation was in no small measure made possible by the excellent work of your troops."

Mayor General Bell said at Camp Upton of the Buffaloes: "I would lead you into battle against any army in the world."

Colonel Moss, a Southerner by birth, said: "If properly trained and instructed, the colored man makes as good a soldier as the world has ever seen."

Provost Marshal General Crowder said in his report of the draft: "One of the brightest chapters in the whole history of the war is the Negro's eager acceptance of the draft, and the small number of them claiming exemption. Thirty-one per cent of registered Negroes were accepted for full military service as against only twenty-five per cent of whites."

NEGRO LOVE FOR THE UNITED STATES.

Roscoe Conkling Simmons, nephew of the late Booker T. Washington, and one of the most forceful leaders of the race, has this to say of Negro loyalty: "We have a record to defend, but no treason, thank God, to atone or explain. While in chains we fought to free white men—from Lexington to Carrizal—and returned again to our chains. No Negro has ever insulted the flag. No Negro ever struck down a President of these United States. No Negro ever sold a military

SHOWING HOW OUR HEROES WERE EQUIPPED TO
MAKE BIRD'S-EYE MAPS AND PHOTOGRAPHS.

map or secret to a foreign government. No Negro ever
ran under fire or lost an opportunity to serve, to fight,
to bleed and to die in the republic's cause. Accuse us
of what you will—justly and wrongly—no man can point
to a single instance of our disloyalty.

"We have but one country and one flag, the flag that
set us free. Its language is our only tongue, and no
hyphen bridges or qualifies our loyalty. Today the
nation faces danger from a foreign foe, treason stalks
and skulks up and down our land. In dark councils
intrigue is being hatched. I am a republican, but a

Wilson republican. Woodrow Wilson is my leader. What he commands me to do I shall do. Where he commands me to go I shall go. If he calls me to the colors, I shall not ask whether my colonel is black or white. I shall be there to pick out no color except the white of the enemy's eye. Grievances I have against this people, against this Government. Injustice to me there is, bad laws there are upon the statute books, but in this hour of peril I forget—and you must forget—all thoughts of self, or race, or creed, or politics, or color. That, boys, is loyalty."

CHAPTER IX.

Some Fair Questions.—Why are the Negroes coming North? How long has the movement been on foot? What are the reasons? Where will it end? What effect did the World War have on this migration?

Knowledge Is Power.—The modern Negro wants to KNOW. He isn't satisfied with the bare statement of facts and conditions. The days when the Negro as a race left his thinking to the white man are past, and let us hope forever. Here, then, is an attempt to throw some light on many of these perplexing questions.

The Beginning.—The real migration of the Negro from the South to the North began as early as 1815, when some states in the North voluntarily abolished slavery. These states became a haven of refuge for oppressed Negroes in the South. In 1810, five years before this time, there were only 102,137 Negroes in the North.

In Spite of the Handicap.—The North at first did not grant the Negro a hearty welcome. His lot was very much like that of a fugitive from justice. The Quakers of North Carolina and Virginia were the first people to make it easy for the slaves to reach free territory. They had long since freed their own slaves, and had become known as the FRIENDS OF ALL HUMANITY by their brotherly attitude.

The Indiana Settlement.—In 1822, at a meeting of North Carolina Quakers, territory now composing the States of Illinois, Indiana and Ohio was selected as most suitable for black colonization, and Negroes were

LEFT TO RIGHT—MR. JULIUS ROSENWALD; WARREN LOGAN, TREASURER,
TUSKEGEE INSTITUTE; THEODORE ROOSEVELT; EMMETT J. SCOTT; E. T.
ATWELL, SECRETARY OF TUSKEGEE INSTITUTE.

(Photo by A. P. Bedou.)

sent there as fast as possible. This colony at once became well known, and served as the true beginning of the movement.

The Fugitive Slave Law.—This law did not interfere with the operation of the Underground Railroad, which grew out of this situation, until about 1850. Rich whites freed their slaves, sent them North, bought land for them, built schools, and provided opportunities to such an extent that the Negro settlements extended finally as far north as Detroit, Michigan.

The Detroit Colony.—Here, in 1860, there were more Negroes in the county than there were whites. Similar settlements sprang up all over Indiana, Ohio and Illinois. The colored people became prosperous and successful farmers. Their homes proved an asylum for fugitive, ill-treated blacks from the South, and thus both aided and promoted that migration which we have under discussion.

Canadian Migration.—Large numbers of colored people migrated in these days even beyond the territorial limits of the United States, through Detroit into Canada. It is of interest to note that in the year 1860 there were over 60,000 Negroes in Canada, 15,000 of whom were free born.

Physical Freedom vs. Economical Freedom.—It will be seen that in the exodus of Negroes before the Civil War, economic conditions did not matter. It was merely a question of liberty. Today those who leave the South do so largely for better jobs, more money, enlarged opportunities, etc.

There Is Alarm in the North as Well as in the South.—Thus began the great movement which in our day and age has become so extensive as to occasion alarm among thinking people throughout the country.

ROLAND W. HAYES, NOTED CONCERT ARTIST.

(C) Bachrach.

How some Negroes failed and some succeeded, how they were liked and disliked, aided and degraded, appears in another part of this history. The thing to remember is that they wanted certain things badly enough to go after them.

Migration in the Civil War.—We come now to the period of the Civil War. In the beginning, as the Union army advanced, the remaining slaves were driven away, freed, or turned back to their owners. Later on they were declared contraband of war and put to work building fortifications for the Union army. In this way slave labor was gradually drawn away from the Confederate forces. The freedmen were concentrated into camps, their own helplessness and a lack of care causing terrible suffering.

Reconstruction.—From 1865 to 1875 as many as 35,-000 Negroes followed the development of the railroad from Georgia and South Carolina to Arkansas and Texas. This same pioneering movement has continued slowly up until the present day.

Immediately After the War there was a return of intelligent, educated Northern Negroes to the South. They came back to carry on the work they had been compelled to give up. This accounts for the total disappearance, in some cases, of an entire Negro colony in the North.

In the Spring of 1879 over 5,000 blacks left Mississippi and Louisiana for the State of Kansas. This happened in spite of every effort on the part of the white population to stop it. They applied illegal methods, persuaded steamboat companies to refuse passage to the Negroes, and in some cases actually cowed the colored men into staying at home. That these measures failed is seen by the fact that in 1880 Kansas boasted of a

CLARENCE CAMERON WHITE, ONE OF THE GREATEST VIOLINISTS THE
RACE HAS EVER PRODUCED.

population of over 60,000 black men. Indian Territory
and other Western sections were invaded gradually.

The Negro in the Mines.—Labor agents at this time
approached the Southern Negro with invitations to come
to the mountain States for high wages at the mines.
That this movement was extensive is evidenced by the
fact that the Negro population in West Virginia, in 1870,
was only 17,000, as against 64,000 in 1910.

**Here Are the Real Reasons Why the Negro Left
the South:**

1.   Political Inequality.—America fought the War of
Independence among other reasons because of TAXA-
TION WITHOUT REPRESENTATION. In practically every State in the South, even where the Negro
pays the bulk of the taxes, he is legally or illegally denied
the right to vote.

2.   Discrimination.—Some Southern States actually
passed laws providing for involuntary servitude on the
part of the Negro population. A pernicious credit system made it necessary for him to borrow money from
white planters, who demanded that he work out the debt.

Lack of Educational Opportunities.—Negroes paid
the taxes to support the WHITE SCHOOLS.

Lynching.—Between the years 1866 and 1919 over
4,000 Negroes have been lynched in the South. Has
Germany any darker page in the history of her atrocities?

What Has Been the Result?—At one time in the history of our country the Negro made up over fifty per cent
of the population IN SIX SOUTHERN STATES. Today only Mississippi and South Carolina have a colored
population larger than the white. During the last ten
years almost every Southern State has had a greater
white increase in population in proportion to the black
increase. It is evident, therefore, that through his ex-

H. COLERIDGE-TAYLOR, SON OF THE LATE COLERIDGE TAYLOR, CONDUCT-ING A RECITAL OF HIS FATHER'S COMPOSITIONS BY THE CENTRAL LONDON CHORAL AND ORCHESTRAL SOCIETY, QUEEN'S HALL, LONDON

tensive migration the Negro has lost his one real opportunity for political supremacy.

During the World War.—The same conditions persuaded Negroes to leave the South during the World
War. Floods and the boll weevil in some cases caused
actual destitution among them. When on top of all this
the South was flooded with labor agents offering fabulous
opportunities for the laboring man in war industries, is
it any wonder that the colored man left his home for
the promised land? Of course the majority of Negroes
will remain in the South. For the first time in history
Southern people are really aroused to the danger of the
situation. They are promising reforms in their efforts to
prevent a labor shortage. It is evident, therefore, that
the movement will benefit not only those that leave, but
those that remain.

It has been said that the Negro as a class was restless,
dissatisfied, always wanting to be on the move. Facts
show that this is not the case. If the Negro had acquired the white man's wanderlust, his same spirit of
pioneering just a little sooner, he would today be in a
position to demand what our Constitution grants him:
life, liberty and the pursuit of happiness.

MRS. BOOKER T. WASHINGTON.

(C) C. M. Battey.

CHAPTER X.

CLUB WORK AMONG NEGRO WOMEN.

Written Expressly for this Work by Mrs. Booker T. Washington.

Until woman made up her mind that her efforts to help in the development of the world's work were not taken into account, there was nothing among us that could be rightly called organization.

Questions relating to the home, the church, the school and the State were all of vital interest to woman. She wanted her home pure and secure. She held the church as a bulwark against indecent living, immoral dishonesty, in favor of moral and spiritual growth and development. She wanted the schools built upon high ground, including in their curriculum lessons in manners, morals and living, as well as those of the three R's. She wanted a citizenship built upon freedom, not license, upon manly courage, and not brute force.

Woman was Interested in the World and its general policies and growth, but how to bring about the thing most desired was the question with her. She finally realized that if she were to be of real service to the country of which she is a part, she must organize her energies, her interest, and her powers, and almost immediately the National Suffrage Association, the National Temperance Association, the National Congress of Mothers, the National Council of Women, the National Federation of Women's Clubs, and other societies of more or less importance were thrown on the screen, and the world began to take notice.

The Colored Woman, like the others, was drifting on in a more or less indifferent way. She had not realized until then that her opportunities had been as great as those of other women: that in the struggle which women were making for recognition in the affairs of the world and men, that she was often not thought of at all. Her home was insecure, her hearthstone held lightly, except by her own immediate family. Her church held standards which she could not tolerate. Schools for her children were too often neglected. Teachers, with little or no education, with little fitness in certain other directions, were employed, and she came to know and to feel that in the citizenship of her State and country she counted little.

The Colored Woman is Conservative, and was slow to believe that she was not counted in; slow to realize that she could not hope to be taken into account, and to keep up with the pace that other women had set for themselves, unless she organized her efforts for social, moral, religious and educational growth, and so forced the world to become acquainted with her, and to see that she is at least interested in her own welfare, which carries with it an interest in the welfare of all other women.

The First National Meeting.—In 1895, in the city of Boston, Mass., was called the first National Body of Colored Women. The call was made by Mrs. Josephine Saint Pierre Ruffin, who had for many years been associated with Mrs. Julia Ward Howe, Susan B. Anthony, Elizabeth Cody Stanton, and other forward moving women, and from whom she had received the inspiration which led her to know and to feel that what one group of organized women could do another with equal chance could also do. For this equal chance Mrs. Ruffin knew all too well that the colored women would have to fight, not separately, but together.

The colored women in 1894 were suddenly awakened by the wholesale charges of the lack of virtue and character made by a Missouri editor in an open letter to an English lady who had manifested great interest in the colored race and in the colored women particularly. Although apparently heretofore quite willing to leave her fate in the hands of others, when they heard of it, instantly woke up to the situation and answered the call which Mrs. Ruffin made to her to come to Boston to appear in public, to plead her own cause, and to prove to all who wanted to know, to all who were willing to learn, to all who had not already made up their minds against her, and there were hundreds of these, not only in the South, but everywhere in the North, who up to date had not had the chance to know anything whatsoever as to the aspirations of the colored women who were their next door neighbors.

Present Membership is 300,000.—So began the American colored women to organize, so came into shape the National Association of Colored Women's Clubs, which now has a membership of over 300,000 women located in every State in the country, including Canada, Liberia, Hayti and Cuba.

Mrs. Josephine St. Pierre Ruffin will live always in the hearts of her women as the pioneer who pointed the way for independent self-development through organization.

Mrs. Booker T. Washington was elected the first president and the association under the leadership of Mrs. Mary Church Terrell, Miss Elizabeth Carter, Mrs. J. Siloame Yates, Mrs. Mary B. Talbert, Miss Lucy B. Thurman, and a host of other strong, fine women, such as Mrs. Josephine Bruce, Mrs. Nettie Langston Napier, Miss Cornelia Bowen, Miss Nannie Burroughs, Miss

1. Mrs. Mary B. Talbert, President National Assn.
2. P. Bruneau.　　　　　3. Mrs. J. Salone Yates.
4. Mrs. Josephine St. P. Ruffin.

Mary Jackson, Mrs. Charlotte Hawkins Brown, who stand ready always to carry the plans laid down by the association; has been able not only to change public opinion in favor of the colored women, but it has changed the colored woman's opinion of herself, her ability to do things, her strength to fortify herself against difficulties, which is a far more important thing.

Mrs. Mary B. Talbert, of Buffalo, N. Y., is now the presiding officer of the association, and during the past few years, under her administration, great strides in civic improvement, in the education of women in general, have been made. Mrs. Talbert has to her credit a piece of work which stands out most prominently: the lifting of the mortgage upon the home of Mr. Frederick Douglass at Anacostia, in the District of Columbia. The mortgage was in the neighborhood of five thousand dollars. Mrs. Talbert raised this money by traveling and speaking in various cities under the auspices of the club women who rallied to her appeal in the finest sort of way.

The Home of Mr. Douglass is now the property of the National Association of Colored Women, and will be used as a memorial to the memory of Mr. Douglass in the same sense, and with the same veneration, as is true of Mt. Vernon, set aside by the national Government as a monument to George Washington, the father of our country.

One aim of the colored club women is to teach race pride, race independence; and the purchase of this home, so long occupied by our great leader, Mr. Douglass, and its permanent maintenance, is a great step in achieving this end; and if our national president does not accomplish anything else, she has done enough by this one effort to put every other woman in the race in her debt all the years that are to come.

Mrs. Rosetta Sprague, the only daughter of Mr. Douglass, during her life was a leading spirit in the club work in the city of Washington, and it was the love and gratitude which the women held for Mrs. Sprague, as well as that they were anxious to show their regard for · her father, that made them respond in this practical manner toward this memorial.

Works Through Departments.—The national association does its work through departments, and these carry on the work through individual clubs. The leading departments are: Woman Suffrage, Patriotism, Education, Conditions in Rural Life, Music, Literature and Art, Gainful Occupation and Business, Better Railroad Conditions, Mothers' Meetings and Night Schools, Health Conditions, Child Welfare and Public Speaking, etc.

The School Question.—How many people realize that even today in many parts of the country the school term for the colored child is not more than four months in a year? How many people in making up their opinion as to the colored woman and her people stop to consider in their comparison that the children with whom the study is made are in school often ten months in the year, and that such conditions are unfair and un-American, and sooner or later colored children, not being given a square deal for growth and all around citizenship, will become a menace and a burden to the community in which they live? No question today is of so vital an interest to the colored woman's club as this one which deals with the schools and the general educational advantages for their children and those of their sister club workers.

The Department of Education has been the one most thoroughly organized because it is that upon which all others are obliged to depend for growth. Our pioneer

MISS CLEOTA J. COLLINS, NOTED LYRIC SOPRANO OF COLUMBUS, OHIO.

women were amongst the chosen of the earth, and at the head stand the following:

Frances Ellen Watkins Harper, Mary A. Shadd, Fanny Jackson Coppin and Charlotte Fortem Grimke, long since numbered with those who have passed into the beyond. They will always be remembered as pioneers in the education of the children of their own race.

Mrs. Harper visited every Southern State, speaking in colleges, schools, churches, and even going from home to home, on the subject of Education, Temperance, Homemaking, Honesty, Morality, and all that went to make up an intelligent citizenship. She was most deeply interested in her women and held many meetings exclusively for them.

Mrs. Harper was the first superintendent of colored workers of the Woman's Christian Temperance Union. She was one of the directors of the Women's Congress of the United States, and so was doubly fitted to help her own women in the higher ideals of living.

The following lines indicate the faith Mrs. Harper had in the future of the success of her race:

> "There is light beyond the darkness,
>   Joy beyond the present pain;
> There is hope in God's great justice
>   And the Negro's rising brain.
> Tho' the morning seems to linger
>   O'er the hilltops far away,
> Yet the shadows bear the promise
>   Of a brighter coming day."

Mrs. Fanny Jackson Coppin was a native of the District of Columbia. She received her training at Oberlin, Ohio. Immediately after her graduation she went to Philadelphia, Pa., and organized what is now known as the Cheyney Training School for Teachers, which institute was presided over by her for nearly thirty years, and was then known as the Institute for Colored Youth.

Mrs. Coppin was an early advocate of industrial education, and made it an important item in building up that institution.

No woman in any race has been a greater credit to its standards of education than has Mrs. Coppin to her race. Her executive ability was recognized by both men and women of prominence as being far above the ordinary, and hundreds of young colored men and women all over the country, South as well as North, call her blessed because she inspired them for an education and to higher ideals of living.

Dorothy H. Greene.—In these later days one does not as often find women willing to consecrate themselves so absolutely to the great cause of education as the three mentioned above, but here, in our midst recently, I came upon a woman who can certainly be classed with the most devoted of teachers, Dorothy H. Greene she is called; a graduate of Selma University.

Miss Greene is a great lover of children, the smaller the better, the poorer the more she loves them. The first year after her graduation she was employed at her Alma Mater. This in itself is an indication of her superiority as a young woman.

Miss Greene was not long in discovering that at the university she was helping and teaching only the children of the well to do, and at the end of the first year she gave up the comforts at the university and went into a most neglected district of a large Southern city, a neighborhood where mothers were so poor that they were obliged to leave their little ones daily and go out to either help make the bread they ate, or to make it entirely.

There can be no more inspiring sight than to see this

good woman, still young, giving up herself absolutely to the care, not only of the minds of these children undeɪ her care, but to their bodies also.   They have little or no other care except as she gives it.

Tribute to White Club Workers.—Dorothy   Greene attributes much of her success to the kindness of two helpfully sympathetic white club women of the city in which she works; and here let us pay our gratitude to many white club women all over the country who stand ready to co-operate with us in every good cause of our educational advancement.

The following shows in what esteem one well known white person, at least, holds our work: "Of all the conventions that have met in the country this summer, there is none that has taken hold of the business in hand with more good sense and judgment than the National Federation of Colored Women's Clubs now assembled in this city (Chicago).   The subjects brought up, the matter of their treatment, and the decisions reached exhibit wide and appreciative knowledge of problems confronting the colored people," and so makes it possible for us to take courage and to press forward as women having our own cause to fight not entirely alone.

Many women in the South, with their friends, and often in the North, are inclined to mistrust the interests of their Northern club sisters, but there are many whose efforts cannot be doubted for one moment, for from the very beginning of our career as organized club workers, which was really begun by a Northern woman and aided largely for years by others, certain Northern women have stood always bravely in the front.   Miss Maria Baldwin, Miss Lucy E. Moten, Miss Elizabeth Carter, Miss Mary Jackson, and a host of others who have had great opportunity for education and leadership, have never tired of working to bring our cause before the country and to insist upon the recognition of other colored women less fortunate than themselves.

"Master" Baldwin.—Miss Baldwin was born and educated in Cambridge, Mass.   In 1882 she was given a position as grade teacher in the public schools of her home city.   For seven years she did her duty as a teacher faithfully and well, and was then made principal, and for nearly thirty-five years Miss Baldwin's position as principal of one of the largest and most influential schools in Cambridge has been unquestioned.

Four years ago the Agassiz was torn down and a building costing in the neighborhood of $60,000 was put in its place.   Miss Baldwin still held her position, and was then known as "Master Baldwin."   There is one other woman master in the Cambridge schools.   This is a position of more than ordinary distinction.   Her school is attended by children of the most advanced families of Cambridge, including those of Harvard professors. Twelve teachers worked under Principal Baldwin, and more than four hundred boys and girls attended daily up to the time of her sudden death on January 9, 1922.

The Massachusetts school's principal did her work so well that it has led the authorities in that State, and in other Northern States, to appoint many colored women in the schools of the North and to give them the recognition their training deserves.

Miss Baldwin was a lecturer also of no mean ability. She was the first woman of any race to give the annual Washington's Birthday memorial address before the Brooklyn, N. Y., Institute.   Her subject was "The Life and Service of the late Harriet Beecher Stowe."

The Brooklyn *Eagle* commented in the following manner upon the address: "She is a type quite as extraordinary in one way as Booker T Washington is in another. Her English is pure and felicitous, her manner reposeful, and her thoughts and sympathies strong and deep, etc."

Miss Elizabeth E. Carter, of New Bedford, Mass., has for years been the only colored teacher in the public schools of that city, and has been one of the most honored of teachers. The past year she resigned her position to take up Y. W. C. A. work in the city of Washington, D. C.

Miss Carter was for years the recording secretary of the national association, and to her credit is now a very accurate statement of work done by the organization and its individual clubs.

Miss Carter early organized the women in the northeastern districts, and so well has she led the women throughout that part of the country that, although for the past two years she has been living in the District of Columbia doing Y. W. C. A. work, they have borne her expenses back and forth to New Bedford, Mass., once every month, so that they might still have her counsel and the inspiration which comes from her presence.

In her part of the country Miss Carter took a deep interest in the large number of women and their husbands and children who went up from the South two or three years ago to seek better living conditions. The club women under her leadership went in person to officials everywhere and secured better homes for these people, more provision in the school for their children.

Miss Carter is the organizer and head of one of the best equipped and well conducted old folks' homes now represented in the National Association of Clubs.

She was for four years the president of the association, and during her administration the women of the

North and South were cemented as never before. We all came to feel that our cause was not sectional, but one big, strong fight of an undivided citizenship.

Lucy H. Moten.—In the early years of our work Miss Lucy H. Moten was making her home in the city of Washington, D. C. Mrs. Cook of that city had many years before carried on work for and with women. There was a chain of a dozen or more clubs which did much of the charitable work of the district. Miss Moten was working in this chain as an individual much of the time. She had by force of character and effort graduated from the Normal School at Salem, Mass.

Soon after returning to Washington from school she was made principal of what was known as the Miner Normal School. Miss Moten assumed the position in the face of the opposition of her own friends. This school is the outgrowth of a work begun before the war by a young white woman who gave up social life and worked continuously through the war times and even afterwards so that we might have the advantages of training, and finally take our place in the world's affairs.

The Miner Normal School has, under Miss Moten, added to its course of study, has grown from two teachers to twelve or fifteen. The enrollment when Miss Moten began the work was the unlucky number thirteen. It is now nearly two hundred. Hundreds of young women all over the country owe their success as teachers to the strong determination of Miss Moten, to make the courses for teachers in her school just as efficient and broad as those in the very best schools of the country.

Tribute to the "Friends."—Here we want to pay tribute to the consecrated efforts of a white woman in the interest of her sisters in black, and particularly to the people called "Friends" scattered throughout the North, who were amongst the very first white people of the country to give of their money, their strength, and even their very lives toward helping the colored people out of the darkness into the light. They stand even today at the head of the list in sympathetic interest and co-operation in all that makes for the highest and best development of a race behind in the race of life because of its late starting.

Mrs. Lucy Thurman.—The Woman's Christian Temperance Union was the early light for us. Mrs. Lucy Thurman, of Jackson, Mich., was appointed by Frances Willard as the second colored woman in charge of the department for colored work in the W. C. T. U., and for twenty years Mrs. Thurman was held in the highest esteem by Miss Willard and her associates because of her good sense and tact in handling a situation often delicate and difficult.

Mrs. Thurman lived in Jackson, Mich., but there is scarcely a hamlet anywhere in the South where she is not now remembered, even though she has passed into the beyond. The women in her city were organized under her inspiration. She was a platform speaker of great personality and force, not only when she spoke on the exciting question of temperance, but also when she advised organization, getting together, standing firmly together for home life, for church life, for school, and finally for our position as women to be reckoned with in the great advance which women everywhere are making.

Mrs. Thurman was at one time our national president, serving one term only, but she drew all women to her, and it often appeared as she stood pleading our cause that she was saying as the Master Himself said: "And I, if I be lifted up, will draw all men unto Me."

1. MARY CHURCH TERRELL.   3. MRS. SYLVANIA F. WILLIAMS.
2. CHARLOTTE HAWKINS BROWN.   4. MRS. JOSEPHINE B. BRUCE.

Mrs. Thurman was a most religious woman, and we who stood by her side and worked with her were often put to shame by her faith in the final justice of man and in the everlasting condemnation by the Father of us all, for the man farthest up who would discredit the one farthest down.

Associated with Mrs. Thurman in her work throughout the country were Mrs. Helen Cook, of Washington, D. C., and Mrs. Elizabeth McCoy, of Detroit, Mich. Mrs. McCoy was the founder of the Detroit Old Folks' Home and was for many years the president of the Society of Willing Workers. This club was the pioneer club of the colored women of the State of Michigan, and perhaps nowhere have we as women found a cleaner atmosphere for advancement than in the home State of Mrs. Thurman, largely because of her fine and noble spirit, her lack of bitterness and her strong Christian spirit of hope, and her abiding faith in one man and woman toward other men and women.

The National Association.—Out of these beginnings came our National Association of Colored Women's Clubs, which is to us what the general federation of white women's clubs is to them. The names were the same at first, but people got us mixed so often that we finally decided to call our federation an association.

A large group of women stand out in the forefront in no small way as leaders in this forward and progressive field of the colored woman's organized efforts in her own behalf—Mrs. Josephine St. Pierre Ruffin, of Boston, Mass., who called the first national gathering of colored women; Mrs. Mary Church Terrell, of Washington, D. C.; the late Mrs. J. Siloame Yates, of Kansas City, Mo.; Miss Elizabeth Carter, of New Bedford, Mass.; the late Mrs. Lucy Thurman, of Jackson, Mich; Mrs. Mary B.

Talbert, of Buffalo, N. Y., our present leader; Mrs. Nettie Langston Napier, of Nashville, Tenn.; Mrs. Mary E. Steward, of Louisville, Ky.; Mrs. Mary Josenberger, of Fort Smith, Ark.; Mrs. Mary Bethune, of Daytona, Fla.; and hundreds of others whose names cannot be mentioned in a short article of this nature.

Six of these women have held the position of presiding officers, and to them and to their followers belong the honor of our present standing and success in club circles.

Colored women's clubs do their work through departments, because we feel that in this way much more effective work may be done. Our various interests are expressed in the Departments of Suffrage, Anti-Lynching, Mothers' Meetings, Education, Railroad Travel, the Country Woman's Position, Health, Business, Literature and Art, Night Schools, etc.

We work in co-operation with all other movements of both men and women of the race: the National Association for the Advancement of Colored People, the Urban League, the Negro Business Men's League, and we lay our plans along the general lines of advance as those of the General Federation of White Women's Clubs, leaving out, of course, their highly social side and paying immediate attention to the more practical and needful things of our homes and civic life as circumstances in our country force upon us.

Suffrage.— Colored women, quite as much as colored men, realize that if there is ever to be equal justice and fair play in the protection in the courts everywhere for all races, then there must be an equal chance for all women as well as men to express their preference through their votes. There are certain things so sure to come our way that time in arguing them is not well spent. It is

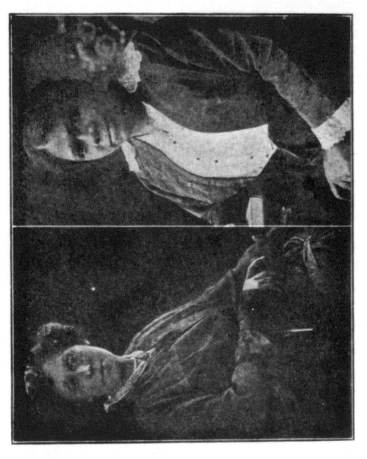

EVA D. BOWLES.

MARY MCLEOD BETHUNE.

simply the cause of right which in the end always conquers, no matter how fierce the opposition. Personally, woman suffrage has never kept me awake at night, but I am sure before this country is able to take its place amongst the great democratic nations of the earth it has got to come to the place where it is willing to trust its citizens, black as well as white, women as well as men, to be loyal to their Government, to be willing to leave the carrying out of governmental offices to the intelligent part of the citizenship. Our Department of Suffrage conducts training classes in the Constitution of the country, and has given time to the study of all governmental affairs, so that women may be prepared to handle the vote intelligently and wisely when it comes to them. Thousands of our women vote in the Northern States where they live, and in no instance have they shown any disposition to assume control of affairs, nor have they presumed anything more than a desire to be counted as a citizen of a country where they are giving the best of themselves in building better homes, better schools, better churches, and finally better citizenship.

"**Anti Lynching.**"—Our club women work incessantly to help mould sentiment against lynching, and although it is a slow process, there is a strong and grow-. ing feeling against this form of punishment for any cause whatsoever.

The Georgia State Federation of White Women's Clubs in their last convention came out strongly in favor of law and order as against mob violence and lynching. When the Women's State Federation of other Southern States take a stand against this evil, the men in authority in these States will see that lynching is put down and not until then will it be done. It is woman's work now as always.

Not long after these women took this position a leading judge in that State gave to the jury this charge: "He who arrogates to himself the authority to enforce the law without the sanction of the law is an enemy to the law and to civilization. Any set of men who take upon themselves to punish a human being, whether they should be meted out the punishment which the outraged law would impose upon them, or whether they escape on account of a false public sentiment, will bear throughout their lives the mark of Cain upon their brows."

What a charge to a Georgia jury! The leading paper in that State, and one of the leading papers in the entire South, follows this charge in the following terms of warning: "If the evil of mob law is not stamped out by the law-abiding element of our population, the time is inevitably coming when the strong arm of the Federal Government will do what the State either fails or refuses to do by the exercise of its own power and jurisdiction." Lynching must cease in a State where there is a strong public sentiment against it, and women need only to keep up the fight.

Public sentiment for law and order, for decent living, is kept before the race by various devices of the clubs: Welfare Work, Traveler's Aid Work, Practical Mission, Protective League, Y. M. C. A. organizations, reform schools, rescue homes, and by small private schools.

Our clubs realize that to every question there is more than one side, and that we must advocate a sentiment amongst our own people for the sacredness of womanhood, for decent living, and for regard for law and order in the smallest detail; and so through our various departments we co-operate with all women toward bringing about that sentiment which will make us all happier and more useful to the community we serve.

Mrs. John Hope, of Atlanta, Ga., has been able in her club work to show that with the proper training in the homes, men's ideals will change.   She has conducted for years a club where women are taught how to direct the education of their boys and girls.   The white women in Atlanta have been of great service to Mrs. Hope in all of her work.

Mrs. Harris Barrett, now the president of the State Federation of Virginia, stands as the organizer and head of one of the finest pieces of club work done by any colored woman.   A farm of a hundred acres of land for $5,200 was purchased more than ten years ago.

So well and so unselfishly have Mrs. Barrett and her followers given themselves to the cause of the untrained, wayward and unfortunate girls of Virginia that the State at large, especially the white citizens, both men and women, have given every assistance in money, in time, and in practical sympathy and advice to these colored club women.

Here is a real home, and a real school, girls learning to care for a home, and going through the first four or eight grades required in the ordinary public schools of the State.

Two years ago these thirty girls raised thirty bushels of peas, sixty-five bushels of potatoes, fifty bushels of corn, whitewashed the trees on the place, the corn cribs, shells, barns, etc., built one hundred and fifty feet of walkway, one-fourth of a mile of roadway and graveled it, cleared forty acres of land of brush, put in posts for two hundred feet of fence, built five gates, cut ten cords of wood, put in flooring in a shed, built a hen house, and at the same time carried on their regular studies and did their daily tasks of homekeeping and homemaking.

Who can doubt that the majority of these young girls will be fully developed, trained and sustained to be wives and mothers of a wise and Christian type, who will give back to the State of Virginia, not in dollars and cents, but in real substantial character and living, every dollar spent upon them, and who will in the years of the future take the place of usefulness now held by Mrs. Barrett and her club followers.

The Mt. Meigs, Ala., Reformatory for Colored Boys is within a stone's throw of the capitol of the State. Fifteen years ago it was founded and carried for years by the women of the Alabama State Federation of Colored Women. There were forty or fifty small boys, now there are in the neighborhood of three hundred young boys, ranging from seven to sixteen years of age.

Four women stand out prominently in this work, Miss Cornelia Bowen, who for more than twelve years was the president of the federation, Mrs. Lillian Dungee, Chairman of the Building Committee, Mrs. Agnes Jenkins Lewis, the corresponding secretary, and Mrs. Irene Hudson, the present secretary.

Just now the Alabama Federation of Colored Women's Clubs is erecting a rescue home for small girls of the State. The foundation has been dug, the material has been laid down, and three thousand dollars to complete the building of it is in the bank.

White people in Alabama, both men and women in all the walks of life, from the highest State official, have helped in all this work, and are still co-operating with it in the finest spirit possible.

These are real schools for the children and not merely workhouses and houses of correction. The course of study for the Reformatory for Boys is made out by the State Superintendent of Education, and Alabama deserves the credit and honor which its colored citizens give it for the interest which it takes in developing that part of its youthful citizens most neglected through lack of parental care.

Club work amongst colored women has developed the women themselves and has led them into fields of usefulness which they would never have dared enter.

Mrs. Mary Bethune is now the president of the clubs in Florida. More than twelve years ago she went through the public schools of South Carolina, graduating from Scotia Seminary in North Carolina, and attended the Moody Bible Institute. She began a small work at Daytona, Fla., with only five small girls and not many more dollars.

She now controls more than twenty acres of land. There is just completed an auditorium costing $40,000. Mrs. Bethune has also been able to fit her school into the life of its community in a very definite way. More than a thousand patients have been cared for in her small but finely equipped hospital.

Mrs. Charlotte Hawkins Brown, one of the secretaries of the national association, came into the State of North Carolina and located at a little town ten miles from Greensboro—Sedalia, they call it.

The people were in debt, their homes were neglected, and the women were discouraged. This little woman went to work with the women of Sedalia. They caught her spirit and soon the entire community was made over— carefully dressed children entered the schoolroom; men and women begun to lift the burden of debt they had carried so long. The little community with its new school, its Sunday school, its church, etc., has taken on new life.

Mrs. Brown a few months ago was invited to speak before the most cultured white women's clubs in Greensboro, N. C.

Miss Cornelia Bowen, of Waugh, Ala., Miss Georgia Washington, of Mt. Meigs, Ala., Miss Nannie Burroughs, of Lincoln Heights, Washington, D. C., all owe their distinction to their long and useful affiliation with the club movement of their own women.

Miss Burroughs organized and conducts the only vocational school for colored women in the world.

She writes and speaks with about the same force and eloquence as she conducts her remarkable school.

Miss Burroughs originated the Negro Picture Calendar, a collection of pictures of homes and incidents in the lives of her people. Truly, it can be said of her, still a young woman, she has come from the bottom of the ladder, and with the spirit of our motto, "Lifting as she climbs," she is still going up.

Other fields than that of teaching, social uplift and welfare have been entered by our club women.

Mrs. Addie N. Dickerson, of Philadelphia, in charge of our Department of Law, is a notary public, and her sign hangs just below that of her husband, who is one of Philadelphia's best known lawyers. All of the law business of our association has been handled by Mrs. Dickerson. The State Federation of Pennsylvania, of which Mrs. Ruth Bennett is president, holds Mrs. Dickerson in high regard.

Miss Carlotte Ray was a graduate of Harvard University, and was the first colored woman lawyer. As early as 1872 Miss Ray had completed her course in law, giving to her sisters of lesser opportunity the advantages of her experience and training. She was with the association in all of its interests.

The business career of women, although not very large, has been developed through their contact with club life.

ANNIE M. POPE MALONE, WHO OWNS AND OPERATES A $50,000 FAC-
TORY AT ST. LOUIS, MO.

A half dozen, perhaps, of our women have done remarkably well in certain lines of business. The late Mrs. Sarah Walker, of Indianapolis and New York, Mrs. Annie Pope Malone, of St. Louis, Mo., Mrs. Maggie Walker, of Richmond, Va., and Mrs. Mary Josenberger, of Ft. Smith, Ark., are amongst the list.

Madame Walker, as she was known to her club friends, was, at her death, which occurred only a few months ago, worth a million dollars. She began her business, that of a beauty specialist, fourteen or fifteen years ago, with no capital worth speaking of. In fact, the first earnings with which to begin her work were made at the most ordinary work. Club women everywhere rallied to her, and she with her indomitable will and faith in herself went up the ladder by bounds.

Her real estate is valued at more than eight hundred thousand dollars, besides stocks and bonds. Her factory and laboratory at Indianapolis is said to be the most complete of its kind in the United States.

Madame Walker traveled in every State in the Union, also in Cuba, Panama and the West Indies. She carried the spirit of the club wherever she went. She was always a conspicuous personage at the national gatherings, and gave liberally to the work of the association.

She led in the contributions for the purchase of the Douglass home. She was truly a product of the club work.

Madame Walker established a school in Africa and provided for its upkeep. No woman loved her own race more than she did, and no one had such abiding faith in the final triumph of the womanhood of her race through its organized efforts.

Mrs. Malone is also a beauty specialist. She has her fifty thousand dollar factory in one of the best localities

PORO COLLEGE, THE $50,000 FACTORY OF MRS. A. M. MALONE AT ST. LOUIS, MO.

of the great city of St. Louis.   There are under her control in the factory more than a hundred women and girls.
The treatment of the scalp, manicuring, chiropody, making of wigs, dyeing hair, manufacturing hair, making
switches, all go to show the wonderful business sense of
this woman, and yet she is a most unassuming person.
She is greatly interested in the Y. W. C. A. of St. Louis.
She remembers the needy.   The club has found many a
woman who would otherwise not have found herself.

Mrs. Maggie Walker was first a school teacher, a
worker for women and an agent for the Women's Union,
then secretary-treasurer of a secret order, which position had been held by a man.   There were few members,
less than a thousand, and little or no money.

At the beginning of her career in this organization
there was less than fifty dollars belonging to the treasury,
with liabilities amounting to $400, and a paid up mem-
bership of less than a thousand members.   In less than
fifteen years the total assets of the order were $116,000,
all debts paid off, 5,694 death claims amounting to
$564,134.   This organization has a paid up capital of
over $50,000.   There is now a membership of men,
women and children of nearly 50,000.   There are nearly
ten thousand children in financial standing in the Juvenile
Department of this order.   The order had no assets;
at present its assets are $150,750.

Mrs. Walker is now the president of the St. Luke Bank.
She is president of the Council of Colored Women, a
leading spirit in the Virginia State Federation.   She is
a trustee of the Girls' Home at Peake, Va., and in every
way possible she lends a strong hand to the woman and
girl waiting to be shown the way.

Mrs. Walker was for years the head of the Business
Department of our association.

ST. LUKE PENNY SAVINGS BANK—MISS MAGGIE L. WALKER, PRESIDENT, AND OFFICERS AT WINDOW.

Mrs. Josenberger, for many years a successful teacher in Ft. Smith, Ark., is a graduate of Fisk University. She is now easily worth $40,000, being an undertaker of no small ability. She owns and controls two large buildings in which she carries on her business.

Mrs. Josenberger leads in the club life throughout the entire State of Arkansas. She is their vice-president; she is now chairman of the Peace Committee of the national association, and is now conducting our business department.

Mrs. Josenberger gives her association with club work as the impetus to all the steps of progress she has ever made.

Mother's Meetings.—The writer of this article has conducted her mother's meetings for twenty years in the village nearest her.

The first day of the class there were five women, today there are more than a thousand, and few are able to read or write their names, but all are wise enough to realize that better mothers are an absolute necessity for better girls and boys of the future. Proper food and dress for the child, orderly and separate sleeping quarters for girls and boys, better bathing facilities for the family for the decent conduct and health of the household. Rights of children for recreation and play, mother's position in the home, relation of mother and father in the home, are all subjects which the women discuss with as much eagerness and intelligence as the average woman.

From these simple lessons have come women who persisted until they learned to read, and to understand the daily lessons which the children bring home from school at night.

Women who have been able by continuous effort to encourage their husbands to purchase property, and to

1. MRS. M. S. JOSENBERGER, A. B.   2. MADAM C. J. WALKER.
3. MADAM MARTHA B. ANDERSON, B. M.

regard his own hearthstone not so lightly as he once did, and to bring about more wholesome conditions in every phase of their life and living.

One club in a certain Southern State organized and has maintained for eighteen years a night school for the women and girls, and men, too, who are not able to attend any school in the day. During these years women and girls have had lessons in cooking, sewing and the general care of their homes, in addition to their lessons in their books. A Y. M. C. A. goes along with this night school; books for the young are distributed and kept in circulation, and women with their families have long since taken an upward trend toward a higher and more wholesome civic and moral life.

This club owns its own rooms and furnishings, and has recently raised nearly a thousand dollars for a home for girls, supplied literature on health subjects to hundreds of country women, held boys' clinics, directed better baby campaigns, held country fairs, and in many ways been able to give cheer and inspiration to thousands of women who otherwise would have drifted away from all that is good and pure.

A modest little woman, Mrs. Dinah Pace, has for many years taken all the children, boys and girls in her neighborhood, who were orphans. They live on a large farm in the summer and do much work, which makes it possible for the family to get through the winters. Mrs. Pace also looks after the mothers in her community who need sympathy and encouragement, and so has come to be a great inspiration to other club women, who, like herself, have had advantages and opportunities above their fellow sisters, and yet have not had the courage to make the step outside of their own doors and circle to lend a helping hand in this great work of uplift.

Our club has made an effort to develop public speakers so that our cause might be brought more clearly and definitely before the country.   Mrs. Mary B. Talbert, of Buffalo, N. Y., Mrs. Mary Church Terrell, of Washington, D. C., the late Mrs. J. Siloame Yates, of Kansas City, Mo., Mrs. Josephine Bruce, of Washington, D. C., Miss Nannie Burroughs, of Washington, D. C., Miss Lucy Laney, of Augusta, Ga., are all women who stand out as the equal of any club women who are in the public eye today.

Nothing has so changed the whole life and personnel of the colored woman and so surely brought her into her own as has the club life to which she has lent herself, inspired by the national association which has for its aim the development of its women, mentally, morally and industrially, as well as along civic lines, and whose motto is, "Lifting as we climb."

> "All swift the cry comes down the world:
>   Take task and take caress,
> But, by our living spirits, we
>   Have other ways to bless.
> Now let us teach the thing we've learned
>   In labor and loneliness.
> We strive with none. We fold man home by
>   The power of a great new word.
> We who have long been dead are alive.
>   We, too, are thy people, Lord!"

14

ALBON L. HOLSEY, SECRETARY TO THE PRINCIPAL, TUSKEGEE INSTITUTE.
EDITOR OF "THE TUSKEGEE STUDENT."

CHAPTER XI.

THE NATIONAL NEGRO BUSINESS LEAGUE.

Written Expressly for This Work by Albon L. Holsey, Secretary to the Principal of Tuskegee Institute.

Introduction.—To see the beginnings of the National Negro Business League in a true perspective, it is necessary to set them against the conditions that existed during the earlier development of Negro business enterprises. When it is recalled that the Negro has come so recently from slavery into the light of civilization, it is expected that he should be slow in assuming a firm place in the shifting and uncertain business world.

The great masses of the Negroes were deprived by the very conditions of slavery of every opportunity to learn the art of business. They were taught, as one of the conditions of slavery, to distrust one another, and the lesson was all too well learned. With this blighting feeling of distrust naturally followed the two "bed-fellows," envy and jealousy; so that with freedom the seeds sprang up and increased wonderfully and constituted for a long time the weeds and thorns in the pathway of the Negro's success in business.

In view of these facts it is no wonder that more progress was made in education and culture, in the acquisition of land, real estate and churches, than in the economic world of business. Then, too, they were face to face with competition of the most efficient kind. Those who would succeed in business had to meet the competition of the white man, with his superior capital and training, and also the distrust and jealousy of many of his own race. Thus he had foes to fight from within and from without. Yet, in the face of these adverse conditions, a

211

very creditable beginning had been made at the time when the National Negro Business League was under consideration.

In 1899, in a very valuable contribution to the study of the Negro in business, Dr. W. E. B. DuBois reported that the capital invested in the various Negro enterprises was approximately nine millions of dollars. The great bulk of these investments, seventy-nine per cent, was in sums less than $2,500, which showed how widely the business interests of the race were distributed and how many Negro men and women were actively engaged in them. While the sum invested in the various enterprises seems small in comparison with the vast investments of the country, or even with the investments of certain Negro enterprises of today, yet when one considers that the Negro had been out of slavery only thirty-five years at the time the league was formed, and that he had started with nothing, the progress seems almost phenomenal.

Dr. Booker T. Washington, in his travels through widely separated regions of the country found so many Negroes engaged in profitable commercial pursuits, came to the conclusion that the time had come to put the Negro business men and women on terms of mutual acquaintanceship and mutual helpfulness. Then with that rare insight which characterized the man's really indisputable genius, he sent out the following appeal, which resulted in a big convention, where the Negro business world should take to itself a voice that must at once impress the white man and encourage the black man.

"After careful consideration and consultation with prominent colored people throughout the country, it has been decided to organize what will be known as the National Negro Business League.

MASONIC TEMPLE, JACKSONVILLE, FLA.

COLORED PYTHIAN BUILDING, NEW ORLEANS, LA.

"The need of an organization that will bring the colored people who are engaged in business together for consultation and to secure information and inspiration from each other has long been felt. Out of this national organization it is expected will grow local business leagues that will tend to improve the Negro as a business factor.

"Boston has been selected as the place of meeting because of its historic importance, its cool summer climate and generally favorable conditions. It is felt that the rest, recreation and new ideas which business men and women will secure from a trip to Boston will more than repay them for time and money spent.

"The date of the meeting will be Thursday and Friday, August 23d and 24th, because it is felt that this is the season when business can be left with least loss. Then, too, nearly all the steamship lines and railroads have reduced their rates to Boston at that time to one fare for the round trip for the entire summer.

"Every individual engaged in business will be entitled to membership, but as far as possible the colored people in all the cities and towns of the country should take steps at once to organize local business leagues, where no such organization already exists, and should see that these organizations send one or more delegates to represent them.

"It is very important that every line of business that any Negro man or woman is engaged in be represented. This meeting will represent a great opportunity for us to show to the world what progress we have made in business lines since our freedom.

"This organization is not in opposition to any

other now in existence, but is expected to do a distinct work that no other organization now in existence can do as well.

"Another circular, giving further information as to program and other details of the meeting, will be issued within a few weeks. All persons, whether men or women, interested in the movement are invited to correspond with,

"Yours very truly,

"BOOKER T. WASHINGTON."

First Meeting of the League.—The meeting in Boston was held on August 23d-25th. Day and evening sessions were held the first two days. The delegates assembled in the large hall of the Parker Memorial Building, which was beautifully and appropriately decorated. The use of the hall was donated by one of the philanthropists of Boston, and the decorations were put up by a business man of our race, Mr. B. F. Washington. On August 25th, which was Saturday, the delegates were given an excursion on a steamer down Boston Harbor by the city government. This was one of the most pleasant features of the week, and the courtesy was thoroughly appreciated by the visitors. Not only in this excursion, but in many other ways were the delegates made welcome. Hon. Thomas W. Hart, the mayor of Boston, himself an eminently successful business man, was present at one of the sessions and made an address which gave the delegates inspiration and encouragement. The people of Boston were unremitting in their efforts to help the visitors in their city to get all of the pleasure and profit out of their stay.

The arrangements for the meeting in Boston were made by a local committee of Dr. S. B. Courtney; P. J.

PYTHIAN TEMPLE, LOUISVILLE, KY.

ODD FELLOW BLOCK, ATLANTA, GA.

Smith; Louis F. Baldwin, real estate; J. R. Hamm, news-dealer and stationer; Rev. W. H. Tomas; Virgil Richardson, gents' furnishings; Captain Charles L. Mitchell; William L. Reed, tobacconist; J. H. Lewis, tailor; Gilbert C. Harris, manufacturer of and dealer in hair goods.

On the morning of August 23d, Dr. S. E. Courtney, the chairman of the local committee, called the meeting to order and read the call of the meeting. Prayer was offered by Rev. Dr. Montague, of Boston. Mr. Louis F. Baldwin, a real estate dealer in Cambridge, was made temporary chairman, and Mr. E. E. Cooper, the publisher of *The Colored American* of Washington, was made temporary secretary. These temporary positions were subsequently made permanent, and the success of this first meeting was in no small measure due to the able and interested manner in which these two gentlemen performed their duties. An address of welcome was made by Hon. John J. Smith, of Boston. There were appointed to serve as a committee of resolutions Mr. W. R. Pettiford, a banker of Birmingham, Alabama; Mr. C. K. Johnson, a real estate dealer of Virginia; Mr. Daniel W. Lucas, a barber of Kansas City, Missouri; and Mr. M. M. Lewey, an editor and publisher of Pensacola, Florida. The permanent organization, effected later, consisted of Dr. Booker T. Washington, president. Vice-presidents, Giles B. Jackson, Richmond; Mrs. A. M. Smith, Chicago. Treasurer, Gilbert C. Harris, Boston. Secretary, Edward E. Cooper, Washington. Compiler, Edward A. Johnson, Raleigh, North Carolina. Executive Committee: T. Thomas Fortune, New York; T. W. Jones, Chicago; Isaiah T. Montgomery, Mound Bayou, Mississippi; Booker T. Washington, Tuskegee, Alabama; George C. Jones, Little Rock, Arkansas; Gilbert C. Harris and Louis F. Baldwin, Boston.

The names given show the widely representative character of the league from the very first, both as regards the territory from which the delegates came, and also the industries represented.

The wide scope of this meeting is best shown in the program which occupied the two days' session. The papers and addresses were short, compact, and to the point. Some of them may have lacked the polish of the rhetorician, but they told a story in every case of what the speaker had accomplished and all present understood. It was not the plan to have formal addresses, but instead to have a person who had succeeded in some business tell how he had accomplished his achievements; to tell what obstacles he had met and just how he had overcome them that others, hearing him, might get information and encouragement which would help them succeed in the things they were doing.

Space will not permit the mentioning of all who spoke at this wonderful convention, but only a few with their topics and a paragraph here and there. Mr. Andrew F. Hillyer, of Washington, D. C., spoke upon "The Colored American in Business." He gave an interesting account of this phase of Negro life and some very valuable data derived from the Government record of 1890.

Mr. Giles B. Jackson, a real estate dealer of Richmond, Virginia, spoke on "The Negro as a Real Estate Dealer." Mr. Jackson showed by the data derived from the report of the auditor of Virginia that the Negroes of that State owned one twenty-sixth of all the land in the State, and one-sixteenth of all the land east of the Blue Ridge. He showed further that they owned one-tenth of all the land in twenty-five of the one hundred counties of the State; one-seventh of the land in Middlesex County. one-sixth of the land in Hanover County, and that in Charles City they owned one-third of all the land. He told how, in the year of 1893, when the city of Richmond needed to borrow money to pay school expenses, the True Reformers Bank, a race enterprise, loaned the city $100,000. Mr. J. E. Shepard, of Enfield, North Carolina, also spoke upon "The Negro in Real Estate."

Mr. M. M. Lewey, of Pensacola, Florida, spoke of the Negro business enterprises in his city. He said that half the population of Pensacola were Negroes, and no less than fifty business enterprises were owned and operated by Negroes. The Negroes were engaged in all forms of business.

Mr. J. W. Pullen, of Enfield, North Carolina, spoke of the business enterprises of this city. Mr. R. B. Fitzgerald, of Durham, North Carolina, was present and made a brief address. As Doctor Washington said, "The mere presence of this man and his wife at the meeting was eloquent with encouragement. Mr. and Mrs. Fitzgerald began the manufacture of bricks in North Carolina several years ago, with unbounded energy and determination, but with so little capital that at first Mrs. Fitzgerald was obliged to wheel away and pile up to dry the bricks that her husband was making. Now they own an establishment that turns out 3,000,000 bricks every year, own much real estate in addition, and Mrs. Fitzgerald runs a drug store."

Dr. A. J. Love, of Chattanooga, Tennessee, spoke for the colored people of his city, and reported that one hundred homes were owned by Negroes and that $243,000 were invested.

Mr. Dungee, of Montgomery, Alabama, spoke as the representative of the Citizens' Commercial Union of that city. Mr. R. B. Hudson, of Selma, Alabama, spoke for the business men of that city. He was followed by Dr.

L. L. Burwell, a druggist of the same city. The latter spoke of the need in the South of competent druggists. The discussion was continued by Dr. E. E. Elbert, of Wilmington, Delaware, and Dr. A. M. Brown, of Birmingham, Alabama.

Mr. Gilbert C. Harris, of Boston, spoke upon "Work in Hair." Mr. Harris came as a young man to Boston from the South, with practically no business knowledge. He secured work in a store where hair goods were sold and learned the trade very thoroughly. Some years later, when the business was up for sale, he bought it.

An excellent address was made by Mrs. A. A. Chesneau, of Boston.

Mr. W. R. Pettiford, president of a colored bank in Birmingham, Alabama, spoke upon "The Negro Savings Bank." He emphasized the importance of the colored people having saving banks of their own and the great incentive these would be for the saving of money and the buying of homes.

Mr. Isaiah T. Montgomery, the mayor of Mound Bayou, Mississippi, spoke very interestingly and instructively upon "The Building of a Negro Town." Mr. Montgomery was a slave of Jefferson Davis, and as a house servant employed about the library and office of Mr. Davis and his brother had an unusual opportunity to acquire an education. In 1887 he made arrangements with a large railroad company to colonize a tract of wild land in the Yazoo Delta. The town of Mound Bayou is the result, a purely Negro community, having churches, a good school, a tributary agricultural population of 2,000, a number of cotton gins and saw mills and several stores, the latter doing a business every year of over $30,000.

Mr. T. W. Walker, of Birmingham, Alabama, spoke on

MONTGOMERY COTTON GIN, MOUND BAYOU, MISS.

OFFICE OF B. A. GREENE, ATTORNEY AT LAW.
Mr. Greene was the first person born in the city of Mound Bayou,
Mississippi.

"A Negro Coal Mining Company." Mr. J. C. Leftwich, of Klondike, Alabama, spoke upon "The Negro of the South and What He Must Do to Be Saved." Mr. W. O. Emery, of Macon, Georgia, spoke upon "Negro Business Enterprises." Mr. J. A. Williams, of Omaha, spoke for the colored people of that city.

One of the best addresses was that made by Mr. J. H. Lewis, a tailor, of Boston. Born a slave, he began work for himself with nothing. His tailoring establishment in Boston not only occupied one of the best stores in the business section of the city, but was one of the finest establishments in the city. He employed a number of men, while the rent of the store was nearly $10,000 a year.

Mr. R. T. Palmer, a tailor and men's furnisher in Columbia, South Carolina, spoke on the business conditions in his part of the country.

Mrs. A. M. Smith, of Chicago, spoke upon "Women's Development in Business."

Mr. Theodore W. Jones, of Chicago, spoke upon the topic "Go Into Business." Mr. Davis B. Allen, of Newport, Rhode Island, spoke upon "Catering," and Mr. H. C. Smiley, of Chicago, read an excellent paper upon "The Afro-American as a Caterer."

Mr. T. Thomas Fortune, at that time the editor of the New York *Age,* spoke upon "The Negro Publisher." Mr. T. H. Thomas, of Galveston, Texas, had a subject "Barbering." Mr. George E. Jones, of Little Rock, Arkansas, spoke upon "Undertaking." Mr. J. K. Groves, of Kansas City, spoke upon "Potato Growing." Mr. A. F. Crawford, of Meriden, Connecticut, had for a topic "The Negro Florist." Mr. E. B. Johnson, of New Bedford, Massachusetts, spoke upon the business conditions of his city. Mr. D. J. Cunningham, a successful grocer of Pensacola, Florida, spoke upon general merchandising there, which subject was continued by E. P. Booze, of Clarkesdale, Mississippi. Mr. J. P. Fowlkes, of Evington, Virginia, explained how co-operative stores were established in his State. Mr. F. G. Steadman, a founder and manufacturer of East Hampton, Connecticut, spoke upon "Bell Making," and presented a beautiful souvenir bell to the league. Mr. J. N. Vandevall, of East Orange, New Jersey, described the business of steam cleaning high grade rugs and carpets.

It is interesting to note that from the beginning one of the most inspiring and helpful features of the league has been the inclusion of colored business women as well as men in the membership. Some of the most helpful and encouraging addresses at all the meetings from the very first at Boston have been made by women, just as some of the most creditable work of the race in business lines has been done by them.

Dr. Booker T. Washington, in his address to the convention, said among many other things:

"We must not in any part of our country become discouraged, notwithstanding the way often seems dark and desolate; we must maintain faith in ourselves and in our country. No race ever got upon its feet without a struggle, trial and discouragement. The very struggles through which we often pass give us strength and experience that in the end will prove helpful. Every individual and every race that has succeeded has had to pay the price which nature demands from all. We cannot get something for nothing. Every member of the race who succeeds in business, however humble and simple that business may be, because he has learned the important lessons of cleanliness, promptness, system, honesty and progressiveness, is contributing his share in smoothing the pathway for this and succeeding

generations. For the sake of emphasis, I repeat that
no one can long succeed unless we keep in mind the
important elements of cleanliness, promptness, system, honesty and progressiveness."

Another interesting and helpful feature of this meeting was the press reports which appeared in the daily
papers at that time. Mr. Henry J. Barrymore, writing
in the Boston *Transcript,* August 25, 1900, said of his
visit to the convention:

"It pleased me to see how brave the Negro could
be and how patient. I waited for outbreaks of
protests against white oppression and especially
against recent white cruelty. I heard none. No one
'cried baby.' The spirit of the whole occasion was
distinctly hopeful. Regarding material advancement
as a basis of every other sort of progress, the convention listened eagerly to accounts of Negroes, once
poor, who had now built houses, bought land, opened
places of independent business, and established solid
bank accounts. Repeatedly it was pointed out that
men born slaves had actually become rich; also that
the total material progress of the race had been accomplished in only thirty-five years—a happy augury
for the future! Such utterances called out tumul-
tuous cheers, mingles with the shrill 'rebel yell' of
the Southerners. Yet there was scarcely any tendency to indulge in racial self-laudation. More than
once the speakers insisted that the commercial superiority of the white man must be frankly recognized and that the Negro must learn to copy the
white man's methods. In general, the convention
deprecated the Negro's desire to flatter the Negro.
'Far from that, let us look the conditions honestly
and courageously in the face. Let us say the things
that will help our people, whether those things are
pleasant or otherwise. To be sure, a good many
of those beneficial deliverances were sheer platitudes,
but the Negro race is in need of platitudes. It is

BOOKER T. WASHINGTON.
Founder and First President of the League.

fortunately developing a relish for platitudes. It has reached the stage of moral and intellectual evolution where it has come to realize the vital importance of plain, homespun, brown-colored truth. It is laying the basis for its social philosophy by making sure of its axioms.' "

AFFILIATED ORGANIZATIONS.

Each year witnesses the tendency to form new groups or organizations affiliated with the National Negro Business League. This, of itself, is evidence of the inspirational value and creative power of the parent body. The National Bankers' Association was the first outgrowth and the first offspring of the business league. Likewise, year by year, there came into existence the National Funeral Directors' Association, the National Negro Press Association, the National Negro Bar Association; the National Association of Negro Insurance Men, the National Retail Merchants' Association, the National Association of Real Estate Dealers. These branch organizations meet each year with the national league and, in addition to special discussions of interest to each group, they conduct highly interesting and instructive symposiums in the main convention of the league.

NATIONAL NEGRO HEALTH WEEK.

One of the most helpful and far reaching efforts of the national league was the instituting of the National Negro Health Week, which started March 21st to the 27th, 1915. This movement was suggested by the president of the league, and had the endorsement of the executive committee. The machinery of the secretary's office was taken advantage of to circulate the idea and keep the country at large in touch with the movement. Circulars based upon the following figures, compiled by

Mr. Monroe N. Work of the Division of Records and Research, Tuskegee Institute, were sent out.   The facts as gathered by Mr. Work are as follows:

> Four hundred and fifty thousand Negroes in the South alone are seriously ill all the time; the annual cost of sickness of these 450,000 Negroes is $75,-000,000.
>
> One hundred and twelve thousand Negro workers in the South are sick all the time; their annual loss in earnings is $45,000,000; 45 per cent of the deaths among Negroes are preventable.
>
> Two hundred and twenty-five thousand Negro workers in the South alone die annually; 100,000 of these deaths could be prevented.
>
> The annual funeral expenses of the Negroes of the South alone amount to $15,000,000; $6,500,000 of this amount could be saved.
>
> Sickness and death cost Negroes of the South alone $100,000,000; $50,000,000 of this amount could be saved.

Some of the special things emphasized in connection with the Negro health organization were: The organization of clean-up committees, special health sermons by colored ministers, health lectures by physicians and other competent persons; the thorough cleaning of premises, including dwelling yards, outbuildings, and making sanitary springs and wells.   The movement was supported by State and city boards of health, State departments of education, county superintendents of schools, white women's clubs, the Federation of Colored Women's Clubs, and ministers and other uplift organizations among the people generally.

No agency at work under the general direction of the National Business League has accomplished so much good in so short a time as this National Negro Health Week Movement.

While there is no disposition on the part of anyone to claim that the National Negro Business League is directly responsible for all of the material progress which has been made by members of the Negro race since its organization in 1900, yet the significant fact remains that the past decades since its foundation have witnessed a more varied and greater amount of economic development than at any other time in its history. In 1900, when the National Negro Business League was organized, there were about 20,000 Negro business enterprises in America; now there are over 50,000. In 1900 there were two Negro banks; now there are 72. In 1900 Negroes were conducting 250 drug stores; now they have 695. In 1900 there were 450 undertaking establishments operated by Negroes; now there are over 1,000. In 1900 there were 149 Negro merchants engaged in wholesale business; now there are over 240. In 1900 there were 10,000 retail merchants; now there are over 25,000. In the twenty years since the National Negro Business League was organized, the total farm property owned by Negroes has shown a remarkable increase. From 1900 to 1910 the value of domestic animals owned by Negro farmers increased from $85,216,337 to $177,273,785, or 107 per cent; poultry from $3,788,792 to $5,113,756, or 36 per cent; implements and machinery from $18,586,225 to $36,861,418, or 98 per cent; land and buildings from $69,636,420 to $273,501,665, or 293 per cent. In the ten years the total value of farm property owned by Negroes increased from $177,404,688 to $492,892,218, or 117 per cent.

CONCLUSION.

While the business league has a distinct purpose (that of promoting the commercial and financial development of the Negro), and does not attempt to prescribe for every racial ill or cover every phase of racial endeavor, yet it is a significant fact that, through the instrumentality of the national body and its six hundred branches or local leagues scattered throughout the country, a very large part of the progress that has been made by the Negro race in the direction of home and farm ownership, banking, insurance, manufacturing and mercantile enterprise, has been achieved since the organization of the National Negro Business League in Boston just twenty years ago. For the wise inception and launching of that movement by Doctor Washington, its founder and life-long president, its continuation by the second president, Hon. J. C. Napier, and Dr. Robert R. Moton, the third president, cannot be too highly praised. For its growth and maintenance as well as its wholesome and wide-spread influence, primarily Dr. Emmet J. Scott, the efficient secretary of the league, together with the executive staff, the members, the press, and other loyal supporters, cannot be too warmly commended.

May the league ever live and grow and be the helping hand of the Negro race.

JESSE BINGA, WEALTHY CHICAGO BANKER.

CHAPTER XII.

PROGRESS IN INDUSTRIES.

FARMS, HOMES AND BUSINESS ENTERPRISES.

By ALBON L. HOLSEY, Secretary to the Principal of Tuskegee Institute.

Progress in Industries.—When we remember that fifty-five years ago the Negro was in slavery it is certainly remarkable to note the progress made in all lines of industry. Keeping in mind some of the difficulties the Negro has had to strive against the progress made in industries is commendable. All throughout the South are found men who stand at the head in the various lines of business. Be it said to the credit of the colored people, and greatly to their benefit, that the race has in its possession a sound means of displaying its progress.

United Efforts.—While much has been done in all lines of business, yet very much more remains to be done before the Negro holds that place in business to which he is entitled. In order to accomplish what should be done in this respect, it is necessary that there be united efforts on the part of the race to assist one another in every business enterprise. Wherever men of the Negro race attempt to increase the advantages of the race there should be found those who stand by them and support them. With the full confidence and patronage of the people the Negro race will have rich merchants and capitalists carrying on rich business enterprises in every section of the country that will demand the respect and recognition of the world.

Fifty Years of Progress in Business.—The following

231

statistics compiled by Mr. Monroe N. Work, director of the Division of Records and Research at Tuskegee Institute, are interesting and also appropriate:

Landmarks in Negro Business Enterprise:

1868   The Fourteenth Amendment to the Constitution adopted. Legalized the right of Negroes, anywhere in the country, to engage in any occupation in which other persons are engaged.

1873   The Freedmen's Saving Bank and Trust Company fails. The loss thereby of many millions of dollars greatly retards the development of Negro enterprises.

1880-85 About this time the operating of Negro beneficial societies developed into a regular business. The operating of industrial insurance companies by Negroes becomes a regular business.

1888-90 First Negro banks organize. 1888, the Capital Savings Bank of Washington begins business. 1889, the True Reformers Bank of Richmond and the Mutual Bank and Trust Company of Chattanooga begin business. 1890, the Penny Savings Bank of Birmingham begins business.

1900   The National Negro Business League organizes.

1912   First old legal reserve (old line) insurance among Negroes, the Standard Life of Atlanta, Georgia, organizes with a paid in capital of $100,000.

Thomas Hudson, Valdosta, Georgia.—Thomas Hudson owns and successfully operates three grocery stores. When Mr. Hudson was requested to tell how he had been able to build up his successful business enterprises, he replied: "We handle nothing but the best and most reliable merchandise, and when the merchandise fails to make good, we make good. My main store acts as a jobbing house and we buy very largely directly from the manufacturer and supply our other two stores at wholesale prices. All credit accounts are handled from the main store. We have worked out our own plan for selecting locations for our branch stores based upon the actual living conditions of our people in that locality."

Sam Charles, Pensacola, Florida.—Sam Charles owns two successful shoe stores. Mr. Charles has been in business for twenty-eight years and his main store is located on the main street in Pensacola, where he employs ten or twelve persons. His business yields him an income of approximately $7,000 a year. His store is patronized by both white and colored people, and in addition to a large mercantile division he also carries a splendid line of shoes. His store is well appointed and would be a credit to any community.

J. W. Wright, Deland, Florida.—Mr. Wright tells the story of his success in his own words: "I was born and raised in Florida, going to Deland when fifteen years of age, twenty-five years ago, with $1.50 in my pocket, which was all the money that I had in the world. I began work for 75 cents per day, but in a short while was raised to $1.00 per day. For four years I saved nothing. Then I got married without a dollar, without a home, and with a $50 debt for furniture, etc. Since that time I have put twenty years into citrus growing, having bought the first five acres twenty years ago. A short while after Florida had been practically wiped out by the freeze of 1894-5, I bought this piece of land for $300, $50 down and $50 a year, with interest. I succeeded in paying more than a hundred a year, at which time I was working for $5 per week. My wife was earning a little and we put our mites together. The place was paid for in less than three years and cared for. I got my trees started, budding them by lantern light at night and doing whatever other work I could do at night. This grove was frozen or killed by the frost three successive winters. Finally I decided to save the trees in spite of the frost. I invited a half dozen or more men to come out and help me bank trees and have dinner with me. We banked those trees with sand, covering up the whole tree. Where the tree was too high we bent it over and covered it anyway. I went home feeling that I had "made safe," but to my complete surprise, when winter was gone and I began to uncover, I found that all of my trees were dead, for they died for want of air. However, I never weakened. Men of my race who doubted the wisdom of my continuing in the citrus fruit growing business would come to me and say: 'The white men who have all the money cannot raise an orange grove; how do you expect to raise oranges, you being nothing but a poor colored man.' Then I was more than ever determined to raise oranges, but decided that my acreage was too much. I ordered lumber and built a wall twenty-five feet high around one hundred trees and a wall through the center the same height, making fifty trees to the lot. This was very expensive for one getting only $28 per month. These hundred trees were fired with pine wood whenever cold enough. At the same time I kept up the trees on the outside of the wall by firing. But after a few years, experience proved to me that Nature must take its course. My trees needed more air and more light, so down went the shed. In reply to the kind suggestion of some of my friends who thought I would never succeed in this business, let me say that I sold the five acre orange grove in question, about eighteen months ago, for $4,000 and reserved the crop, for which

I received $1,800. As soon as I began to realize a small profit on this grove, I began to buy more, purchasing a seven acre grove next, and so on from year to year until I now own two hundred and fifty acres of land, sixty acres of which are devoted to citrus fruit growing. These sixty acres of citrus fruit trees consist of forty-five acres of bearing trees and fifteen acres of trees newly set; or, in other words, I have 3,150 bearing trees and 1,050 young trees."

Mr. J. R. Barreau, New Bedford, Mass.—Twenty-eight years ago when I was a boy, fourteen, and living in New Haven, Conn., I tried to learn the photographer's business, but could not get an opportunity, even though I offered to work for nothing, but being one of two children of a widowed mother, I had to get some work and finally got a job in a wholesale and retail store where window shades, curtains, rugs, oil cloth, etc., were sold. My first work was nailing caps on shade rollers. I worked about three-quarters of the day at that, and having filled the place where the boss told me to put them, I asked him where I should put more. He told me he never had a boy to fill that place before, and would give me other work to do. Well, in a little while they found out my ability to hang curtains tastefully, and put me to work making and hanging curtains. When I was nineteen the foreman whom I worked under was discharged, and the boss asked me if I thought I could hold the job down. I told him I would try, and he said he would give me a chance.

I worked for him seven years, until he went out of the retail business, then for nine months ran a little work shop of my own, until I got a job as foreman of the drapery department by convincing the owner of "The Thompson Shop"—which was then a wall paper store—

that he should specialize in draperies and rugs as an "Interior Decorator," which term was just then coming into use. I worked for him three years, and then accepted a position offered me in New Bedford as foreman of workroom in a large house furnishing store. I remained with them fifteen years, part of the time as foreman, and the last few years, as buyer and manager of their drapery department. At the end of that time my present partner, who is a white man, and I, both thought we would like to try doing business on our own account, so we entered into partnership and for three and a half years have done business for the best families in our town as "The Decorative Shop," and have specialized in wall papers, curtains, rugs, furniture, upholstering, aesthetic novelties and in interior decorating.

Mr. J. L. Whitlow, Farmer, Tuskegee, Alabama.— I started in life very small, had no one but myself to help me; was born and raised in Alabama. I worked for a white man at the start, plowing three days and hoeing three days, and going to church on Sunday, for I believe in worshiping God who gives us everything we have, who gives us strength to work, and if we lean on Him in business He will hold us up and we will prosper. I married early in life, worked hard to make a living, and am the father of fourteen children. I paid $800 for the first land I bought, which was soon after President Lincoln freed the slaves, and all my friends thought I was foolish to start in buying land, for it was said at that time that every slave that was freed would soon be given forty acres and a mule, but I paid no attention to it and went on and bought my land, paying part cash and the balance on time. My wife worked right along with me and shared my hardships, stuck by me through thick and thin, and we not only bought and

HENRY H. PACE.
Secretary-Treasurer, Standard Life Insurance Company, Atlanta, Ga.

DR. WILLIAM PICKENS.

paid for that land, but since then we have been adding on to what we had and today I own 1,537 acres of land near Tuskegee Institute, Alabama, raising mostly corn and cotton; have my own steam gin where I gin my own cotton as well as for other cotton raisers; own my own sawmill, and have built my own house for my family and myself to live in, which is comfortable, and we are getting along pretty well.

Standard Life Insurance Company.—Concerning the organization of the Standard Iife Insurance Company, Mr. Harry H. Pace, Secretary-Treasurer, says:

The first attempt to organize this company was made over five years ago when Heman E. Perry, born on a Texas ranch, where his vision became great by necessity.; who had eagerly read every word that had ever fallen beneath his eyes that was written about life insurance; who at spare time had sold life insurance for the Mutual Reserve, the Fidelity Mutual and Equitable; who had drifted to New York and had studied life insurance at first hand in the offices of these companies as an employe; who had formed the acquaintance of actuaries of national reputation and distinction; and who had dreamed of an institution of insurance owned and operated by Negroes, came down to Atlanta, on the red hills of Georgia, and told a group of business men gathered at the Y. M. C. A., that he purported to start a hundred thousand ($100,000) dollar life insurance company. Some of those who were present sat up and gasped. Surely this young man was crazy, they thought. Some of them did not hesitate to even say so. When he outlined to them his plans, told them his dream in a simple, straightforward, earnest way, and explained to them that the least amount with which they could begin would be $100,000 paid-in capital, which must be invested in bonds

BOYD BUILDING, NASHVILLE, TENN.

and deposited with the State treasurer for the protection of the policy holders of the company, they could hardly believe their ears. These men who had been in business and in the professions in Atlanta for many years, many of whom had grown wealthy in the one usual way (through investment in real estate), who had been accustomed to seeing big things done in their own little wonderful city of Atlanta, by white men, were not prepared to see a Negro with an idea as big as this. They began to ask questions; they did not understand the meaning of those words "paid-up" and "$100,000." They really wondered if he didn't make a mistake and meant $10,000 instead, and when they finally became convinced that this serious, sober, earnest young man meant every word he said, some of them went home to think the matter over. Some few of them never came back, but the talk of that one meeting and what had been said was destined to live.

Little by little the idea grew, and men and women in every walk of life became interested in what this stranger was trying to do. Finally, when the subscription list opened, there were many who subscribed in good faith; who made the first payment, and gave their notes for the balance. There were some others of our folk, and we have a good number of them among us, who are professional subscribers, who put their names to everything that comes along, and who never really intended paying. All of them, however, saw the possibilities of an organization backed by a capital of $100,000, and operated along conservative insurance lines, but they didn't believe that that much money could ever be raised by and among colored people, except at a rally to build a church.

Finally a charter of incorporation was secured, in

16

January, 1909. Then began the real struggle. Up and down the length and breadth of the entire Southland, through every State from Virginia to Texas, Mr. Perry traveled at his own expense during the two years that immediately followed, "selling stock," as he used to say, in the "Standard Life Insurance Company." Tireless and unceasing, he endured all of the hardships of Southern Jim Crow travel, obsessed by his dream, and the idea that he could succeed in raising $100,000 to establish an old line legal reserve insurance company among Negroes. There was a provision in the subscription blank which we offered to every subscriber, that not one penny of the money paid in should be used for the expenses of the organization; that if the company was not launched every dollar received with four per cent interest should be returned to the subscriber.

Berry O'Kelly, Merchant, Method, North Carolina.— I will endeavor to state in a few words what I have been attempting to do and what I have accomplished along the line of wholesale merchandising. In order that you may have some idea of the character of merchandise handled, let me say that I am a wholesale dealer in groceries and general merchandise, including flour, hay, corn, oats, cotton-seed meal, hulls, dairy feed, etc., maintaining a warehouse on the Southern Railroad. The president, in introducing me, stated that I was from Raleigh, North Carolina, but really my place of business is three miles from Raleigh. I was born in Chapel Hill not far from that place; I am now located at Method, North Carolina.

I began business with five dollars. First I was an orphan boy, being deprived of both father and mother early in life, and went to live with my kind-hearted aunt who raised me; it is to her I owe a great deal in shaping

my career. Before going into business I went to work
for $5 a month. Sometime later on I was persuaded
to change my employment and was hired by a railroad,
where I worked for fifty cents a day as "water toter."
I went there but did not stay there long because conditions were such I could not stay there; I did not like that
kind of life, so I went back to the same lady and continued working for her at the handsome salary of $5 a
month. Of course I was young then and at first my
aunty got all the money I made, all I made was hers,
but later on, as I grew older, I made $5 of my own
money and though I kept on working for only $5 a
month, by denying myself I managed to save something
each month, if only a little, until I had saved up one
hundred ($100) dollars, which was a LONG TIME.
After I got $100 saved up there was a man, Mr. C. H.
Woods, a liveryman who lived and his business was
located very close by. One time he was sick and he asked
my aunty to let me stay there with him, which she did.
He soon became attached to me and finding out that I
had $100 he induced me to become a partner of his. I
bought half interest in his business, paying the $100
cash down and the balance on credit. Afterward I went
into the grocery business by myself, and I found that
in order to succeed in the grocery business was to give
the people the same value for their money as any other
groceryman was able to give. After making up my
mind and determining to follow that method, I found
no trouble in getting people to deal with me. My only
trouble was to get money enough to buy what they
wanted in order that they might deal with me. I merely
mention this because I have heard some colored business
men complain that their race don't patronize them, when
they themselves have not taken the proper steps to win

or deserve their trade. Today my business is prospering, my customers are colored as well as white, and to many of them I ship in carload lots.

Negro Business Progress in Kansas.—At a recent meeting of the National Negro Business League the following facts regarding Negro progress in Kansas were presented:

Mr. John Salem, of Hill City, Kansas, has founded a large Negro colony out there and the colony is called Nicodemus; it is one of the oldest Negro colonies in this country; I know that because they went there by night, or some night after Nicodemus went there. He reports that he is sixty-nine years of age; was born in Kentucky, and, by the way, when you look up the records, you will find that a very large number, if not the majority, of the inhabitants of Kansas were born in other States. Kansas is distinguished by the fact that it is settled by men from all parts of the country who evidently found there better opportunities to live and prosper than were available in their own native States. Kansas, as you know, is further famous for being the great initial battleground between Freedom and Slavery in the time of John Brown, the immortal hero of Ossawatomie. This man was born sixty-nine years ago in Kentucky, where he got a good wife and came out to Kansas in 1884, with a family of nine children; he has been a practical farmer for thirty-four years, and among the difficulties he had to overcome were seven years of drouth, so that he had to live on corn meal, broom corn coffee and in a dugout (which is a hole in the ground covered with trees and mud to keep out the wind and weather; he reports that he holds property amounting to $10,000 in land, money and live stock, in addition to drawing a pension from the Government.

Green Keith, of Lawrence, Kansas, reports that he is sixty-five years of age; born in Alabama; he came to Kansas in 1871—came from Alabama to Kansas and got rich. He worked for thirty-eight years, and now has a general income of $1,400 a year; total wealth $18,000 in land, dwelling, produce and live stock; made it all by hard work.

Mack Henry, of Speed, Kansas (that's out in Nicodemus district), is fifty years of age; born in Pennsylvania; came to Kansas in 1871; took up a homestead and grew up with the country; he has accumulated since, in forty-one years, an estate valued at $50,000, and has a general income of $3,000 with expense account $600, his wealth being in land, money and stock.

W. E. Ross, of Logansport (out there in western Kansas where it doesn't rain much); he reports that he is thirty-eight years of age; born in Topeka, Kansas; has an income of $800 a year; his wealth consists of land valued at $10,000, made by working land.

Wesley Page, of Estey, Kansas, is fifty years of age; born in Tennessee; came to Kansas in 1880; worked fifteen years as a farmer; now has a yearly income of $3,000; expense account $1,800; his total wealth amounts to $15,000 amassed by hard work, toiling in the land.

J. Beverly, of Speed, Kansas, reports that he is sixty-nine years of age; born in Virginia; has ten (10) children barring other wealth; came to Kansas in 1876, worked twenty years; has about $20,000, made by farming and stock raising.

George W. Kerfoot, of Atchison, Kansas, is fifty-two years of age; born in Kentucky; came to Kansas in 1879 looking for health; having failed in business because of sickness he came to Kansas from Kentucky, mark you, and found health and prosperity; his general wealth is

$28,000; yearly income $2,800; in Kansas he accumulated $15,000 in three years' time, being in the quarry business at Atchison, Kansas.

W. L. Sayres, Hill City, Kansas (that's out in Nicodemus district, too), is forty-one years of age; born in Nebraska; came to Kansas in 1887 and commenced teaching; later he was elected clerk of the District Court at the age of twenty-two; assistant county attorney at the age of twenty-eight; county attorney at the age of forty, and at the end of his present term will have been county attorney for four years; he is county attorney of Graham County. His father died when he was only twelve years of age, since which time he has not only taken care of himself, but helped to take care of the family; he has a general income of $3,000 a year; total wealth of $15,000, represented in land and other property, with some money invested in mercantile business, and he enjoys a very good law practice.

James M. Wright is one of the most interesting characters in Kansas; he is forty-six years of age; was born in Oregon; came to Kansas in 1870, and his answer to the question, "What special difficulties have you over-come?" was this: "I learned to hold my job anywhere." He has a yearly income of over $2,000; total wealth $8,000, represented in farming land, other real estate and stock in a fraternal insurance company. Mr. J. M. Wright states that what he has is the result of systematic saving, and that is a valuable lesson for all of us to learn; his career is similar to that of Mr. Sayres, of whom I spoke a while ago; in 1892 Mr. Wright taught school, since which time he has held the following positions: Clerk, U. S. postoffice at Topeka; deputy county treasurer of Shawnee County, headquarters at Topeka, for eight years; city treasurer of

Topeka for two years—he occupied that position when I went to Kansas; at present he is deputy county clerk of Shawnee County; he was raised on a farm; received a high school education, a business education, and specialized in accountancy; he is also the founder and president of one of the leading fraternal insurance companies of our State. Mr. Wright has also recently established in the city of Topeka a fine moving picture theatre that is meeting with abundant success; it is one of the cleanest and best places of amusement in that city.

Mr. W. V. Smith, a bachelor, came to Kansas from Mattoon, Illinois, many years ago; worked for fifty years as a farmer, and has a yearly income of $2,000 as the result of knowing the value of manure and the best fertilizer; though an unlettered man, he is said to be worth over $30,000 in farming land, live stock, and other property which he accumulated by "knowing how to manage."

A. C. Howard, Shoe Polish Manufacturer, Philadelphia, Pa.—As a railroad porter I had saved up something like $180; with that $180 I started in business. I began by selling my blacking to railroad porters, and I had a host of friends among the fellows I used to work with; that was why I placed my photograph upon all of the boxes, tins and cartons containing my blacking and polish, because I was very well known among the railroad fraternity, and in that way a number of them recognized my goods. Of course some of my friends did not think that a black man could get any farther along in life than a railroad man or a Pullman car porter, but it seems that other people made demands for A. C. Howard's Shoe Polish and Leather Dressings. My first output was only one dozen boxes, which I delivered with my own hands. I used to thank shoe dealers and proprietors of bootblack stands very profusely for even giving my goods a place on their shelves, but now there is a widespread demand for all the shoe polish, leather dressings and dyes, and bootblack supplies that my factory can produce. The A. C. Howard Shoe Polish Company has a plant at 349 Fourth Street here in Philadelphia that is fitted up with the latest improved filling machinery, and we have demonstrated our ability to prepare as good an article as "Whittemore," or any of the oldest and best known blackings make. I started preparing my goods in a woodshed, which was on the alley back of my home. I used to use an old tin box for mixing purposes; now we have a factory well equipped, and in all the big department stores of Chicago, Philadelphia and New York Howard shoe polish has won its place with the standard stock. We are selling our polish in large orders to the United States Government; it is being used at Fortress Monroe, Fort Todd and Fort Hamilton. I sold in Philadelphia one order alone amounting to $2,500. We were awarded first prize at the Paris Exposition in 1900, and also the first prize at the Jamestown Exposition in 1907.

Henry Kelley, Successful Farmer.—My first experience in working land or on a farm was, when I was a boy, about ten or eleven years old. In 1886 I married and bought a farm for myself. My farm had about 520 acres of land in it; there were about thirty-five acres of that land in a state of cultivation at the date I bought it; after which I thought it would pay us well if we would begin and clear it up. I began to cut down the trees, got a plenty of logs and built houses for a year or two, and in 1889 I bought my first steam gin to gin cotton for ourselves and the general public.

Jonas W. Thomas, Farmer and Merchant.—I bought

JAMES & ALLEN DRUG CO., CHATTANOOGA, TENN.

DRUG STORE, W. H. BALLARD, LEXINGTON, KY.

an old horse for $45.75, rented a small farm of thirty acres for 1,800 pounds of loaned cotton, thus starting out on the farm sea of life. I continued in this way for four years before I was able to clear enough money to buy a mule. At the expiration of four years I became able to buy a mule for $69, then I increased my farm seven acres, making thirty-seven acres in cultivation— this increase was rented land, of course.

After farming five years I rented another farm, and after managing two farms successfully the next year I increased it one more, and continued to increase as I saw that I was able to get means and labor. Along with my farming I began to run a commissary, or as some people call it, a "grab."

From a rented one-horse farm twenty-two years ago, I am today running fifty-two plows with a good many running on my own places; and from a "grab" I am now running a store and carrying regularly a stock of goods valued at $4,500. These goods are in my store, of course; one built at a cost of $8,520.

Windham Brothers, Contractors and Builders, Birmingham, Alabama.—Mr. B. L. Windham: We employ, on the average, one hundred (100) men all the year round. Sometimes more and sometimes a little less; seldom less. Our payrolls average two thousand dollars ($2,000) a week. Our yearly contracts amount to from $250,000 to $300,000 per year. We have commercial credit in the banks of Birmingham. We can procure the necessary funds and finance our work to the extent of fifty thousand dollars ($50,000) without any real estate security.

Mound Bayou, Mississippi, a Negro Town.—Mound Bayou was founded by Isaiah T. Montgomery and Benjamin T. Green in 1887. From a few settlers on a few

LIBRARY - Allegheny Campus

MOUND BAYOU OIL MILL, MOUND BAYOU, MISS.

INTERIOR VIEW MOUND BAYOU OIL MILL.

hundred acres it has grown to an agricultural community of 30,000 acres, a rural population of six or seven thousand and a town of 1,500 or more. It struggled along as a small railway stop and no business connections or stores of consequence until the opening of the Bank of Mound Bayou in 1904. Since that time it has steadily grown in importance as a commercial factor in the business life of the county. It has now an A. M. E. church edifice costing $25,000, First Baptist Church costing $17,000, an Episcopal Church, Christian Church and M. E. Church. It has a Carnegie Library, one public school and two Normal schools, operated and under the auspices of the Baptist and A. M. E. respectively. The Y. & M. V. R. R. employs all Negroes here, the agent, R. J. Gardner, a graduate of Walden University, Nashville, having two Negro girls as his assistants, one porter and night watchman. The receipts of this office were $9,000 for the month of October.

Mound Bayou ranks sixth in the county as a cotton shipping point, handling upwards of 6,000 bales. The express office is handled by a Negro, L. E. Jones, who has one assistant. The Cumberland Telephone Company maintains an exchange, employing all Negro girls and has nearly a hundred subscribers. The postoffice is a presidential office. Mrs. M. C. Booze, a graduate of Straight University, is postmistress, and employs three assistants. C. F. Bolton is president of the bank, and D. A. Carr, a graduate of the State School at Alcorn, is cashier. F. H. Miller, a successful farmer, is vice-president. The bank had aggregate resources of $259,681.30 on October 31st. B. H. Creswell, manager of the Mound Bayou Supply Company, a store composed of one hundred farmers, is mayor; R. L. Clegg is marshal; J. W. Francis, S. A. Allen, E. O. Powell, J. L. Lee and L. E. Jones compose

MOUND BAYOU STATE BANK.

OFFICE MOUND BAYOU COTTON COMPANY.

the board of aldermen.   Jake Parker, United States Government demonstrative agent, is treasurer.

B. A. Green is city attorney, as well as the only attorney of the community, and enjoys a good and growing practice.   He is a graduate from the law school of Harvard.   Drs. W. P. Kyle, J. A. Banks and W. H. Broomfield are the physicians.

The town and community have recently voted a bond issue of $100,000, and will erect a $70,000 school building for a consolidated school district, build teacher's home and purchase truck or car to be used in transporting children to and from school who live too far to walk.

The Mound Bayou Oil Mill was completed in 1912, the late Dr. Booker T. Washington and Mr. C. P. J. Mooney, editor of the *Commercial Appeal,* being the speakers on the occasion of the opening.   The plant is considered by competent authorities as one of the best in the State, and is the only one owned by Negroes in the United States, and perhaps the world.   It is engaged in the manufacture of cotton-seed oil and by-products, and would cost today to build over $250,000.   The mill was designed by a Negro, Thomas Cook, using all Negro labor and financed by a Negro, Charles Banks.   The manufactured output per day is around five to seven thousand dollars.

The Farmers Mercantile Company is the leading store of the town, managed by E. P. Booze.   The principal stockholders are I. T. and M. R. Montgomery, Charles Banks and E. P. Booze.   Rev. A. A. Cosey, pastor of the First Baptist Church, is the leading minister, having lived here for several years and has contributed largely to the substantial growth of the town and community. Other prominent ministers are F. R. C. Durden and S. P. Felder.   The consolidated school is under the man-

ISAIAH T. MONTGOMERY, STANDING; CHARLES BANKS, SITTING.

agement of Prof. J. H. Mosley, of Alcorn. Mound Bayou has three newspapers—the *News-Digest,* W. N. Lott, editor; the *Advance-Dispatch,* Dr. A. A. Cosey, editor; the *Gazette,* Prof. R. M. McCorkle, editor.

Mound Bayou has many beautiful residences that will compare favorably with similar neighboring towns. Has two moving picture shows, the Casino, F. H. Miller, proprietor, having a seating capacity of nearly one thousand. It has recently let contract for concrete sidewalks and now receiving gravel for its principal streets. It has electric lights, supplied by a near-by town, Shelby, and has pure water from a flowing artesian well of 160 gallons per minute, several auto repair shops, pressing shops, billiard rooms, drug stores, and one manufacturer of hair and face preparations.

Most of the cotton firms maintain colored representatives here as buyers, Charles Banks being the only Negro cotton broker, who also employs a Negro buyer. These buyers are all experts in their line, and their classifications of grades and staples of cotton pass satisfactorily with Eastern spinners. There are four cotton ginneries, one each owned by I. T. Montgomery and R. M. McCarty; the Farmers Gin Company, J. A. Powell, manager; and the Christmas Gin Company, O. J. Christmas, manager.

The relations between the Negroes of Mound Bayou and their white neighbors are pleasant and friendly. There has never been a clash or disturbance between them, and in all their efforts in self-help the whites have manifested a helping hand. Perhaps the one white man standing out above all others who has done more for Mound Bayou than any other white man, and contributed most largely to the harmonious working and relations between the races, not only in Mound Bayou,

17

but the entire county, was the late Hon. Thos. S. Owens, a resident of the county seat, Cleveland. Mr. Owens died during the flu epidemic in 1918, and so dearly was he esteemed by the Negroes of Mound Bayou that the floral design by them was considered by some the most beautiful one to rest upon his bier.

Charles Banks, Financier, Mound Bayou, Mississippi.—Charles Banks who born in Clarksdale, Coahoma County, Mississippi, in 1873. He was educated in the public schools of the county and Rust University, Holly Springs, Mississippi.

While Charles Banks has shown exceptional ability as a business man by the organization of practically all of the enterprises of Mound Bayou, yet the thing that stands out paramount, which marks him as a genius in this respect, is shown by his successful efforts in the rehabilitation and reconstruction of the Mound Bayou State Bank and the Mound Bayou Oil Mill and Manufacturing Company, both of which went out of business by reason of the general depression at the outbreak of the war in 1914. Being the founder of the first bank at Mound Bayou, when it failed in 1914, undismayed or discouraged, he set about establishing a new bank, and in less than eighteen months he had raised eleven-twelfths (11/12) of the entire capital necessary to start a new bank, opening its doors for business October 1, 1915, which today is one of the strongest institutions in the county. His rehabilitating the oil mill is even more marvelous. This plant, which is valued today something like a quarter of a million dollars, had been thrown into the hands of a receiver because of the financial embarrassment of the lessee. Mr. Banks succeeded in disposing of the receivership, arranged to satisfy and pay off the bonds held by Mr. Julius Rosenwald, the head of Messrs.

Sears, Roebuck & Company, who, out of his goodness of heart, had carried them for years without pressing the payment, helping the Negroes to hold the plant until they could get it on a firm foundation. After negotiations and several trips to Chicago, Mr. Banks arranged a basis of settlement with Mr. Rosenwald, paid him the money required and then arranged for the operation of the plant, formed with one of the strongest connections in the Delta, which from present indications assures a successful operation of the plant, and removing all possibility for loss to the stockholders in the future. The plant now is running night and day, giving employment to a large number of people. Mr. Banks organized the Mound Bayou Supply Company a little over a year ago with one hundred of the substantial farmers, the purpose of which is to take care of advances to farmers by the year, which is now largely done by merchants in nearby towns. He has recently purchased something over two thousand acres of fertile land in the St. Francis Basin in Arkansas, and is now developing it into a magnificent plantation. He also was largely instrumental in starting another Negro colony south of Pine Bluff, Arkansas, under J. A. Patterson, having secured around 40,000 acres for this project. He owns considerable real estate in Clarksdale and Memphis, as well as considerable farm lands in and around Mound Bayou. He subdivided and platted two principal subdivisions of the town, known as Banks Addition, and Banks and Francis Addition. He was a delegate-at-large to the republican national convention in 1908-12, and is today the leading factor in republican politics among the Negroes in the State. He is a trustee of Campbell College, which owns one thousand acres near Mound Bayou, being their rental agent, and has collected this year $8,000.

Boley, Oklahoma.—The exclusively Negro town of Boley is located on the Fort Smith and Western Railroad, in the heart of one of the most fertile sections of Oklahoma. It was founded in 1904 by Mr. T. M. Haynes, a sturdy Negro pioneer. There are from ten to fifteen thousand people around Boley. In the township proper there are three thousand. The town is incorporated and has its own electric light plant and waterworks. Many substantially built and attractive residences, principally frame structures, reflect credit upon the home life of their Negro owners. Boley has one bank with a capital stock of $20,000; three cotton gins; a telephone outfit; eighty-two business concerns; a city hall; a chamber of commerce; a splendid two-story brick, stone trimmed high school, built at a cost of $15,000; several good churches; a Masonic Temple for the State of Oklahoma, worth $35,000; a public recreation park; cement sidewalks; a Negro mayor, a Negro postmaster, Negro lawyers, Negro doctors, Negro school teachers, a Negro ticket agent and telegraph operator, etc. Boley is, in many respects a substantial evidence of the ambition, thrift and ability of the Negro to look out for himself if given a fair chance. Its citizens have shown rare pluck and "stick-to-it-iveness." Blessed with such a citizenry, with railroad facilities, productive soil, etc., it is bound to grow and attract to itself thousands of other Negro inhabitants who would themselves enjoy and give to their children unlimited chances for development.

T. J. Elliot, Merchant, Muskogee, Oklahoma.—Mr. T. J. Elliot is owner of three successful stores which carry a full line of men and women's clothing, shoes and furnishings. His main store is located in Muskogee and is situated on the main business street, and is handsomely decorated with modern equipment of every kind. He carries a full line of up-to-date and stylish merchandise. His other two stores are located in Tulsa and Okmulgee, Oklahoma.

S. S. Favor, Farmer, Shiloh, Oklahoma.—I claim that it is only the exceptional man who can raise cotton year after year at anything like a satisfactory profit, because among other things there are seventeen (17) different varieties of cotton and seventeen (17) different kinds of insects and enemies to destroy your cotton while it is growing and maturing. It doesn't pay to depend wholly on cotton or any one kind of crop for your success as a farmer. I claim that no farm is complete unless you have on it some hogs, some cattle, a few mules, some chickens and some calves, and unless you are able to raise feed for your live stock and a nice kitchen garden for your own use. I have made farming pay on two hundred (200) acres of land; on this land I raise alfalfa, clover, corn and other grain feed, together with from 50 to 75 head of cattle, 20 to 50 mules, from 100 to 150 head of hogs, and I don't feel like I have done anything unless I sell upwards of $3,000 worth of live stock every year. We keep close to the market on hogs, and sell them when the market suits us best. As a farmer I find no prejudice against our hogs, for we go to market with the best.

Mr. C. P. Combs, Practical Farmer, Oak Grove, Louisiana.—Although I never worked at the carpenter's trade, I can build a frame house valued anywhere from $1,000 to $3,000, and I can paint the same three coats and give satisfaction in every particular. Instead of twenty-five acres I now own two hundred and forty (240) acres of land. I raise plenty of corn for my stock, about 40 to 50 bushels and sometimes 60 bushels to the acre; we have a fine farming country down there around

Oak Grove, Louisiana. Farm land sells now for about $50 an acre; it is kind of hilly land, a good deal of it, but the soil is very deep and rich and black. I have a pretty good house, built it myself, and painted it myself; it cost me about $2,000 to build.

Mr. H. P. Ewing, Truck Farmer, Kansas City, Missouri.—I am a truck farmer and have been following that business for a good many years. We have a combination of Negro truck farmers in Kaw Valley, the region round about Kansas City, where we have banded together for mutual benefit. We have 25 acres of potatoes to dig this year; 5 acres of cabbage heading up; 5 acres in onions, 2 acres of onion sets, 2 acres in carrots, besides a number of other things actually growing and maturing each day, and we have actually paid to members of our own race, mostly school boys and girls, $1,166.65 for labor performed; this was paid to them in cash money. Farmers near by have depended largely for labor upon people who go to the country, work on the farm during the day and come back to the city every night. We furnish work for the colored boys and girls who attend the city schools and work for us during their vacation and at odd times, thus helping along as many as we can accommodate. We keep two men and five boys on the farm regularly, and our tomato crop this year will bring us in something like $2,000.

Mr. C. W. Gilliam, Merchant, Okolona, Mississippi.— Mr. Gilliam has had a most interesting career, starting in as a bell boy at a hotel in Memphis at $15.00 per month. This was in 1886, when he left his home in Okolona to make "his fortune." After working at the hotel for a considerable period, he returned to his home with $65.00, and later purchased a small stock of groceries from Mr. T. W. Gregory and started business on the

JAMES T. ROBERTS, EVANSVILLE, IND.

C. W. GILLIAM, MERCHANT, OKALONA, MISS.

main street. Mr. Gilliam says concerning his business:
"I soon put in a small line of drygoods and that fall
I went to Memphis, Tennessee, to market with Mr. P.
McIntosh, who introduced me. I wish to say that Mr.
McIntosh is supposed to be the oldest Negro merchant
in the State of Mississippi and one of the most successful
in this country. I bought $2,000 worth of dry goods,
clothing and notions, bought $500 worth or more of
shoes from a St. Louis shoe firm. My business continued
to grow. In 1900 Mr. P. McIntosh and I formed a co-
partnership; the first year we did about $38,000 or $40,-
000 worth of business. Being a little ambitious, I thought
I could do better by myself, so Mr. McIntosh and I dis-
solved partnership on perfectly friendly terms and remain
strong friends to this day."

He is said to be rated in the Dun and Bradstreet
agency as a good credit risk up to $20,000.

J. T. Roberts, Furniture Dealer, Evansville, Indiana.
—I started my third year's business with a stock of $500
with a splendid outlook for an increased business over
the previous year. Having calls for cheap articles of
hardware, etc., I decided to add to my business a five-
and-ten-cent counter, which paid me well, and at the end
of 1911 I had done $6,188.84 worth of business. I
started my fourth year with a stock of $650 and ended
the year 1912 with $7,399.00 worth of business, with
larger quarters, a well-stocked warehouse, two horses and
wagons, increased hired help and a second-hand clothing
department annexed. I started my fifth year's business
with a $1,000 stock, purchasing a larger store and ware-
house at No. 1 Lincoln Avenue, Evansville, Indiana, in
which to conduct our main business and using the old
site as a "New and Second-hand Clothing Store" and
extra warehouse. The five-and-ten-cent counter had

grown so I decided to open a five-and-ten-cent store adjoining the furniture store.   In it we have ice cream, a soda water fountain, cigars, tobaccos, stationery, hardware, tinware and almost any small article our customers want.   We did $10,425.66 worth of business in 1913, and now the sign on the building reads: "We Trust the People."

Robert L. Smith, Banker, Waco, Texas, says concerning the Negro banks and banking institutions in the country for Negroes: To my way of thinking, the history of our Negro banking institutions reveals more than any other business or profession, the great and wonderful progress our race has made since the war.   The very idea that men and women who were chattels about fifty years ago, or whose mothers and fathers were denied an education and were owned and sold as slaves, without previous apprenticeship or experience in banking, have been able to establish and conduct successfully nearly sixty (60) Negro banking institutions now operating in this country—I say such a record of progress has no parallel in the annals of human history.   Instead of being put up for a loan or sold as a chattel, like horses, cattle and hogs, they have made good use of their liberty by engaging in almost every line of industry and practically every kind of business enterprise in which white men— their former owners—are now engaged, including even the complex and intricate business of banking.   They have taken advantage of educational opportunities, and instead of the Negro race being almost wholly ignorant and illiterate, they have become for the most part intelligent and, according to official figures, the great majority of them can read and write; instead of being put up for a loan and being sold themselves, as chattels, they are lending money, making deposits, owning and selling stocks

HON. FREDERICK DOUGLASS.

and chattels and dealing in bonds and many other forms of securities. From former slaves or sons of slaves, some of them have become presidents of banks which are owned, operated and sustained by Negroes and Negro capital. That is the biggest change that has come, the most wonderful miracle that in my opinion has been wrought among the Negroes of the United States. It shows or reflects more clearly than anything else the wonderful progress we have made in but fifty years of opportunity, and we give God credit not only for our emancipation, but also for this most wonderful miracle which he has subsequently performed.

David Chiles, Farmer, Topeka, Kansas.—I started when I was about eight years old; I was raised on the farm; I worked for a man for wages for a while until I wanted to start out by myself; when I went to the man I was working for to get some horses he never said "No," and when I started in to buy a piece of land, the man I bought from didn't even take mortgage on that land, and I paid him every cent I owed him within a year's time. That was in 1868—at Nashville, Tennessee, just out from the city. The next year I had a little better sense, and made up my mind to buy a little more land. And then I started increasing from year to year, sometimes I would rent land and raise a crop until I was able to buy it. I would raise different kinds of truck or vegetables and would hire the little boys and girls of my neighbors to pick my crops until I got so I was paying out to them alone as high as $25 a day for picking and gathering in the stuff. I had no trouble in selling all I raised. When I first started out land was worth $15 an acre, and now you'll have to pay $200 an acre for the same kind of land.

Finally I made up my mind to move out West, so I

come out to Kansas; sold out what I had in Tennessee and moved out to Topeka, where I bought land on the Kaw River. The first year I raised twenty-eight carloads of as fine a watermelon as you ever tasted and sold them all at something like $150 a carload.

Mr. George W. Cox, Manager, Negro Insurance Company, Indianola, Mississippi.—The Mississippi Beneficial Life Insurance Company, of Indianola, Mississippi, of which I am the assistant general manager, of which the late W. W. Cox was the founder and financial supporter, has hammered and continued to hammer away on these things until today it can say more than any other company can say—whether owned and operated by white or black, doing business absolutely on the lives of our people, that is, in Mississippi alone—it has upon its books over 70,000 paying policy holders, all satisfied, representing an actual premium income of $100,000 a year. Upon its books is $1,000,000 worth of business in force, all of this upon the lives of Negroes. Our company carries two separate departments, "The Sick and Accident," and the regular "Old Line Legal Reserve Department," which enables us to hang our policies upon the walls of every Negro home, however humble, for we write from five cents to five thousand dollars. Sometimes when our people are located on the plantations of the whites, they object to Negro agents coming on their farms, but we fix this all right without a hitch.

We give employment to over 500 men and women in our State. We paid them last year in commissions and salaries over $35,000. We enabled the sick to secure the best medical treatment to the sum of $30,000 last year. We paid the undertakers of the State something like $5,000 for taking care of the dead. That's good, but the best of all is the most remarkable mortality that existed among our risk last year, and including this year to date.

Mr. N. C. Bruce, Winner of World's Corn Prize at the Panama Exposition.—Mr. Bruce is principal of the Bartlett Agricultural School. He tells in his own words how he won the world's corn prize at the Panama Exposition:

In 1912, by deep plowing-in of green crops, cowpeas, red top clover and other legumes in the fall, by re-breaking disc harrowing, smooth harrowing and careful check row planting in the spring, after getting pure bred Boone County white seed corn, and by frequent cultivations in 1913, our school won the highest contest yield premium of $400, producing 108 bushels to the acre. This was at the Missouri Corn Grower's Show where there were over two thousand (2,000) small and large white farmers competing at the Missouri University in January, 1914.

This 1914 top-notch record yield made it necessary that His Excellency, our governor, Elliott W. Major, appoint us as Missouri's Top-Notch Competitor to meet the world's corn champions by States at the Panama-Pacific International Exposition at San Francisco in 1915. Mindful of the previous year's experience, our school set to work early with barnyard manure, cowpeas and red clover, with our muscles and brawn to beat our 1914 yield. At times our work ceased not by day or night. The result was that from our sixty-two (62) acre field we pushed the yield on some acres to 114 bushels and exceeded 100 bushels on many acres, and among the world's corn growers at San Francisco we won the WORLD'S GRAND CHAMPION MEDAL and have secured since over three thousand dollars ($3,000) in cash premiums, together with the praise and applause of our governor and of very eminent people.

The Progress of the American Negro in the industrial field is significantly reflected in the action taken by the American Federation of Labor at its Montreal convention in June 1920.

A resolution was adopted instructing all affiliated organizations to eliminate the color line and to admit the Negro worker to membership on the same basis as the white worker.

Two Factors have contributed to this policy of human justice—first, the increasing efficiency of the Negro as an industrial worker; second, the fact that under the disabilities of the color line the Negro was too readily available as a strike breaker. The first factor was strongly reenforced by the second.

THE NEGRO AND THE THEATRE.

In spite of the bitterest opposition, the progress of The Race on the stage has not been without its cheering aspects. The Negro was not wanted in legitimate drama, and everything possible was done to keep him out of it. Nevertheless the career of the distinguished actor, Ira Aldridge (1810-1867), ranked him as the greatest tragedian of his time. He played before kings, princes and potentates throughout Europe and was showered with honors and decorations wherever he went.

Other Celebrities.—There have been many other Negroes on the stage, both as performers, playwrights, and composers, among them Robert Cole (1868-1911), Bert Williams (see biographical sketch, page 449), and Ernest Hogan, but their efforts were necessarily limited to minstrelsy, light musical comedy, and vaudeville. In the motion picture field Noble M. Johnson has starred in such films as "Intolerance," "The Death Warrant," etc.

True Negro Drama.—Thus an honest presentation of Negro character has been somewhat of a dream—a dream nevertheless that must some day come true. Evidences of its coming are seen in "Granny Maumee" and other plays by Ridgely Torrence, produced in New York City by a company of colored players, also in "The Exile," "The Star of Ethiopia" and other Negro plays produced by Negro actors with remarkable success.

Charles Gilpin, as "Emperor Jones," in Eugene O'Neill's play of the same name, stirred the country by his magnificent acting, his imagination, and his impersonation. The play was first produced by the Provincetown players (white) in Greenwich Village and later moved to an uptown theatre in New York, where it ran with packed houses for many months. Mr. Gilpin proved in a startling way that a Negro can act, and he proved the fact for all time to come.

The Shuffle Along Company was another of the forward steps of 1921. This company of players had phenomenal success wherever they went.

A Chain of Negro Theatres.—Barney Oldfield once gave Clarence Bennett of New Orleans a diamond ring. Early in 1919 Bennett hocked this ring for $1,000.00, bought the Lyric Theatre there, and opened it as a playhouse exclusively for Negroes. Out of this venture has grown what is known as the Theatre Owners' Booking Association, which controls over fifty theaters throughout the country, catering to ten million Negroes, and representing an investment of over $5,000,000.00. It has inspired and encouraged the development of an immense amount of astonishingly good talent in the Race that was never before suspected.

1. HENRY D. DAVIDSON, Principal Centerville Industrial Institute.
2. W. M. HUBBARD, Principal Forsyth Normal and Industrial School.
3. W. R. BANKS, President Texas College, Tyler, Tex.
4. J. E. MILLER, President Baptist Normal and Industrial Institute.
5. B. F. ALLEN, President Turner College.

CHAPTER XIII.

EDUCATIONAL PROGRESS.

In spite of most severe restrictions against teaching the Colored people in the South to read and write every effort was made on their part to secure an education by stealth— a desire to learn has been, from the beginning, one of their outstanding characteristics. Today we see the results in an intelligent, useful, truly American citizenship.

During the Civil War under the Freedmen's Bureau there sprang up hundreds of schools all over the South devoted to the training of the Negro population. The teachers came from the North with truly altruistic motives and the progress was remarkable.

Almost immediately normal schools and academies for higher education came into existence. Atlanta University, Fisk University, Straight University, Howard University, and Hampton Institute are among the nationally known institutions which came about through these missionary efforts. Incidentally there evolved the Peabody, Slater, Hand, Jeanes funds and others to aid and maintain the already high standard of education.

The common schools of the South came into existence through the political power of the Negro vote in the reconstruction of the new state governments after the Civil War. Expenditure of time and money on Negro schools has been hopelessly inadequate when compared with the white schools, but the following statistics indicate a decided change for the better. In 1890, 39 per cent of the Negro population was illiterate. In 1900 the rate dropped to 30 per cent and according to the latest government

18

SCENES FROM OKOLONA INDUSTRIAL SCHOOL.

1. Home of the President.   4. Boy's Dormitory.

2. Ball Team.   3. Main Building.

5. 70.2 Bushels Oats to the Acre.

figures the illiterates now number only 18 per cent of the entire Negro race in America. The records of Phi Beta Kappa show that at least 36 Negro students have been honored with membership in this exclusively honorary organization in competition with white students in our higher educational institutions. The total number of Negro college graduates is now over 7000.

RECENT PROGRESS IN NEGRO EDUCATION.

The Past Year has witnessed considerable progress in the field of Negro education, despite adverse conditions brought about by the war. Probably the most significant event of the year was the appointment in Texas of a state supervisor of rural Negro schools, whose salary and expenses are paid entirely by the state. Short terms, poor schoolhouses, and low salaries continue to hamper the work of the public schools, but the problem of Negro education has been called to the attention of the white South by the recent exodus of Negroes from that section, and some improvement has already been made. While there has been a considerable increase in the actual amounts appropriated by the Southern states for salaries of Colored teachers, the Negro still receives no greater proportion of the sums expended for teachers' salaries. The official reports of State superintendents of public instruction show that these officials are trying to increase the school facilities for Negroes and are calling the attention of the public to the matter.

Jeanes Industrial Teachers.—The number of Jeanes industrial teachers has increased, and their work has been so effective that one state superintendent recommends in his official report that similar supervisors be employed for white schools. The cooperation of the General Education

Board has enabled these teachers to organize home makers' clubs during the summer months.

In doing this home club work the teachers give demonstrations of cooking, canning, and preserving. The General Education Board has also cooperated with the states in maintaining supervisors of rural schools and in furnishing equipment for county training schools. The county training schools, supported by the counties with the aid of the Slater fund, have passed the experimental stage, and only the high cost of labor and materials prevented the building of additional schools during the year. The Rosenwald fund has made possible the erection of a number of rural schoolhouses. The Phelps-Stokes fund, which financed the investigation of Negro education, continues to cooperate with the Bureau of Education. Its work has been the maintenance of an information bureau, giving expert advice to schools and keeping before the public the educational needs of the Negro. The table here given shows the extent of the work done by the Jeanes fund and how it is financed:

NEGRO RURAL SCHOOL FUND, JEANES FOUNDATION, 1918-19.

States	Number of Teachers	Number of Counties	Paid by Jeanes Fund	Paid by Public Fund
Alabama	24	23	$5,223.00	$3,806.83
Arkansas	20	19	2,928.75	7,750.00
Florida	4	4	1,055.00	612.00
Georgia	24	24	3,810.00	3,060.00
Kentucky	9	9	1,995.00	1,065.00
Louisiana	15	14	4,185.00	2,848.00
Mississippi	26	25	4,110.00	6,535.00
North Carolina..	39	39	5,815.00	7,665.00
South Carolina..	14	14	3,465.00	1,708.00
Tennessee	20	21	3,557.50	5,110.00
Texas	6	6	1,540.00	1,300.00
Virginia	16	18	2,973.00	3,132.00
Total.........217		216	$40,657.25	$44,591.83

State Supervisors.—At present 10 states, with the assistance of the General Education Board, maintain

SWIFT MEMORIAL COLLEGE—SENIOR NORMAL CLASS.

SAW-MILL MEN OF TUSKEGEE INDUSTRIAL INSTITUTE.

BIRD'S-EYE VIEW OF THE CAMPUS AT TUSKEGEE INSTITUTE, ALABAMA.

supervisors of Negro rural schools. Oklahoma and Florida are the only states with a considerable proportion of Negroes that have no special supervisor. In Texas the supervisor is paid entirely by the state.

The work of the state supervisors may be briefly summarized under four heads: (1) The improvement of school facilities, by urging county superintendents and boards of education to extend school terms, pay better salaries and provide better houses. (2) The development of county training schools, maintained by the counties with the help of the Slater fund. The first object of these schools is to train teachers for the rural schools. In offering some high-school work and industrial training, these schools are rendering a large service. (3) The improvement of teachers in service by conducting county institutes, and cooperating with State normal schools and summer schools conducted by private institutions. (4) The promotion of home-makers' clubs. In North Carolina and Mississippi the state supervisor has a Colored man to assist him in his work. In North Carolina the salary of this assistant is paid by the State Colored Teachers' Association; in Mississippi it is paid by the state. The work of these assistants has been of great value.

County Training Schools.—At present there are 77 of these institutions and several others will be erected as soon as the abnormal price conditions of war times have passed. They are divided among the states as follows: Alabama, 11; Arkansas, 5; Florida, 1; Georgia, 5; Kentucky, 2; Maryland, 1; Louisiana, 4; Mississippi, 3; North Carolina, 14; South Carolina, 6; Tennessee, 6; Texas, 5; Virginia, 8. These schools are built and maintained by the combined efforts of the public-school authorities, the Slater Fund, the Colored people of the country and the local white friends of Negro education.

SCENES FROM ROBERT HUNGERFORD NORMAL AND INDUSTRIAL SCHOOL, MAITLAND, FLORIDA.
Mrs. M. C. Calhoun, Principal.

One of the greatest immediate needs is for even fairly competent teachers in the small public schools. The Slater fund has contributed much to the preparation of teachers, but in the past its contributions in this direction have been mainly to the larger and higher institutions. There is now great need for the preparation of teachers in a lower grade of advancement. The immediate conditions under which such work must be done may be far from ideal, but the effort faces facts as they are. It is a fact that a very large majority of the teachers in the small rural schools for Negroes have got what they have of education and training in their own neighboring county. Many superintendents are showing interest in the improvement of some central school in the county, which may serve the purpose of supplying a somewhat better grade of teachers.

Aid from the Slater fund is given on the following simple conditions:

First. That the school property shall belong to the state or county, thus fixing the school as a part of public-school system.

Second. That there shall be an appropriation of at least $750 from the public funds for maintenance.

Third. That the teaching shall be carried strictly and honestly through at least the eighth grade, including industrial work, and in the last year some training, however elementary, for the work of teaching.

Under these conditions the Slater fund has agreed to appropriate $500 for maintenance, and in the first year, where new buildings or repairs may be necessary, to aid in supplying these in cooperation with amounts raised from other sources.

Rosenwald Schools.— The Rosenwald fund is available for assistance in constructing model Colored school buildings, in cooperation with local communities and

WOMEN'S CONFERENCE, 1918, DAYTONA NORMAL AND INDUSTRIAL INSTITUTE.

county authorities. This fund is offered for the purpose of encouraging the construction of modern model school-houses. Such houses will doubtless improve the kinds of residences of the people and tend to elevate the moral and civic ideals of the people.

Upon compliance with the following conditions, participation in the Rosenwald fund is possible:

1.   The schoolhouse is to be for country children, and small towns may be interested.

2.   From two to five acres of land are to be secured by the Colored people, at a place approved by the school board, and the property is to be deeded to the board of education for Colored school purposes.

3.   The county superintendent, the patrons, and the Rosenwald fund are to agree upon a plan of building.

4.   The superintendent of schools shall handle the funds and direct the construction of the building.

5.   The community and county authorities must guarantee the completion and equipment of the building. The house shall be painted inside and outside with at least two coats of paint; each classroom must contain at least 20 lineal feet of good blackboard and have suitable desks for pupils and teacher; the building must contain at least two cloakrooms, a workroom and a small kitchen. The smoke flues must be built from the ground.

6.   Two closets, properly located, must be built.

7.   It is understood that the school shall be run at least five months each year.

Propositions.—For a one-teacher schoolhouse the community and county authorities must raise in cash, material and labor, $750. The Rosenwald fund will contribute $400.

For a two-teacher house the community and county

THE MYRTILLA MINER NORMAL SCHOOL, WASHINGTON, D. C.   MISS MOTEN, PRINCIPAL.

PALMER MEMORIAL INSTITUTE, SEDALIA, N. C.

RUST COLLEGE, HOLLY SPRINGS, MISS.

authorities will raise, as above, $1,000. The Rosenwald fund will give $500.

In cases of consolidation of two or more schools the Rosenwald fund will contribute more.

The Rosenwald fund is handled by the extension department of Tuskegee Institute. According to the latest available information a total of 501 schoolhouses have been built at a cost of $726,000.00 of which Mr. Rosenwald has contributed $193,616.00. Additional expenses paid by Mr. Rosenwald amount to about $25,000.00.

Phelps-Stokes Fund.—For the past five years the Phelps-Stokes fund has financed a staff of workers in the Bureau of Education. One member of the staff who is trained in business methods and accounting gives all his time to the improvement of accounts and records in the schools. Schools have been given assistance in their efforts to adapt their courses to the needs of their pupils and community. Fraudulent Negro schools have been exposed, and the needs of worthy institutions brought to the attention of interested persons. A bureau of information has been maintained. Campaigns for the teaching of gardening and for the improvement of living conditions in dormitories have been carried on. The fund's agents have kept in touch with educational boards of the various churches, other educational funds, the public-school authorities in the several states, independent schools and land-grant colleges, and have endeavored to have these agencies coordinate their efforts. Individual schools have been given financial aid for maintenance. Fellowships for the study of the race question have been established at two state universities in the South.

PUBLIC SCHOOL FACILITIES.

The public schools for Negroes in the South, especially

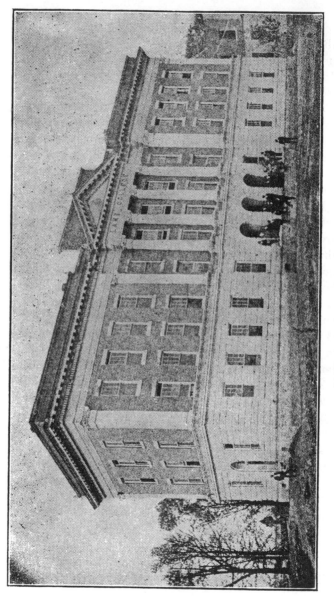

LANE COLLEGE, JACKSON, TENN.

in those counties where the Negroes outnumber the white people, are not doing efficient work, because of the small salaries paid to teachers, short terms, and poor school buildings. In the annual report of the Alabama Department of Education we find the statement that :

The amount paid for salaries in the public schools of the state amounts to $3,145,604 for white teachers—an average annual salary of $431 for each man and $363 for each woman, almost precisely what they were the year before, and despite the fact that the high cost of living is constantly increasing. In the schools for negro children last year 641 men and 1,931 women were employed. There was a slight decrease in the number of both men and women due to the egress of Negroes to other states. There was expended in the form of salaries upon the teachers so employed $399,970, a decrease of $20,185 from the preceding year. The average salary paid to each man was $167, and to each woman $152, and the length of the school term was 104 days.

From the above quotation it will be seen that the superintendent of education in Alabama explains the decrease in the number of Negro teachers and pupils by the migration of Negroes from the South. The white men and Colored men who have investigated the movement are agreed that the poor public-school facilities were among the most important causes of the exodus.

The following table shows the increases in the amounts appropriated for the salaries of Negro teachers in five of the Southern states. It will be seen that, while in every case there has been an actual increase, there has been very little increase in the proportion of the total salaries, and in the case of Florida and North Carolina there has been actual decreases in the proportion. In considering the figures in the table it should be remembered that between

19

DAYTONA NORMAL AND INDUSTRIAL INSTITUTE, MARY MCLEOD BETHUNE, PRINCIPAL AND FOUNDER,

A SPECIAL CLASS IN BASKET MAKING.

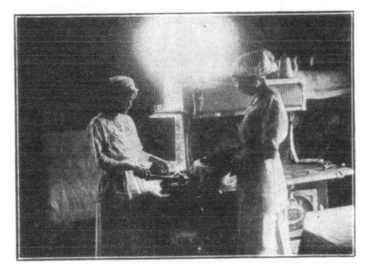

TEACHING COOKING, CENTERVILLE INDUSTRIAL INSTITUTE, CENTER-
VILLE, ALABAMA.

FISK UNIVERSITY, NASHVILLE, TENN.

VIRGINIA HALL.—HAMPTON INSTITUTE.

293

1900 and 1910 the white population of the southern states increased faster than the Colored and it is only reasonable to assume that this has been the case since 1910:

INCREASE IN SALARIES OF NEGRO TEACHERS IN FIVE STATES.

States	Date of report	Salaries	Per cent of total	Date of report	Salaries	Per cent of total
Florida	1910-11	$167,381	14.2	1916	$214,291	11.6
Georgia	1911-12	483,622	14.3	1917	555,822	14.8
Louisiana	1911-12	211,376	7.0	1915	263,515	7.6
North Carolina	1910-11	340,856	16.6	1916	563,273	14.1
Virginia	1911-12	421,381	13.2	1916-17	626,555	14.7

Recent Publications.—From time to time various state departments of education issue pamphlets showing the progress that has been made in Negro education. As representative of these, Bulletins 9 and 10 of the Georgia Department of Education may be cited. These leaflets contain the reports of the Home Makers' Club workers and the Jeanes Industrial Teachers. The Department of Public Instruction in North Carolina issues a "Monthly Progress Letter" reporting the activities of field workers in that state. The most significant publication of the year is one issued by the Louisiana Department of Education entitled "Aims and Needs in Negro Public Education of Louisiana." It is a frank and fearless discussion of the problem.

It may be well to point out here that in some sections of the state the Negro is not receiving for the education of his race the direct school taxes that he contributes. To fail to grant him this amounts to confiscation. Segregation of funds or taxes for the two races is undesirable, but let us allow him what he is clearly entitled to. Surely this includes a just share of state taxes, a just share of corporation taxes, all fines that his race pays, and the indirect school taxes that he pays as renter and as laborer in helping to produce the wealth of the state. In dealing

PINEY WOODS COUNTRY LIFE SCHOOL, LAURENCE C. JONES, PRINCIPAL.
Student Body Marching to Chapel Led by the Band.

MARTIN LUTHER GRAVES HALL, UNION UNIVERSITY, RICHMOND, VA.

MORRIS BROWN COLLEGE, ATLANTA, GA.

PHILLIPS HALL, TEXAS COLLEGE, TYLER, TEXAS.

NEW ORLEANS COLLEGE, NEW ORLEANS, LA.

with this question we must learn to apply the same standards of honesty and fairness that we use in dealing with the different white schools and white communities. Only through the exercise of justice and fair play may we expect justice and fair play in return, and as a result of this, good feeling and good citizenship.

Educational Meetings.—The National Association of Teachers in Colored Schools held its fifteenth annual meeting at Harper's Ferry, W. Va., July 31 to August 2. This was the most important educational gathering of the year. A number of state teachers' associations met during the year. These associations have worked to raise the standard of the teaching profession, and have cooperated with state superintendents in many ways. On account of war conditions, the Association of Colleges for Negro Youth was unable to hold its annual meeting.

Church Boards.— The American Baptist Home Mission Society has adopted the policy of concentrating its efforts at one or two schools in a state, and has therefore withdrawn its aid from some schools where the public school facilities become adequate, and increasing the support of other institutions. The Freedmen's Aid Society of the Methodist Episcopal Church has discontinued its appropriation to Walden College, at Nashville, Tenn., and the property of Walden has been given to Meharry Medical College. The board has decided to sell the property of New Orleans College, at New Orleans, La., and of Gilbert Industrial Institute, at Baldwin, La. Only one school will be maintained by this board in Louisiana. It will be located in a section where a secondary school is needed.

The Christian Woman's Board of Missions now maintains five schools and property has been purchased for another one. The Presbyterian Board of Missions to the Freemen reports new presidents at two schools maintained

LECTURE HALL, UNION UNIVERSITY, RICHMOND, VA.

BENEDICT COLLEGE, COLUMBIA, S. C.
Above and Below—Campus Scenes.
Center—Nurses and Superintendent.

by the board. The Society of Friends has determined on the policy of enlarging the Cheyney Training School for Teachers, at Cheyney, Pa. The American Church Institute for Negroes of the Protestant Episcopal Church reports a growing appreciation of the importance of accurate accounting and businesslike administration in the schools under its control.

The educational boards of the African Methodist Church, the A. M. E. Zion Church and the Colored Methodist Episcopal Church have given evidence of their willingness to improve the accounting, buildings, and supervision of students in the schools under their control.

Private and Denominational Schools.—Most of the secondary schools for Negroes in the South are supported by private philanthropy. These schools are largely denominational and have some assured, though inadequate, support from the churches back of them.

Some Negro schools are well known and have many influential friends. But many worthy schools both of the academic and industrial type have no income except from donations. They need money urgently, not only for the necessary work they have been doing for years, but particularly to provide the special training imperatively needed for large numbers of Colored people in the reconstruction emergency.

First Research Grant.—The National Academy of Sciences operating under the Congressional Charter, the highest scientific body in America, has just announced that it will provide a grant for the research of Dr. Ernest E. Just in the field of Physiology of Development at Howard University. This is the National Research Council's first grant in the field of biology. It is in signal honor to the Negro people of America, because it reminds us once more that the competitions of intellect know no color line. Dr.

Just, concerning whom more appears in another section, has made a remarkable record in his chosen work. He is a member of Phi Beta Kappa and was awarded the first Spingarn Medal by Gov. Whitman in 1915.

Knowles Building.   Boys' Hall.   Stone Hall.   Girls' Hall.   Model Home.

ATLANTA   UNIVERSITY.

TYPES OF MODERN NEGRO ARCHITECTURE.

NEW HOME OF THE SUNDAY SCHOOL PUBLISHING BOARD OF THE NATIONAL BAPTIST CONVENTION, U. S. A.

This convention presided over by Dr. E. C. Morris was organized in 1880 and has 3,116,325 members. The publishing house supplies literature to over 12,000 Sunday schools.

CHARLES M. MELDEN, PRESIDENT NEW ORLEANS COLLEGE, NEW
ORLEANS, LA.
Author of Chapter XIV.

CHAPTER XIV.

RELIGION AND THE NEGRO.

Written Expressly for This Book by Charles M. Melden, D. D., President of New Orleans University.

A common fallacy against which a writer should guard himself is that of drawing universal conclusions from particular premises. Generalizations are frequently based on very narrow inductions. This is apt to be the case in dealing with peoples and races. Types, representative of the whole, are not so plentiful. The typical American, the typical Briton, Frenchman, German, exists only in the fertile imagination of the person who uses the term. The old proverb "ab uno disce omnes" cannot without great qualification be applied to ethnic traits. This is peculiarly true of the Negro.

Many Negro Races.—The Negro is not one but many, not simple but complex, not local but widely distributed, not homogeneous but divergent. The old song "They All Look Alike to Me" reveals the superficiality of the observer rather than describes the monotony of the subject. There is the same variety among Negroes that we find among other races. The word Negro has a wide denotation. It embraces all dark-skinned peoples whose original home is in the inter-tropical and sub-tropical regions of the Eastern hemisphere, stretching roughly from the Senegambia to the Fiji Archipelago lying north and south between the extreme parallels of the Philippines and Tasmania. From this can be seen how numerous, widespread and complex the Negroid races are. They differ in appearance, in color, in physical development, in degree of civilization, in temperament, in intellectual ability and attainment, in morals and religion. Mr. Smythe, United

307

BISHOP I. B. SCOTT.   (C) C. M. Battey.

States Minister to Liberia, says he has personal knowledge of two hundred tribes on the west coast of Africa
alone, and describes them as more unlike in their characteristics than the French and German. These differences have been transferred to America and perpetuated.
Moreover, there has been quite a large intermixture of
Caucasian blood, carrying with it the faults and excel-
lencies of the strain.

These considerations show how difficult it is to char-
acterize the colored people as a whole. Too often no
attempt is made to differentiate, and all Negroes are
grouped indiscriminately together. The man of culture
of high ideals, of upright life, of polished manners, is
confounded with the lowest and most ignorant, the most
degraded and brutal. This works a grave injustice to
the aspiring and advanced members of the race.

In treating of the religion of the Negro these facts
must be borne in mind. It will be difficult, if not impossible within the limits of a chapter, to discuss exhaus-
tively this important subject. To do this would require
researches into tribal and national customs for which we
have not the space. Nevertheless, in spite of individual
traits, we may discover certain general characteristics
which may help us. There are racial qualities. However individuals may differ in physical appearance, they
still have sufficient resemblance to identify them with
their race. Thus we may trace among the mental and
moral peculiarities of individuals certain racial characteristics. In this lies our hope as we attempt to study
the religion of the Negro.

We can better appreciate the present religious condi-
tion of the people if we glance at their history. The
American Negro looks to Africa as his ancestral home.
His forefathers lived very largely along the west coast

of that continent. He has inherited many of his religious beliefs and customs from them.

Religion Founded on Superstition.—The religion of the native African was a kind of animism or fetichism. "The world is full of spirits—spirits, of the rivers, the mountains and the woods. Most important were the ghosts of the dead who had power to injure or help the living and who were therefore propitiated by offerings at stated periods as well as on occasions when their aid was specially desired." (Bryce.) This sense of spirit presences, malevolent and benevolent, developed a persistent fear upon which the medicine man or witch doctor played. He claimed supernatural powers. By means of charms and incantations he withstood the attacks of evil spirits and protected his favored ones. This gave him great influence over the ignorant and simple-minded people which he used for his own preferment and emolument.

The Over God.—From out the all but universal darkness one may catch a gleam of light, dim, it is true, and uncertain, but apparently coming from the original source, viz., certain tendencies toward polytheism and even monotheism. Miss Kingsley says, "The African has a great Over God." Nassau, the missionary, affirms, "Standing in the village street surrounded by a company whom their chief has courteously summoned at my request when I say 'I have come to speak to your people.' I do not need to begin by telling them that there is a God. Looking on that motley assemblage of villagers the bold, gaunt cannibal, with his armament of gun, spear and dagger; the artisan with rude adze in hand, or hands soiled at the antique bellows of village smithy; women who have hasted from the kitchen fire with hands white with the manioc dough or still grasping partly scaled fish;

BISHOP C. H. PHILLIPS, NASHVILLE, TENN.

(C) C. M. Battey

BISHOP GEORGE W. CLINTON.

(C) C. M. Battey.

and children checked in their play with tiny bow and arrow, or startled from their dusty street pursuit of dog or goat. I have yet to be asked, 'Who is God?'"

This conception of the "Over God" has nothing of the Christian content in it. He is remote and to be disregarded or feared rather than loved and worshipped. Weatherford thus sums up his study of the African's religion: "A God who created man and is supreme but who has gone away into a corner of the universe and is no longer interested in his creation; an infinite host of spirits, good and bad, which hold the destiny of man in their grasp and whose favor must, therefore, be won; witch doctors and medicine men who conjure certain spirits and keep the people in constant awe; fetiches which are the habitats of spirits used for protection; and with the practice of black art with all its murderous motives and deeds. Of course there are elements of moral power in this religion, but so much of it is so degraded that one wonders if God has been able to reveal himself in the smallest degree to these people."

Voodooism.—When the Negro came to this country he brought his crude conceptions of religion with him. They found expression in the West Indies and in the South in superstitions and the excesses of Voodooism. During the days of slavery this persisted, and it is to be feared that it has not entirely passed away. Among many, belief in hoodoos, witchcraft, ghosts, "hants," as they are called, is still strong. It resists the influence of Christianity. Doubtless it will require many generations of Christian training before it is entirely eliminated. This, perhaps, is only what we should expect when we remember that centuries after their conversion to Christianity Anglo-Saxons burnt at the stake persons accused of witchcraft, and even now individuals, professing to be intelligent, will carry a horse chestnut in their pocket as a guard against rheumatism.

Religion in Slavery.—In judging the religion of the Negro, this dark background must not be forgotten. The mighty influences of heredity must be taken into account. It should be remembered also that this environment for two hundred and fifty years in this country was not such as to develop the highest type of intelligent Christian character. It is true that some owners took an active interest in the religious welfare of their slaves, but many did not care. Besides this the severe laws against acquiring learning, and in some States against assembling even for religious meetings, militated against any intelligent conception of the obligations of a Christian life. Their preachers, while sometimes men of a great natural ability, nevertheless were illiterate. They had the power to sway their hearers, but necessarily their range of thought was limited. They could stir the emotions but not inform the mind. This is essential. A clear conception of duty must be at the basis of a Christian character. But in spite of their disadvantages, Bishop Haygood was able to say: "I know that the religious life of the colored people in the days of slavery was not what it ought to have been, yet among them were the holiest men and women."

A Natural Emotion.—Imperfectly as they may express themselves, everyone who knows the Negro people must admit that they are naturally religious. This is clear from even our brief glance at their history. Their rich emotional nature responds to the appeal of religion. Converted to Christianity they have a simple but mighty faith, a vivid and powerful sense of the supernatural. God is very real to them. And while it must be admitted that their religion is sometimes mixed with superstition, it is also true that by it they are saved from infidelity

CLINTON METROPOLITAN A. M. E. CHURCH, CHARLOTTE, N. C.

and materialism. In the dark hour of their servitude it sustained and cheered them. Says Doctor Blyden: "By that mysterious influence which is imparted to man independently of outward circumstances, to not a few of them the preaching of the gospel, defective as was its practical exemplification, opened a new world of truth and goodness. There streamed into the darkness of their surroundings a light from the Cross of Christ, and they saw that through suffering and affliction lay a path to perfect rest above this world; and in hours of the most degrading and exhausting toil, they sang of the eternal and unseen."

Religion Shown in Song.—If the songs of a people are an index to their character, then the Negroes are worthy of all praise. They reveal much of the Christ spirit. We may frequently catch the minor tone, but never a vengeful note. There is plenty of pathos, but no rancor. They pray for blessings upon themselves, but not for curses upon their oppressors. This is in sharp contrast to the Hebrew Psalms, many of which call down the most fearful imprecations upon the heads of their enemies. They pray for Christlike qualities, for love, gentleness, long suffering, patience, kindness. "To be more like Jesus in my heart." They may be violent upon provocation, but are quick to forgive. They do not harbor a vengeful spirit. They are not good haters. In their songs they turned away from hardships and privations of their lot and found comfort in personal communion with their Saviour and the contemplation of their heavenly home. "Steal away to Jesus," "Dem Golden Slippers," and other melodies for the time lifted them out of the sordid life they were obliged to lead into the realities of the spirit world. As one has said, "The captive Jews did not sing by the waters of Babylon, but the Negro, in the dark

LEADERS OF THE NATIONAL BAPTIST CONVENTION OF THE UNITED
STATES OF AMERICA.

1. C. H. PARRISH, D.D., President of Simmons University.
2. R. B. HUDSON, A.M., Secretary.
3. J. D. CRENSHAW, Editor Nat'l Baptist Voice.
4. A. M. TOWSEND, D.D., of the S. S. Publishing Board.
5. E. C. MORRIS, D.D., President.

dungeons of American slavery, made themselves harps and swept them to some of the most thrilling melodies."

Among the more intelligent, old time superstitions have been outgrown. It is true even yet that with many religion is simply or largely an emotion. It arouses the feelings but does not influence conduct. It is dissociated from morality. Perhaps this is not an exclusive characteristic of colored people. Every pastor finds one of his greatest problems to be to get the moral life of certain parishioners to correspond with their professions. There are always some who cry, "Lord, Lord!" while they do not the things that He commands. It therefore is not strange that we find the same inconsistency between profession and conduct among these undeveloped people. Emotionalism is not to be crushed, but controlled and directed. Like fire it is a useful servant, but a terrible master. Unrestrained emotionalism will degenerate into all kinds of excess, and religious meetings instead of being mounts of vision are turned into unspeakable orgies. The more intelligent among pastors and people are setting their face against this degradation of a divine quality. Many religious gatherings are conducted with decorum, their worship orderly and reverent. The emotions, the rich soil out of which spring the peace that is like a river and joy that is a perennial fountain, are not to be extirpated but intelligently cultivated.

The writer after an experience of nearly a quarter of a century of close association with the colored people is glad to bear testimony to the great advance which multitudes have made. Their religion is mighty inspiring, molding influence in their lives. They understand that genuine religion fruits in a holy life. The discrepancy between profession and conduct disappears. Their characters reflect the excellences of the Master whose they are and whom they serve. These individuals are the leaven. They will gradually affect the masses. They are leaders who will guide the people out from the wilderness of sin and ignorance into the Promised Land.

Early Churches.—The religious life of the Negro finds organized expression through the church. During slavery colored people usually worshipped with the white congregations. Some effort was directed toward their evangelization. In exceptional cases preachers of their own race ministered unto them, but generally speaking assemblies of colored people, even for religious purposes, were discouraged and in some States forbidden by law. However, here and there churches were organized among them. The Baptists seem to have led in this movement, organizing a church in Williamsburg, Va., in 1776, and one in Savannah, Ga., in 1788. After this churches began to multiply.

The history of religious denominations among the colored people as among other races reveals a much to be deplored tendency to division. Not only are the greater denominations represented among them, but these are divided and subdivided into many petty groups which represent nothing except the idiosyncrasies of some individual and the few he may be able personally to influence. They are weak in members and resources, without moral standards and contribute little or nothing to the welfare of the community.

Baptists.—The type of religious experience and plan of church government of this great denomination make a strong appeal to the colored people. They are attracted by the somewhat spectacular method of baptism by immersion, and enjoy the liberty which is the inviolable possession of the individual church. There is no organization with centralized authority over the

THE NATIONAL BAPTIST PUBLISHING HOUSE, NASHVILLE, TENN., THE LARGEST OF ITS KIND. DR. R. H. BOYD IS THE FOUNDER AND PRESENT HEAD.

denomination as a whole. However, through the convention, the publishing houses, missionary and other organizations a certain uniformity of creed and practice
is maintained.

The National Baptist Publishing House at Nashville
is one of the most successful enterprises of its kind in
the country. It issues most of the literature used in
Negro Baptist churches. Through its organized missionary societies the denomination is doing most praiseworthy work, both at home and abroad. It reaches five
foreign countries where it has established mission stations, some of which have developed into organized
churches. The statistics are unreliable and probably the
figures given are not justified by the facts. However,
according to the Negro Year Book, there are more than
two million regular Baptist besides several thousands
scattered among other Baptist churches.

The African Methodist Episcopal.—This branch of
American Methodism was organized in Philadelphia, in
1816, by a number of colored members who withdrew
from the Methodist Episcopal Church in search of larger
freedom of action. Rev. Richard Allen was elected as
its first bishop. In doctrine and policy this church does
not differ materially from the body from which it sprang.
It has an itinerant and a local ministry, and its territory
is divided into annual conferences. It has a general
conference meeting once in four years. Its affairs are
administered by bishops elected for life, by presiding
elders and pastors. It has a probationary system for
new members, exhorters, class leaders, stewards and
stewardesses.

Since the Civil War the denomination has grown
rapidly. It has covered the Southland and in some of
the larger cities has very strong societies. Its foreign

21

missionary work was organized in 1892. Its publishing interests are extensive and exert a wholesome influence upon the membership. There are several educational institutions supported by the church, among which Wilberforce University is easily first. The last available statistics give 6,647 churches, 620,000 members, property valued at $14,000,000.

African Union Methodist Protestant.—This body, which has a few congregations divided among eight States, came into existence at about the same time the African Methodist Episcopal Church was organized (1816), differing from the latter chiefly in objections to the itineracy, to a paid ministry, and to the episcopacy. It has two annual conferences, with 40 organizations, 69 church edifices, church property valued at $183,697, and 5,592 communicants.

African Methodist Episcopal Zion.—A congregation of colored people, organized in New York City, in 1796, was the nucleus of the African Methodist Episcopal Zion Church. This congregation originated in a desire of colored members of the Methodist Episcopal Church to hold separate meetings, in which they "might have an opportunity to exercise their spiritual gifts among themselves, and thereby be more useful to one another." They built a church, which was dedicated in 1800, the full name of the denomination subsequently organized being given to it. The church entered into an agreement, in 1801, by which it was to receive certain pastoral supervision from the Methodist Episcopal Church. It had preachers of its own who supplied its pulpits in part. In 1820 this arrangement terminated, and in the same year a union of colored churches in New York, New Haven, Long Island and Philadelphia was formed and rules of government adopted. Thus was the African Methodist Episcopal Zion Church formally organized.

EDWARD P. JONES, B. S. D. D., EVANSTON, ILL., PRESIDENT, NATIONAL
BAPTIST CONVENTION, UNINCORPORATED, A SPLIT-OFF FROM
THE REGULAR NATIONAL BAPTIST CONVENTION.

The first annual conference was held in 1821. It was attended by nineteen preachers, representing six churches, and 1,426 members. Next year James Varick was chosen superintendent of the denomination, which was extended over the States of the North chiefly, until the close of the Civil War, when it entered the South to organize many churches.

In its policy lay representation has long been a prominent feature. Laymen are in its annual conferences as well as in its general conferences, and there is no bar to ordination of women. Until 1880 its superintendents, or bishops, were elected for a term of four years. In that year the term of the office was made for life or during good behavior. Its system is almost identical with that of the Methodist Episcopal Church, except the presence of laymen in the annual conference, the election of presiding elders on the nomination of the presiding bishop, instead of their appointment by the bishop alone, and other small divergences.

Its general conference meets quadrennially. Its territory is divided into seven Episcopal districts, to each of which a bishop is assigned by the general conference.

Colored Methodist Episcopal.—The Colored Methodist Episcopal Church was organized in 1870, of colored members and ministers of the M. E. Church, South. Before the war this church did a large evangelistic work among the Negroes. Many of the Negro slaves received the gospel from the same preachers and in the same churches as their masters, the galleries or a portion of the house being assigned to them. For those who were not privileged to attend organized churches, special missions were begun as early as 1829. In 1845 there were 124,000 members of the slave population, and in 1860, 207,000 members. In 1866, after the opening of the

South to Northern churches had given the Negro members opportunity to join the A. M. E. Church, the A. M. E. Zion and other Methodist bodies, it was found that there were only 78,000 members left. The general conference of 1866 authorized these colored members to be organized into separate conferences, and in 1870 two bishops were appointed to organize the colored conferences into a separate and independent church. This church has the same articles of religion, the same form of government, and the same discipline as its parent body. Its bishops are elected for life.

Bishop Holsey declares that the great aim of the church is to evangelize the Negro, and to educate and elevate him. There are 23 annual conferences, 240,798 members. There are 3,196 church edifices. Valuation of property $3,500,000.

Congregational Methodists (Colored).—This body consists of congregations of colored members organized into conferences by presidents of the Congregational Methodist Church, to which it corresponds in all particulars of doctrine, policy and usage. The only difference in the churches of the two bodies is that they are composed of white and colored persons respectively. There are in all 156 organizations and 11,960 communicants, church property $459,500.

There are in addition to these churches several others which share the allegiance of the colored race. For the most part they are similar in doctrine and polity to the larger denominations from which they have sprung. It would be vastly better for them and for society if they would forget their differences and unite themselves with their parent bodies.

In some of the so-called white churches there is a large Negro membership. For example, the Methodist

Episcopal Church has a Negro membership of 350,000, 5,750 local and itinerant ministers and church property valued at $6,000,000. The colored members are represented on all the boards of the church, and in the general conference. They hold high official positions as secretaries, college presidents, etc. As a result of the recent Centenary the church is devoting millions of dollars for work among the colored people, both North and South. In Chicago and other large cities strategic centers have been occupied and extensive preparations made to care for the multitudes who have migrated since the beginning of the exodus of Negroes from the South.

The Presbyterian Congregationalists, Northern Baptists and some others are doing a similar, needed and praiseworthy work.

The Roman Catholic Church has never obtained a great hold upon the colored people. Recently, however, an active propaganda has been undertaken especially in the naturally Catholic sections of the South. States have been districted, cities like New Orleans have been divided into colored parishes, churches have been established, schools opened and every evangelizing agency employed. These efforts are meeting with some success.

There are various religious sisterhoods and brotherhoods which are doing a helpful benevolent work in the various communities where they are organized. The Young Men's and Young Women's Christian Associations afford a fine opportunity for religious activities. Young men and women of executive ability have been developed and are active in pushing forward these organizations. In several cities monumental buildings have been erected and are serving the people. This work has been greatly stimulated by the generosity of Mr. Julius Rosenwald, of Chicago, who in January, 1911,

A. M. E. BIG BETHEL CHURCH, ATLANTA, GA.

announced that he would give $25,000 to any city in the
United States which would provide the remaining $75,000
toward a $100,000 building for colored Young Men's
Christian Association work. Taking advantage of this
generous offer, buildings have been erected in Washington, D. C., Chicago, Philadelphia, St. Louis, Los Angeles,
Atlanta and various other places. The colored people
themselves have contributed liberally toward these enterprises.

Under the auspices of the associations various great
meetings are held, such as the students' conferences at
Kings Mountain, Atlanta, etc. These are centers of instruction and inspiration. The white secretaries cheerfully co-operate and by counsel and material assistance
help the work. Strong men of the colored race have been
appointed as international secretaries, and talented women
are engaged in pushing the work in the cities and the
schools.

Sunday school work, missionary enterprises, publishing interests, all afford opportunities for the expression
of the religious life and activities of the Negro people.
As one has said, "They have done remarkably well, considering all the circumstances, in the matter of educational, missionary, charitable and philanthropic work;
many of their religious institutions of learning being
managed by Negro boards of trustees, taught by Negro
teachers, and supported largely or entirely by themselves.
They are also represented on the boards and in the faculties of the schools maintained by Northern benevolence.
The aggregate amount which they pay annually toward
the education of their children in Christian institutions
is a very considerable sum. They have their local, State
and national educational and missionary organizations,
and are year by year making progress in the art of
organization and administration.

CHAPTER XV.

WHO'S WHO IN THE NEGRO RACE

Written Expressly for this book by W. M. Dogan, D. D., President
of Wiley University.

Aldridge, Ira, tragedian, born in the fall of 1810. At an early age he was brought into contact with a Mr. Kean, who was the great tragedian of the time. Kean induced him to accompany him to Europe in 1826, where he was permitted to appear as Othello. He appeared in this role at Covent Garden in 1833 and in Surrey Theatre in 1848. He ranked as one of the greatest tragedians of his time on the Continent. He received singular honors at the hands of the king of Prussia, the Emperor of Austria, the Emperor of Russia, and other crown heads of Europe. He was elected a member to a number of scientific societies, among them the Prussian Academy of Arts and Sciences; member of the Imperial and Archducal Institution of Our Lady of the Manger in Austria; a member of the Russian Hof-Versamburg of Riga; Honorary member of the Imperial Academy of Arts and Sciences in St. Petersburg, etc.

Alexander, Archie Alphonso, was born at Ottumwa, Iowa, May 14th, 1888. He graduated from the Oak Park High School in 1905. He entered the State University of Iowa and graduated with the degree of Civil Engineer. He was employed by the Marsh Engineering Co. of Des Moines and later was given charge of the bridge construction work on the Minnesota and Iowa Road. In 1914 he severed his connection with this company and entered business for himself. While at the University of Iowa he was a member of the football and track teams.

The modesty of many men and women has prevented a record of their noble lives. In other cases the names did not reach us in time.— THE AUTHOR.

He is also a member of Kappa Alpha Psi Fraternity and The Square and Compass.

Anderson, Charles William, was born at Oxford, Ohio, April 28th, 1866. He was educated at the public schools of Oxford and Middleton, Ohio. He took courses in the Berlitz School of Languages, Worcester, Massachusetts, and the Spencerian Business College of Cleveland, Ohio. He was appointed United States gauger in the second district of New York in 1890. From 1893 to 1895 he was the private secretary of the State Treasurer of New York and from 1895 to 1898 Chief Clerk in the State Treasurer's office. From 1905 to 1915 he was the Collector of Internal Revenue in the Second District of New York, a position which he held until 1917. Mr. Anderson has served on many important committees in New York City among which are: The Committee to Welcome Admiral Geo. Dewey and the fleet upon its return from the Philippine Islands, The Citizens Committee to welcome Admirals Wm. T. Sampson and Winfield S. Schley when the two returned from Cuba, The Hudson Fulton Celebration committee, The Committee to welcome Theodore Roosevelt from his trip in Africa; and a permanent member of New York City Independent Day Commission. He was Republican Alternate Delegate at Large to the Convention at Chicago, Ill., in 1908 and 1912; is a member of the National Geographical Society, The Metropolitan Museum of Art, the Academy of Political Science, and New York Peace Society.

Anderson, Mrs. Martha Broadus, was born in Richmond, Virginia. Her early literary training was obtained in the public schools of Washington, D. C., where she also began her musical training. She studied under Professor John T. Layton and under his direction she mastered the rudiments and technique of music. At the tender age of twelve she had so completely mastered the fundamentals of her art that she was appointed the director of the chorus of the Second Baptist Lyceum. At the completion of her course in the high school she sat for the civil service examination, passed and was appointed to a position in the printing department of our National Government where she remained for a number of years.

In 1898 Mrs. Anderson moved to Chicago and entered more vigorously into the study of music. She placed herself under the direction of such private teachers as Pedro Tinsley, Herbert Miller and in addition to that matriculated in the Chicago Musical College. In 1908 she graduated from this institution with the degree of Bachelor of Music. She maintains a studio in Chicago where vocal as well as instrumental music is taught. She is also the director of the choir of Bethesda Baptist Church.

Banks, Charles,* was born at Clarkesdale, Mississippi, in 1877. He went to Rusk College and left before his graduation. He entered in the mercantile business at Clarkesdale with his brother in 1891. In 1903 he organized the Mound Bayou Bank and was the cashier until 1914. He organized the Mound Bayou Oil Mill and Manufacturing Company and became its general manager. He is a trustee of Wilberforce University, Campbell College, a director of The Union Guaranty Company, Jackson, Mississippi, and the Mississippi Beneficial Insurance Co. He was delegate to the Republican National convention in 1908 and delegate at large in 1912.

Banneker, Benjamin, inventor of the first striking clock in America. His father and mother were born in Africa and he in Maryland. He constructed his clock with rude tools using his watch as a model. He became

* See Chapter XII.

an astronomer and devised the first almanac in America. This almanac was adapted to local requirements of Pennsylvania, Virginia and Maryland and published from 1792-1806. It contained the motion of the sun and moon, the motions, places and aspects of the planets, the rising and setting of the sun; and the rising, setting, southing, place and age of the moon, etc., and is said to have been the main dependence of the farmers in the district covered. He was also engaged as the assistant to the commissioners in laying out the lines of the District of Columbia. A copy of his almanac was sent to Thomas Jefferson who thanked him in a personal letter.

Barnett, Ida B. Wells, was born at Holly Springs, Mississippi. She received her education at Rusk University, Mississippi, and married Ferdinand L. Barnett, assistant state attorney, in Cook County, Ill., June 27th, 1895. Mrs. Barnett has been connected with a number of newspapers and was the editor of the "Free Speech," Memphis, Tenn. She has devoted a number of years agitating against the lynching of her people both in this country and in England. She is one of the most influential women of her race and is a genius at organization. She has organized a number of clubs and societies, among which are the following: "The North-side Women's Club," "The Ideal Club," and "The Douglass Center of Chicago;" "The Ida B. Wells Club," also of Chicago; "The Woman's Era Club" in Boston, Mass., and "The Woman's Royal Union" in New York and Brooklyn. She also organized "The Negro Fellowship League" in 1908, and is an honorary member of a number of these clubs. In 1913 she was appointed probation officer for the city of Chicago. In 1915 she was elected vice-president of the Chicago Equal Rights League and in the winter of 1919 was elected by that body to represent it at the Peace

Conference in Paris. She is a trustee of the Amanda Smith Industrial School for girls and takes active part in politics. Mrs. Barnett is the mother of four children, Alfred, Ida, Aked and Herman.

Billups, Henry Lee, was born at Goliad, Texas, January 10th, 1867. He received his academic education at Wiley University, from which institution he received his B. S. degree in 1888; and his M. S. in 1892 and his Ph. B. in 1905. He is subsequently a graduate of the University of Michigan, where he pursued a course in the law department. He received his LL. B. from the Carnegie Law School in Rodgers, Ohio, in 1914. Mr. Billups has spent a number of years in the teaching profession. He was a member of the faculty of Wiley University for thirteen years and twelve years at the George R. Smith College, Sedalia, Mo. In 1901 he was appointed to the educational work at San Juan, Porto Rico. In 1902 he was admitted to the Missouri Bar and subsequently formed an association with Bouron in a law firm which came to be known as Bouron & Billups of Kansas City, Mo. Mr. Billups is a member of the Knights of Pythias, Mosaic Templars, and was three times elected delegate to the M. E. General Conference.

Bond, Scott, came into this world as a slave in 1852, in Mississippi, and settled down in Madison, Arkansas, after he had attained his majority. Mr. Bond relates the story of his arrival in Madison in a somewhat dramatic manner. It is enough to say that when he found himself in Madison, his entire possessions did not amount to five dollars.

He began life in Madison by renting a little farm on which he raised cotton. The entire income from his little farm went to pay the rent. By consistent application to work he was able to save a few dollars, which he in-

1. SCOTT BOND.
2. BISHOP ALEXANDER P. CAMPHOR.
3. JOHN WESLEY BOWEN.
4. REV. R. H. BOYD.

vested in a small tract of land, part of which was a wash-out in a creek bottom. Little did he dream that this very creek would form the basis of a substantial income. His friends laughed at him for what they called his foolish-ness, but "Unc" Scott as he is intimately known did not murmur. An opportunity came to him one day when the Rock Island Railroad Company's agent, who was out looking for gravel, found that the gravel deposit on his land was the quality of gravel for which he had been looking. Negotiations were begun with him which culminated in a contract between him and the railroad company for the supply of gravel. The income from this contract he has invested in farm lands which he rents to tenants.

Mr. Bond owns over four thousand acres of fertile soil, owns and operates one of the largest cotton gins of that community as well as a saw mill. His entire hold-ings is valued at $280,000 which also includes a co-oper-ative store.

Bowen, John Wesley Edward, was born in New Orleans, La., December 3rd, 1865. He received his A. B. from the University of New Orleans in 1878 and his A. M. in 1886. He entered the Divinity School of Boston University and received his B. D. in 1885 and Ph. D. in 1887. The honorary degree of D. D. was conferred upon him by Gammon Theological Seminary. Dr. Bowen served as a teacher in a number of schools in various parts of the country among which are Morgan College, Baltimore, Md., Professor of Church History and Syste-matic Theology, Howard University, Washington, D. C., Professor of Hebrew and Theology. Dr. Bowen was elected president of Gammon Theological Seminary, Atlanta, Ga., a position which he is now holding.

Bowles, Eva D., was born in Columbus, Ohio, the

daughter of one of the early Negro migrants to Ohio.
She received her early education in the public schools of
Columbus, Ohio. She entered the Ohio State University
and at her graduation entered the teaching profession.
She selected the South as her field of educational activities and for eleven years she toiled among her people in
that section of the country. She was attracted by Y. W.
C. A. work and became identified with the organization
after leaving the South. She won recognition by her
work and was appointed General Secretary of the New
York City branch of the organization. In 1913 she was
elected National Secretary of the Negro branch of the Y.
W. C. A. Under her leadership the association has taken
a new life and a new meaning so far as the people of
color are concerned. One notices a steady increase in the
number of cities with branches of the organization. Miss
Bowles was called upon by the War Work Council of the
National Board of the Y. W. C. A. to take up the work as
Executive Secretary of War Work among the colored
people during the war. She did so and brought order in
what before her appearance was chaos. She organized
the Hostess Houses in the various camps and in the
cities near the camps. Miss Bowles is chairman of the
Northeastern Federation of Colored Women's Clubs and
an ex-president of the National Association.

Boyd, Richard Henry, was born in Mississippi about
the 15th of March 1843 or 1844 of slave parents. When
the Civil War broke out he went with his owners and
younger master with the Confederate Army. After the
war closed, he went back to Texas and was a cow puncher
on the plains of Texas. Then he went to farming and
from farming he worked as a sawmill hand and from
the sawmill back to the cow trail. During this time he
made several trips to Mexico. He was ordained as a

Baptist preacher about 1874 or 75. He has pastored in Willis, Grimes County, Texas, where he held one church for thirty years; at Palestine, Anderson County, Texas, for ten years; at San Antonio, Bexar County, Texas, for about six years. He founded the National Baptist Publishing Board's plant and started the operation of the institution in 1897 at Nashville, Tennessee. The plant is now valued at over three hundred fifty thousand dollars.

Brady, Doctor St. Elmo, is a product of Fisk University, Nashville, Tenn., and Tuskegee Institute. He received his A. B. degree from Fisk University after which he became identified with the faculty of Tuskegee Institute. From Tuskegee he entered the graduate school of the University of Illinois and specialized in chemistry. From the very beginning he won admiration of his instructors for his original research work. His achievements in that line were rewarded by his election to the two honorary national scientific societies, Sigma Chi and Lamda Nu. In the spring of 1916 he received the degree of Doctor of Philosophy in Chemistry.

Immediately after his graduation Dr. Brady was appointed head of the department of Science at Tuskegee Institute, Ala.

Braithwaite, William Stanley Beaumont, was born in Boston, Mass., December 6th, 1878. Mr. Braithwaite is an eloquent example of a self made and self educated man. The death of his father compelled him to leave school at an early age to help support his mother. This fact, however, did not dampen his ardor for knowledge. He continued his studies and developed a fondness for poetry which found expression in a complete abandonment to the pursuit of this form of literature. Today he is reaping the fruit which he had sown under such a great handicap for he is now the literary critic for The

22

Boston Transcript, and an authority on American Poetry and Literature.

Mr. Braithwaite is the author of a number of books and articles among which are: "Lyrics of Life and Love," "The Book of Elizabethan Verse," "The House of Falling Leaves," "The Book of Victorian Verse." He contributes frequently poems and articles to Scribners, Forum, Lippencott, Century and other periodicals.

Brawley, Benjamin, was born in Columbia, South Carolina, April 22nd, 1882. He received the A. B. degree from Morehouse College in the spring of 1901 and five years later, 1906, received a similar degree from the University of Chicago. He subsequently entered the graduate school of Harvard and in the spring of 1908 the degree of Master of Arts was conferred on him by that institution. Since his graduation he has pursued further graduate studies at the University of Chicago.

In the fall of 1902, Brawley was called to Morehouse to fill the chair of Instructor of English and in 1906 was appointed professor of English in that institution. He held that position until 1910 when he severed his connection with Morehouse to become professor of English in Howard University, Washington, D. C. From 1910 to 1912 he labored assiduously at Howard and succeeded in raising the literary tone of the institution. He displayed such unusual ability as an executor that in 1912 Morehouse, his Alma Mater, called him back to fill the responsible position of dean of the college, a position which he has filled with credit to himself and his Alma Mater. In addition to his regular duties at Morehouse Brawley finds time to teach in the Hampton Summer school and lecture before various institutions.

In 1919, Brawley was elected president of the association of colleges for negro youths, a position of honor and distinction.

It is as a writer, however, more than an educator that Brawley is known to the public. The following are some of his more important publications:

"A Short History of the American Negro," The Macmillan Co., New York, 1913, revised 1919.

"The Negro in Literature and Art," Duffield & Co., New York, 1918.

"Africa and the War," Duffield & Co., New York, 1918.

"History of Morehouse College," published by the College, Atlanta, Ga., 1917.

"New Era Declamations," (Edited) The University Press, Sewanee, Tenn., 1918.

"Women of Achievement," Woman's Amer. Bapt. Home Mission Society, Chicago, 1919.

Numerous booklets of verse, especially "The Seven Sleepers of Ephesus," and various articles on Hymnody, Pre-Raphaelitism, Richard Le Gallienne, and other literary topics in "The Dial," "The Sewanee Review," "The South Atlantic Quarterly," etc.

Brooks, Walter Henderson, was born at Richmond, Va. His mother and her six children were sold as slaves in 1858. Young Walter received his early training in Richmond and at Wilberforce Institute, Carolina Mills, R. I. He entered Lincoln University and received his B. A. degree from that institution in 1872. He was a student in the Theological School in 1872-3 and fifteen years later received his M. A. degree from his alma mater. Other degrees conferred upon him are: D. D., Rogers Williams University, Howard University, State University, Louisville, Ky. He was ordained in the Baptist Church in 1876 and served as pastor of the Second Baptist Church, Richmond, Va., 1877-80; Sunday School Missionary, New Orleans, La., 1880-2; and has been

1. HARRY T. BURLEIGH.
2. WILLIAM HENRY BROOKS.
3. BENJAMIN BRAWLEY.
4. WILLIAM S. BRAITHWAITE.

pastor of the Nineteenth Street Baptist Church, Washington, D. C., since 1882. Doctor Brooks was a delegate to the International Sunday School Convention, London, England, in 1889. Dr. Brooks is one of the most interesting and distinguished ministers of the African Baptist Church. The fact that he has been attached to that church for over thirty years attests his capabilities.

Brooks, Dr. William Henry, was born September 6th, 1859. He entered Morgan College, Baltimore, Md., and subsequently Howard University, Washington, D. C. He felt the need of a more thorough training for the ministry and in the fall of 1898 he entered the Union Theological Seminary, New York, and terminated his connection with this institution two years later. From 1903 to 1906 he was a student in New York University where he pursued his courses in philosophy and the natural sciences. Dr. Brooks joined the M. E. Annual Conference in 1879 and received his first appointment as pastor at Talcott. Other charges which he held subsequently were in Spring Creek, West Virginia, Harper's Ferry, Md., and in Washington, D. C. He was ordained minister of the church in 1884 and in 1892 to 1897 was presiding elder in the Washington District and went from there to take up his work as pastor of St. Mark's Church in New York City.

Dr. Brooks has been eminently successful as a churchman and pastor and in recognition of his services to his people and his church the degree of Doctor of Divinity was conferred upon him by Wiley University, Marshall, Texas, in 1897, and by Morgan College, Baltimore, Md., in 1917. He was sent by the church in 1910 as a delegate to the World's Conference at Edinburgh, Scotland. After this conference he went to France and took special courses in the University at Dijon. Dr. Brooks was

Fraternal Delegate to the General Conference of the C. M. E. church in 1902 and a delegate to the General Conference in 1896. He has traveled extensively both in Europe and in this country.

Brown, Samuel Joe, was born in Keosauqua, Iowa, July 6, 1875. At the completion of his high school course he entered the University of Iowa, Iowa City, and graduated four years later with honors. He was elected to the Phi Beta Kappa, the National scholarship fraternity, while in college. He entered the Law School of the University at the completion of his college course and graduated in 1901, and in 1902 received his Master degree from the same school. Before taking up the practice of law Mr. Brown spent one year as principal of the public school of Muchakinock and one year as professor of ancient languages at Bishop College, Marshall, Texas. He is now engaged in the practice of his profession in Boston and Des Moines, Iowa, as member of the firm of Woodson & Brown. He has been singularly honored by his state and county by appointments to serve as a member of the committee of 300 citizens that drafted the commission plan of government for the city of Des Moines, commissioner from Iowa to National Half Century Anniversary of Negro Freedom in Chicago, Ill., in 1915. Mr. Brown was defeated for councilman in 1910 by a narrow margin. Mr. Brown holds membership in Kappa Alpha Psi fraternity, Negro Business League, Iowa State Bar Association, Mason, Eastern Star, ex-president of the Interstate Literary Association of Kansas City and the west.

Bruce, Senator Blanch K., was born a slave in Prince Edward County, Virginia, in 1841. In his young days he was trained with his master's son and when the day of freedom came he migrated to Missouri and for several years was engaged in teaching. He took special courses at Oberlin College, Ohio, to supplement the training which he had received from his master. He soon became tired of teaching, consequently he returned to the South and took up farming in Bolivar County, Mississippi. He was successful in his new occupation and became a prominent man in that section. In recognition of his ability he was elected superintendent of schools in his county and then as sheriff and finally as senator from the state of his adoption. He served in the senate from 1875-1881. At the expiration of his term he was appointed register of the treasury by President Garfield and was reappointed by President McKinley in 1897. He died while still in office in 1898. Mr. Bruce married Miss Josephine B. Wilson of Cleveland, Ohio, on June 24th, 1878 and by this union an illustrious son, Roscoe C., survives.

Bruce, Roscoe Conklin, was born in Washington, D. C., April 21st, 1879. He received his early education in the public school of the District of Columbia, and entered Harvard in 1898, and graduated with honors in 1902. While an undergraduate at Harvard he was elected a member of the Phi Beta Kappa, the college scholarship fraternity. At his graduation Mr. Bruce became the director of the Academic department of Tuskegee Institute and continued in that capacity until 1906. In 1906 he became the supervising principal in the 10th district of the public schools of the District of Columbia. He gave up this position to become assistant superintendent of instruction in the colored schools in the District of Columbia in 1919. Mr. Bruce is prominent in the educational world and devotes a great deal of his time in the study of educational problems especially as they are related to Negro schools and Negro education. He holds membership in the Sigma Pi Phi fraternity and the Mu-So-lit Club.

Buchanan, Walter Solomon, was born at Troy, Alabama, February 8th, 1882. He attended the public school of Troy and later entered Tuskegee Institute, Ala., and finished in 1899. At the completion of his course at Tuskegee he went to Boston, Mass., and entered the Sloyd Training School and completed the course in 1902. He prepared himself to enter Harvard by attending the Y. M. C. A. night school. He matriculated at Harvard and graduated with the degree of B. A. S. in 1906.

President Buchanan began life as a teacher in the Schofield Normal and Industrial Institute. Upon his graduation from Harvard he was appointed southern agent for Tuskegee Institute. He served for two months when he resigned to accept a position as principal of the Corona Industrial Institute, Corona, Alabama. He remained in this position until 1909 and then resigned to become president of State Normal School, Normal, Alabama.

President Buchanan is also connected with the Standard Life Insurance Company as director and holds membership in the following societies: American Academy Political and Social Science, National Geographical Society, Mason, Knights of Pythias. He is one of the editors of "The Competitor."

Burleigh, Harry T., was born in Erie, Pennsylvania. He came into contact with musicians of note at an early period of his life and on his graduation from the high school he entered more actively in the preparation of himself for a musical career. He obtained a scholarship which was offered by the National Conservatory of Music through the influence of a white woman whom he had served on a previous occasion in his home city. In appreciation of the rare opportunity which befell him he made good.

In 1894 he led in a competition for a baritone soloist conducted by the St. George's Church, New York City, and received the appointment and from that day he has been identified with that church. Mr. Burleigh is not only a singer of distinction but also a composer of national prominence. Some of the products of his pen and imagination are sung by artists of note the world over. Among his most popular selections are: "Deep River," "The Soldier," "Jean," "The Gray Wolf," "Ethiopia Saluting the Flag." In recognition of his contribution to the world he was awarded the Spingarn prize in 1917 and the M. A. degree from Atlanta University.

Burroughs, Nannie Helen, was born in Culpeper, Va., May 2, 1879. She took a business course in 1902 and returned to her home and became a bookkeeper and stenographer in a manufacturing house.

Miss Burroughs became a private secretary of Dr. L. G. Jordan, secretary of Foreign Mission Board, and when the Women's Convention Auxiliary was inaugurated she was one of the leading figures.

On October 19, 1909, the doors of the National Training School for Women and Girls were opened to the Negro women of the nation by Miss Burroughs. This institution represents the efforts of this conscientious woman for the betterment of her sex. She is identified with a number of organizations, among them the Douglass Improvement Co., of which she is secretary. She is corresponding secretary of the Woman's Auxiliary of National Baptist Convention; secretary Young Women's Department of the National Association of Colored Women's Clubs. She holds membership in the following organizations: Ladies Union Band; St. Lukes'; Saturday Evening Club and Daughters of the Round Table.

In 1905 she went to London as a delegate to the

World's Baptist Congress and addressed the Assembly on "Woman's Part in the World's Work."

Camphor, Bishop Alexander P., was born in Orleans Parish, La., August 9, 1865. He received his early education in New Orleans University and subsequently at Columbia University, New York, and the University of Chicago. After completing his course of study he entered the teaching profession and spent many years teaching in New Orleans. He was ordained a minister of the church and was assigned to a church in New Orleans. From New Orleans he went to Africa and served as president of the College of West Africa from 1898-1908. Returning to the United States at the expiration of his term as president of the African institution in 1909, he became the president of Central Alabama Institute.

Carrothers, James Davis, was born at Calvin, Michigan, July 2, 1869, the son of James R. and Maggie Carrothers. His mother died at his birth and left him in the care of his father. It is said that Mr. Carrothers has in his veins Negro, Scotch-Irish and Indian blood. His education was received at South Haven, Michigan, from 1874-1883. He entered Northwestern University in 1890 and continued his course of studies there until 1893. In the interval between 1883, the date on which he finished his elementary training, and 1890, his time was spent working in sawmills, lumber camps and similar places. He spent a year at Bennett College in Greensboro, N. C. He was ordained a Baptist minister in 1894. Mr. Carrothers is a voluminous writer and his contributions appear in the leading periodicals of the country. His poems are well received and elicit honorable mention from critics. Among his literary productions are: "The Black Cat," which appeared in 1902. His book of "Selected Poems," which appeared in 1907. "A Man

That Did Not Know," appeared in 1913, "The Dream and the Song" in 1914. Mr. Carrothers has also written his autobiography with the preface written by Ray Stannard Baker, editor of the American Magazine. He also wrote the sketch of Dr. C. Albert Findley for the Associated Sunday Magazine.

Carter, Edward Albert, was born at Charlotteville, Va., April 11, 1881. At an early age he moved to Oskaloosa, Iowa, where he attended high school. 'Upon his graduation he entered the State University of Iowa and received his degree of B. Ph. in 1903. Not satisfied with this degree which he had just earned he re-enrolled in the medical department of that institution from which he graduated four years later. At his graduation Dr. Carter went to Buxton, Iowa, and affiliated himself first with Dr. L. S. Henderson and then with Dr. C. B. Powell (both of them white) and became the partner of the latter. He was appointed health physician for Bluff Creek township and the local surgeon for the Consolidated Coal Company and the C. & N. W. Ry., of Buxton. In all these he is acquitting himself with satisfaction to his employers and with credit for his race.

Dr. Carter holds membership in the following organizations: Kappa Alpha Psi, Mason, National Medical Association, Monroe County Medical Society and Knights of Pythias.

Chandler, Dr. Edward Marion Augustus, was born in Ocala, Florida. He received his early literary training in his native home and in the A. and M. College of Florida. He later entered Howard University, Washington, D. C., and graduated from the College Department in 1913. He was awarded a scholarship to Clark University, Worcester, Mass. He entered Clark in the fall of that year, specializing in chemistry and received his

Master of Arts degree in 1914. In the fall of 1914 he secured a Fellowship to the University of Illinois, entered at that institution specializing in chemistry. Dr. Chandler distinguished himself as a research scholar in chemistry and was elected to the two honorary scientific societies. In 1917 he graduated with the Ph. D. degree.

Immediately after his graduation he secured connection in the chemical laboratory as research assistant in an industrial plant in Chicago.

Chestnut, Charles Waddell, was born in Cleveland, Ohio, June, 1858. Young Chestnut received his preliminary education in the public schools of Cleveland, Ohio, and later in those of North Carolina, where his father returned after the Civil War. At an early age he began to teach and served in various capacities as teacher in both North and South Carolina. He was chosen the principal of the Fayetteville Normal School where he had been teacher, and served for three years, at the end of which time he moved to New York City, where he engaged in some form of journalism in Wall Street. From New York Mr. Chestnut went to Cleveland, Ohio, the state of his birth, and entered the service of the New York, Chicago and St. Louis Railroad Co. as stenographer. He studied in the legal department of the company, to which he had been transferred, and was admitted to the Ohio bar in 1887. His activities as a stenographer and court reporter however have kept him so busy that he has devoted but little time to the practice of law.

For the past twenty-five years he has devoted his time to reporting, assisted by a corps of stenographers. Among his literary productions, most of which have appeared in "Atlantic Monthly," are: "The Wife of His Youth and Other Stories," "The Conjure Woman," in 1889, "The

House Behind the Cedars," 1900, "The Marrow of Tradition," 1901, "The Colonel's Dream," 1905, and the "Life of Frederick Douglass" which forms a part of Beacon's Series of Biographies of Eminent Americans.

Mr. Chestnut is identified with the following organizations: The Chamber of Commerce, The Rowfant Club, The City Club, The Cleveland Bar Association, The Western Reserve Club, and the Council of Sociology. Mr. Chestnut has often appeared on the stage in interpretations of his stories and on these occasions has won the applause of the public.

Coleman, Julia P. H., was born in North Carolina. She received her early education in Scotie Seminary, Concord, N. C. She entered the Pharmaceutical Department of Howard University, Washington, D. C. and received the Phar. D. degree in 1897. She subsequently entered the Pennsylvania College of Pharmacy in Philadelphia where she pursued graduate courses in pharmacy. For ten years after her graduation she was engaged in the drug business both in Philadelphia and in Washington, D. C. About six years ago she became identified with the hair preparation business and organized the Hair-Vim Chemical Co., Washington, D. C., of which she is the president and manager. Mrs. Coleman has recently established a branch of her business in New York City, housed in her own property which is said to have cost her $30,000.

Conrad, George Washington Bryant, was born at Xenia, Ohio, June 22, 1867. He received his early education in the public schools of Xenia, and at Richmond, Indiana, where he pursued a course in business. He subsequently entered Oberlin College in Ohio and later matriculated in the law department of the University of Michigan, from which institution he graduated with the

CLASS IN CHEMISTRY, ATLANTA BAPTIST SEMINARY.

LL. B. degree in 1902. Mr. Conrad has been connected with the Pennsylvania Railroad system for a number of years, serving in the capacity of stenographer and telegraph operator and private secretary to Colonel J. F. Miller, vice president of the railroad. At his graduation from the law school he was employed by that company and assigned to the claim department as assistant.

Mr. Conrad was one of the United States Commissioners at the Louisiana Purchase Exposition held at St. Louis, Missouri, from 1903-4.

Cook, Will Marion, is a musician of international reputation. His musical compositions have thrilled the hearts of music lovers in both continents. As director of the New York Syncopated Orchestra he has helped materially to attract attention of the white public to the excellence of Negro-composed music and the skillfulness of Negro artists. Some of the compositions which have come from his pen are: "Bandana Land," "The Casion Girl," "Cruel Popupa," and other popular pieces. He has just returned from a season engagement in London, England, where the excellence of his work and that of artists under his direction has elicited favorable comment from the music critics of London.

Cotter, Joseph S. Jr., was born in Louisville, Ky., September, 1895, the son of Joseph S. Cotter. He graduated from the Central High School of that city, and entered the class of 1915 in Fisk University. At the close of his second year he was compelled to give up his studies on account of ill health, but not before he had been chosen president of his class, and made brilliant records in scholarship and as a member of the football team.

He served in an editorial capacity with the Louisville Leader and the Courier-Journal but later turned his at-

LIBRARY = Allegheny Campus

tention to the writing of poetry. He attained a degree of literary merit which led Cole Young Rice to rank his work with that of Paul Laurence Dunbar and James Weldon Johnson.

In the spring of 1918, The Cornhill Company, (Boston), published his "The Band of Gideon and Other Lyrics." At the time of his death, February 3, 1919, he left two unpublished books, one of verses "Out of the Shadows," and a collection of "One Act Negro Plays" which is soon to appear.

Cotter, Joseph S., Sr., was born in Kentucky in 1861, and with the exception of two short terms of night school he is entirely self-educated. He began to teach school at the age of twenty-three, and is today the principal of the S. Coleridge Taylor School in Louisville, Ky.

Mr. Cotter has been called the South's premier Negro poet and a worthy successor to the late Paul Laurence Dunbar. Among his best known writings are "Caleb, the Degenerate," a play in four acts, "Sequel to the Pied Piper of Hamlin," "Negro Tales," "I'm Wondering," "The Christmas Tree," and "June Breezes and Roses." His story telling ability is well known throughout the country. Some of his best poems were written to his son, Joseph S. Cotter, Jr., the invalid.

Cottrill, Charles A., was born at Findlay, Ohio, December 3, 1863. He was educated in the public schools of Toledo, Ohio, and the Ohio State Business University. He studied law under John F. Kumber of Toledo, Ohio, while he was chief deputy recorder of Lucas County, Ohio.

Mr. Cottrill began his public career as clerk in the internal revenue service in 1881 and was advanced from

THE LATE JOSEPH S. COTTER, JR.

one position of responsibility to another. In 1878-9 he was bookkeeper in the Treasury office, from 1888-1893 he was corporation clerk in the State department of Ohio; was chief deputy recorder of Lucas County from 1893-1910; in 1911 he was appointed collector of internal revenue for the United States for the District of Hawaii. He served in that capacity until 1915.

Mr. Cottrill was identified with a number of clubs and fraternity organizations among them being, The Ad Club of Honolulu, Mason, Knights Templar, Knights of Pythias, Odd Fellows and member of the Central Union church of Honolulu. Mr. Cottrill is making his home in Honolulu, Hawaii.

Crabb, Edward Joseph, was born at Tuscaloosa, Alabama, December 24, 1865. He received his early education in the private schools of Furman and Jeremiah Barnes and at Talladega College. From 1882-85 he gained his knowledge of electricity through the correspondence course of the International Correspondence School of Scranton, Penn. This course was pursued while he was working in the Birmingham shops of the Louisville & Nashville Railroad. In 1890 he was advanced to the position of utility man. He served in that capacity for a year when he severed his connection with this company to become an instructor in the Westinghouse Air Brake Co., of Pittsburgh, Penn. His duty as instructor took him all over the United States and Canada. Mr. Crabb's efficient work as inspector was recognized by his employers and they appointed him air brake inspector. He occupied this position for two years (1901-3) and then became connected with the Erie railroad as foreman of electricians in the lighting department.

Craig, Arthur Ulysses, was born at Weston, Missouri,

December 1, 1871. His grammar school training was received in the public schools of Weston and his high school training in Atchison, Kansas. He entered the Electrical Engineering School of the University of Kansas in 1892, and completed the four year course in three years, receiving his B. S. degree in 1895. Mr. Craig had the honor to be the first colored man to graduate as an electrical engineer in the United States.

Following his graduation Mr. Craig went to Sweden and studied the Sloyd System under the famous master Herr Otto Solomon, the founder of the system. While in Europe he studied industrial training in London, England, Stockholm and Goteberg, Sweden. On his return he entered Columbia University and specialized in psychology and manual training.

Mr. Craig is turning his training to a profitable account. He has been identified with a number of industrial activities both in and out of the school room. His first connection was with the Tuskegee Institute in Alabama. He remained with this institution from 1896 to 1901. He was night principal of the Armstrong Training School in Washington, D. C., three consecutive years, 1904-5 and 6. He was identified for a time with F. B. Stearn & Co., automobile manufacturers. It was he who introduced mechanical and architectural drawing in the colored schools of the District of Columbia and helped to formulate manual training courses of study in a number of city schools. He originated the public play grounds of the District of Columbia and for three years was superintendent. He is in a great measure responsible for the establishment of the Colored Social Settlement house of Washington, D. C., and the introduction of moving pictures in churches for educational and religious purposes. He is also responsible for the movement to convert Frederick Douglass' home into a memorial.

He holds membership in the following organizations: American Negro Academy, Mason, Teachers' Association of Washington, D. C., National Educational Association and the National Association for the Advancement of Colored People.

Creditt, Dr. William Abraham, was born at Baltimore, Maryland, July 14, 1864. At the age of twenty-one he received his A. B. degree from Lincoln (1885) and the A. M. degree a year later. He received his S. T. B. degree in 1889 and had the honor to be the class orator. Dr. Creditt was ordained a minister in the Baptist church immediately after his graduation and has been engaged in preaching and teaching ever since. He was a teacher in the State University, Louisville, 1890-1900, in the State Normal School, Frankfort, Ky., 1890-1, and pastor of the church in that community. He was elected pastor of the Berean Baptist Church in Washington, D. C., in 1892 and served for five years. He resigned this position to become the pastor of the Cherry Street Baptist church in Philadelphia, Penn. Under his influence the church was reorganized and a $100,000 edifice was erected to take the place of the old building. While pastoring in Philadelphia Dr. Creditt conceived the idea of establishing an industrial training school for the colored youths of the North. He communicated his idea to John S. Tower, and in 1905 the Downingtown Industrial Training School was established in Downingtown, Penn., and Dr. Creditt became its president. In 1915, the demands of the institution for his undivided attention was so great that he resigned his position as pastor to devote his time to the building of the institution. Dr. Creditt has not confined his activities within the church and school-room. He has to his credit the organization of the Cherry Building and Loan Association and the Reliable Mutual Insurance Co.

In recognition of his service to his people and to humanity at large his Alma Mater has seen fit to confer upon him the D. D. and LL. D. degrees.

Crogman, Dr. William Henry, was born at St. Martins, Danish West Indies, May 5, 1841. Dr. Crogman entered Atlanta University, Atlanta, Ga., and received his A. B. degree in 1876; three years later the master degree. He became identified with Clark University in 1876, the year of its organization, and has continued in the service of that institution until today. From 1903-1910 he was president of the institution and since that time Professor of Ancient Languages. His Alma Mater saw fit to confer upon him the degree of Doctor of Letters in 1901 and Clark University the honorary LL. D. On July 10, 1878, Dr. Crogman married Mavinid C. Mott, of Charlotte, N. C., and of this union eight children have been born.

Dr. Crogman is a charter member of Clark University and Gammon Theological Seminary and the secretary of the board of trustees. He has been superintendent of the Sunday School of Clark University and has been for three times a member of the General Conference. He has held offices of distinction in his church, among them, member of the University Senate, and the Commission for the Unification of the Book Concern. Dr. Crogman is a member of the American Philological Association, American Geographical Society and the author of "Talks for the Times."

Cummings, Harry Sythe, was born in Baltimore, Md., May 19, 1866. His early intellectual training was received in the public schools of Baltimore. He entered Lincoln University, Penn., and received his B. A. degree in the spring of 1886. Three years later he received his LL. B. from the University of Maryland. That very year

1. James B. Dudley, LL.D.
2. Charles Waddell Chestnut.
3. William H. Crogman, LL.D.
4. Mathew W. Dogan, D.D.,
    President Wiley University.

he was admitted to the bar of Maryland and began practicing in Baltimore.

Mr. Cummings has been a member of the city council of Baltimore since 1891, and has been instrumental in fighting a number of segregation ordinances which are brought up in the council from time to time. He is the director of the House of Reformation for Colored Youths. In 1892 and in 1904 he was one of the delegates from Baltimore to the Republican National Convention in Minneapolis and Chicago repectively and in 1904 he seconded the nomination of Theodore Roosevelt.

Mr. Cummings is identified with the following organizations: Knights of Pythias, Masons and Odd Fellows.

Curtis, Austin Maurice, was born in Raleigh, N. C., January 15, 1868. He received his early training in the public schools of Raleigh and his preparation for his medical course at Lincoln University, Penn. He received his A. B. degree in 1888. He entered the medical department of the Northwestern University at Chicago, Illinois, and received his M. D. degree in 1891. A year after his graduation he was appointed attending surgeon of Provident Hospital, Chicago, Illinois. In 1896 he was appointed an attending surgeon in the Cook County Hospital. From Provident Hospital Dr. Curtis went to the Freedman's Hospital as the Surgeon-in-Chief, and served from 1898-1902. Since that time he has been connected with the hospital and medical department of Howard in various capacities. He has served as associate professor of clinical surgery in the Medical Post Graduate School and Professor of Surgery. He is also attending surgeon in the Freedman's Hospital. Dr. Curtis' success as a surgeon is well known in the medical world and his work in the hospital has received recognition. He holds membership in the following organizations: Mason, Mu-So-

Lit, National Medical Association, American Medical Association, Medico Chirurgical Society of the District of Columbia and the Physician Reading Club.

Davidson, Shellry James, was born at Lexington, Kentucky, May 10, 1868. He received his preliminary education in the public schools of Lexington and Louisville, Ky., and his A. B. at Howard University in the spring of 1893. At his graduation Mr. Davidson secured a clerical position in the postoffice department of Washington, D. C., and studied law under Colonel William A. Cook during his spare hours.

While in the postoffice Mr. Davidson made a special study of adding machines and invented a rewinding device for totalling and tabulating accounts with an attachment to total money order reports to the Postmaster General. He was commissioned by the Treasury authorities to study the use and operation of adding machines at Detroit, Michigan.

Mr. Davidson was admitted to the bar of Washington, D. C., three years later to the courts of appeals to the District of Columbia, and in 1912 to the Supreme Court of the United States. Mr. Davidson is connected with the following organizations: Masons, Odd Fellows, Colored Bar Association, District of Columbia and Mu-So-Lit Club.

Davis, Benjamin Jefferson, was born in Dawson, Georgia, in 1870. While still in his teens he joined the Grand United Order of Odd Fellows, and became interested in the development of the order. His zeal and initiative were soon recognized and in 1891 he was made past officer of the order and a year later a member of the District Grand Lodge. His promotion from this time was rapid. In 1900 he was elected District Grand Treasurer; in 1904, Grand Director of the North Branch

JUDGE SCIPIO A. JONES.

BENJAMIN JEFFERSON DAVIS.

in Columbus, Ohio; Grand Treasurer of the North Branch in 1906; Chief Justice of the Supreme Court in 1910, in Baltimore, Md.; District Grand Secretary, a position which he held for sixteen consecutive terms, and finally the General Manager of the Corporation of the Order in America.

Mr. Davis' greatest constructive service to the order is the part he played in the erection of the Odd Fellows block in Atlanta, Georgia, and the substantial increase in the wealth of the organization. Of equal importance as a beneficial contribution is his establishment of a bureau of endowment for widows and orphans. To put his plan into effect it was necessary to amend the constitution whereby every member was to carry a death benefit of at least $200 and not more than $500.

Mr. Davis is also the publisher of "The Atlanta Independent," a weekly paper with a wide circulation. He is a Republican and has served as delegate-at-large to the Republican National Convention.

Dett, R. Nathaniel, was born at Drummonville, Ontario, Canada, in 1882. He received his preliminary education in Drummonville. He subsequently entered the Niagara Falls Collegiate Institute and graduated in 1903. Five years after the completion of his course at the institution he received the Bachelor of Music degree from Oberlin Conservatory of Music. He also took special courses in music in Oliver Halstead Conservatory of Music.

Since his graduation Mr. Dett has devoted his time to the teaching of music, and has served as director of music to a number of Negro schools, among them, Lincoln Institute, Jefferson City, Mo., Lane College, Jackson, Hampton Institute, Hampton, Va.

Mr. Dett is the author and composer of a number of

musical selections among which are: "Listen to the Lambs," a choral work; "The Magnolia Suite," parts one and two; "In the Bottoms," a suite for piano also. "The Album of a Heart" appeared in 1911 and received favorable mention. He is the director of the Choral Union of Hampton and is identified with all literary and musical activities of the institution. He is a member of the Musicians League of America.

Diggs, James Robert Lincoln, was born in Upper Marlboro, Md., on November 7, 1866. He attended Wayland Seminary, Washington, D. C., and completed the preparatory, Normal and Theological courses. He matriculated at Bucknell University, Lewisburg, Tenn., and received his B. A. degree in 1898 and a year later his M. A. degree.

His desire for thoroughness in the educational world led him onward. He entered Cornell University in New York where he pursued special courses and a year later he entered Illinois Wesleyan University in Bloomington and three years later (1906) received his Ph. D. degree. Doctor Diggs was singularly honored while in Bucknell University for his high scholarship. He was president of the Theta Alpha Literary Society. Twice represented his Alma Mater in successful inter-collegiate debates and won the prize in the Junior debate. He was an honor man of the University.

Dr. Diggs entered the teaching profession first as a public school teacher and subsequently as a college professor and dean. At Virginia Union University he was professor of Latin, Economics and Philosophy. He served respectively as president of State University, Louisville, Ky., 1906-8; Virginia Seminary from 1908-11; Dean of the College Department of Selma University, 1911-14; and president of Clayton Williams University, Baltimore, Md., 1914. He is also pastor of Trinity Baptist Church of Baltimore.

Dr. Diggs holds membership in a number of organizations, among which are American Academy of Political and Social Sciences, Negro Academy, American Geographical Society, The N. A. A. A. C. P., the Alumni Associations of Bucknell, and Virginian Union University.

Dogan, Dr. Mathew Winfred, was born at Pontotec, Mississippi, December 21, 1863. His early training was received in his native town and later he entered Rust University, Holly Spring, Mississippi. He graduated from the preparatory department and later entered the college department and graduated at the head of his class in the spring of 1886. At the completion of the college course Mr. Dogan was appointed to a place on the faculty of Rust University and five years later, 1891, he was elected teacher of mathematics in the Central Tennessee College, Nashville, Tenn., now known as Welden University. From Welden University he went to Wiley in 1896, as president of that institution and has held that position ever since. Dr. Dogan is one of the most influential men in the M. E. conference. He has represented his conference as a delgate to the General Conference since 1904 and has just been elected for the fifth time to that great office. Dr. Dogan's social as well as his educational value to the church has been recognized by those in high authority. He has been appointed a member of the Board of Education, a board which determines the educational policies of the schools of the church. His responsibilities as the chief executive of Wiley University and as a leading member of his church have not lessened his interest in the other activities of life. He was president of the Standard Mutual Fire

Insurance Co., president of the Texas State Teachers' Association and an active member of the Knights of Pythias.

Perhaps it is as an educator that Dr. Dogan is best known. As the president of Wiley he has succeeded in raising the status of the school to an enviable position among the Negro schools for the higher education of the youth of the race. Under his supervision there has just been erected a new Administration building, the most modern and beautiful in the Freedman's Aid System, and a new refectory. The College Department has been rejuvenated by an excellent corps of accomplished teachers from the Northern institutions of learning all of which serve as a testimony of Dr. Dogan's capacity for accomplishing big things. In recognition of his service to his fellowmen his Alma Mater conferred upon him the degree of Ph. D. in 1904, New Orleans University the degree of Doctor of Divinity in 1910. Dr. Dogan is a member of the Advisory Board of the National Cyclopedia of the Colored Race, the first volume of which made its appearance in 1919.

Dorsey, Reverend Father John Henry, was born at Baltimore, Md., in the year of 1873. He was baptized in the St. Francis Xavier Catholic Church, the oldest in Baltimore, and received his early literary training in the public schools of Baltimore. At an early age he showed a leaning toward the ministry. He came under the influence of the very Reverend Father John Slottery who encouraged and started him on his career. His first instructor was the most Reverend Archbishop John Ireland of St. Paul, Minn. He studied under him for a year, 1888-1889. He subsequently entered Epiphany College and graduated in 1893. In the fall of that same year he enrolled for colored missions at St. Joseph's Seminary,

Baltimore, but on account of his failing health was forced to withdraw and seek less strenuous work. He became a teacher in the public schools of Maryland and Virginia; this line of work he pursued for four years, at the end of which he returned to the Seminary and resumed his studies for the priesthood. Upon the completion of the courses offered in the Seminary he was ordained a priest in the Roman Catholic Church in the Cathedral at Baltimore by his Eminence James, Cardinal Gibbons, the 21st of June, 1902. Father Dorsey was appointed pastor of the Colored Catholic Church of Pine Bluff, Arkansas, where he served a year. He was subsequently appointed a missionary priest among the Southern Negroes and the director of Knights of Peter Claver, an organization for Colored People of the Roman Catholic faith.

Douglass,. Joseph Henry, was born in Washington, D. C., on July 3, 1871. He was the grandson of Frederick Douglass, the most distinguished propagandist against slavery and the leading Negro figure among the Abolitionists. He received his preliminary education in the public schools of New York and Washington, and his musical training in the New England Conservatory of Music, Boston, Mass.

Upon the completion of his course he was appointed an instructor of violin at Howard University, Washington, D. C. He severed his connections with Howard after a number of years to enter into the activities of a concert soloist. In that capacity he has appeared before audiences both white and black all over the country, receiving the commendations of the musical critics of the daily papers wherever he appears. The Victor Talking Company recognized his skill on the violin and have asked him on several occasions to make records for them.

Dubois, Doctor W. E. Burghardt, was born in Great

DR. W. E. B. DU BOIS, EDITOR OF THE "CRISIS," THE WORLD'S GREATEST
NEGRO MAGAZINE.

Barrington, Feb. 23, 1868. He was educated at Fisk University, Harvard University and the University of Berlin. He was two years a fellow at Harvard and holds her degree of Ph. D. He has taught at Wilberforce, Ohio, the University of Pennsylvania, and in the Atlanta University.

Dr. Dubois is the author of "Suppression of the African Slave Trade," also "Harvard Historical Students No. 1," "Souls of Black Folk," "The Negro," "John Brown," and a number of articles contributed to the leading magazine of the country. "Darkwater," his latest volume, is just off the press.

Dr. Dubois is at present Director of Research for the National Association for the Advancement of Colored People and the editor of the Crisis Magazine, the organ of the association.

As the official correspondent of the Crisis, Dr. Dubois visited France and the battlefields of Flanders. While in Paris he was instrumental in having an International Negro Conference for the consideration of problems which affect the people of color all over the world.

In the field of Sociology Dr. Dubois takes his place in the front ranks. He is one of the best informed men on questions relating to the Negro in America. Through the pages of the Crisis, he is conducting a propaganda for the social, political and economic emancipation of the Negro.

Dudley, James Benson, was born at Wilmington, N. C., on November 2, 1859, the son of John Bishop and Annie Dudley. He was a student for a period in Shaw University, Raleigh, North Carolina. In 1897, the honorary degree of Master of Arts was conferred upon him by Livingston College and the LL. D. degree by Wilberforce University in 1900.

Mr. Dudley began his career as an educator in the rural schools of Wilmington and step by step he rose to the position as head of the State Agricultural and Technical College, Greensboro, N. C. He founded the Metropolitan Trust Company and the Pioneer Building and Loan Association of Greensboro, N. C. He is president of the North Carolina Teachers' Association; trustee of the National Religious Training School; Advisory member Board of Directors Inter-State Church Association for Whites and Negroes; President of the North Carolina Anti-Tuberculosis League; Chairman of the Negro Railroad Commission. He is a Mason, a member of the Knights of Pythias and Odd Fellows.

Dunbar, Paul Lawrence, born at Dayton, Ohio, June 27, 1872, died at Dayton, Ohio, February 9, 1906. Dunbar's greatest service to the race perhaps lies in the articulate expression which he gave to the language of his people. Of him, Wliliam Dean Howells wrote: "Some of these (poems) I thought very good. What I mean is several people might have written them, but I do not know anyone else at present who could quite have written his dialect pieces. They are derivations and reports of what passes in the hearts and mind of a lowly people whose poetry had hitherto been inarticulately expressed, but now finds for the first time in our tongue, literary interpretation of a very artistic completeness.

Dyson, Walter, was born at Paris, Illinois, September 14, 1882. At the completion of his preparatory training he entered Fisk University, Nashville, Tenn., and received his Bachelor of Arts degree in 1903. Not satisfied with the training which he had received at Fisk, he entered Yale University where he pursued supplementary courses in history, economics, etc. This institution conferred upon him the degree of A. B. in 1905. Immedi-

24

ately after his graduation he received an appointment to teach in the public schools of his native town. He left this position to fill the chair of History at Howard University, Washington, D. C. Professor Dyson, always eager to enlarge his storehouse of knowledge, enrolled in the Post Graduate Department of Chicago University Summer Session and received his Master's Degree in 1913. In 1914-1915 he was graduate student in History and Economics in Columbia University, New York. Professor Dyson is the author of a "Syllabus of the United States History," which made its appearance in 1908; a "History Text Book Review Chart," which was published in 1912; "The District of Columbia in the Civil War," published in 1913 and articles relating to the subject of history in some of the National Magazines. Professor Dyson is an authority on Ancient History.

In addition to his work as an educator he is a zealous worker in the Sunday School and the International Bible Study of the Y. M. C. A. Professor Dyson is identified with the following organizations: The National Association for the Advancement of Colored People, Mason, and the History Teacher's Association of the Middle States and Maryland.

Ellis, George Washington, was born at Western, Platte County, Mo., May 4, 1875. His preliminary training was received at Western and his high school training at Atchison, Kansas. He graduated from the Atchison High School in 1891 and entered the law department of the University of Kansas. In 1893 he received his LL. B. from that institution and began the practice of law. He spent four years while in the actual practice of law, pursuing courses of study in the college department of the University of Kansas. Finishing his work in this institution he went to New York and took up graduate work in the Gunton's Institute of Economics and Sociology. While in New York he took advantage of the opportunity to qualify himself as a stenographer and entered the Gray School of Stenography and Typewriting. After the completion of his course in stenography Mr. Ellis went to Washington, D. C., and spent two years pursuing courses in Philosophy and Psychology at Howard University. In 1900, after successfully passing an examination, he was appointed clerk in the Bureau of Census Department of the Interior. Two years later (1902), President Roosevelt appointed him secretary of the American Legation at Liberia. He served for eight years in that capacity. Since his return he has been engaged in the practice of law in Chicago. While in Africa he made an ethnographical study of Africa communities and gathered numerous specimens which he has loaned to the National Museum in Washington, D. C. Mr. Ellis is a voluminous writer, all his work receiving international recognition. He was elected Fellow of the Geographical Society of Great Britain, African Society of London, American Academy of Social and Political Science, American Political Science Association, American Sociological Society, American Society of International Law, Cook County Bar Association, Knight Commander of the Luther Burbank Society, and the National Independent Equal Rights League. He was elected president of this organization in 1915. Among some of the literary works which have come from his pen are: "The Leopard's Claw," "Negro Culture in West Africa," "The Psychology of American Race Prejudice," "Negro Achievement in Social Progress," "Liberia in the Political Psychology of West Africa," "Dynamic Factors in the Liberia Situation," "Islam as a Factor in the West African Culture,' "Education in Africa," "Political Institutions in Liberia," "Morality in the African Black Belt."

Mr. Ellis is as ardent in his religious activities as he is in his secular activities. As a member of the Methodist Church he has been elected a delegate to the General Conference 1912-1916. His name appeared in the Who's Who in America in 1912—one of the less than half dozen names of Negroes to appear in this work; the Book of Chicagoans, 1917, and the National Encyclopedia of American Biography.

Farmer, Dr. J. Leonard, was born in Williamsburg County, South Carolina, June 12, 1885. Prepared for high school at the age of twelve, but for certain reasons gave up school until 1905, when he entered Cookman Institute, graduating therefrom in 1909. Entered Boston University 1909, graduating with A. B. degree in 1913, having been awarded four scholarships of $100.00 each. Entered Boston University School of Theology 1913, graduating, S. T. B. in 1916, in the meantime pursuing studies in the Graduate School; 1916-1917 studied in the Graduate School of Boston University and Harvard. Reading assistant in the departments of Old Testament and philosophy in Boston University School of Theology. Candidate for Fellowship for a year's study abroad, the entrance of the United States into the war making it impossible for a Fellow to go abroad and causing the election to be given up. Ph. D. (magna cum laude) Boston University 1918, the subject of the doctor's dissertation being "The Origin and Development of the Messianic Hope in Israel, with Special Reference to Analogous Beliefs among other People." Held charges at Marshall and Galveston, Texas. Professor of philosophy and economics, Wiley, editor Sunday School department of Southwestern Christian Advocate.

Floyd, Dr. Silas Xavier, was born at Augusta, Ga.,
October 2, 1869. He received his preparatory school
training in the schools of Augusta and his A. B. degree
at Atlanta University, Atlanta, Ga., in 1891 and the A. M.
degree in 1894. After the completion of his college course
he began to teach and became the principal of the third
ward school in Augusta. From 1893-1896 he was the
principal of the Mange Street School and 1903-1908 was
principal of the first ward school and editor of the
Augusta "Sentinel," and departmental editor of "Voice
of Negro." Dr. Floyd was ordained in the ministry
(Baptist) and was appointed pastor of the Augusta
Tabernacle Baptist Church. He has been the Vice-President and Auditor of the Georgia Mutual Life and Health
Insurance Co., Vice-President American Benefit Association, Secretary of the Negro Fair Association; Colored
Y. M. C. A.; advisory member on the board of the Standard Life Insurance Co., field worker for the Inter-
national Sunday School Convention, Sunday School
Missionary of the American Baptist Institute. In ad-
dition to these organizations he is a member of the
American Historical Association, American Social
Science Association, Secretary of the National Association of Teachers in Colored Schools.

French, Clifton G. A., was born at Topeka, Kansas.
His elementary training was received in his native city
and his high school training in the Kansas City High,
Kansas. Upon completion of his high school training he
went to New York where he entered the College of the
City of New York. He subsequently matriculated in
New York University where he received his B. S. degree.
He entered the Law School of this University and received
the degree of LL. B., and in 1912, the degree of Master
of Law. At the completion of his law course Mr. French

settled and began the practice of law in New York City
as a partner in the firm of French & French. He was
a member of Co. C., 23rd Regiment of the Kansas Volunteers and served as Chief Clerk of General Courts-
Martial. He has traveled extensively in South and
Central America and the West Indies. Mr. French is
numbered among the successful lawyers of his race and
has served as chairman of Election Board on two occasions in the city of New York. Mr. French married
Minnie M. Walker of Kansas, October 28, 1900. Mrs.
French is a prominent soprano soloist and has appeared
in concerts in Europe, Africa, South and Central America
and the West Indies. In Madagascar she sang frequently
before the Prime Minister. Some of the songs she
sang in her concerts were her own compositions.

Fuller, Meta Vaux Warrick, was born in Philadelphia, Pennsylvania, June 9, 1877. She attended the
public schools of Philadelphia and subsequently the
school of Industrial Art of Philadelphia. She sailed for
Paris, France, in 1899 and there entered the Academic
College and later the Academic Colarossi. She spent
three years in France, 1899-1902, and then entered the
Academy of Fine Arts in Philadelphia. The products of
her chisel and mallet have been exhibited in the best
salons in Paris and other exhibits have been: Jamestown
Exposition, Emancipation Exposition in New York,
1913; Annual Exhibits Academy of Fine Arts, Philadelphia. Private exhibits: Paris, 1901; Woman's Paint-
ers and Sculptors, 1902; Framington, Massachusetts,
1914. Her work has received flattering commendations
from art critics in France and in the United States. She
is a member of the Society of Arts and Crafts of New
York.

Furniss, Dr. Henry Watson, was born in Brooklyn,
New York, February 14, 1868. He matriculated at

Howard University in the department of medicine and graduated in the spring of 1891. Two years after his graduation he enrolled in the graduate school of Harvard and pursued courses in surgery and the following year, 1894, he was pursuing a similar course in the New York Post Graduate School.

Dr. Furniss' first appointment was to a position of assistant surgeon in the Freedman's Hospital, Washington, D. C., in 1894. His connection with this hospital terminated, he went to Indianapolis, Indiana, and began the practice of medicine. In 1898 he was appointed Consul at Bahia, Brazil, and served until 1905, when he was transferred to Haiti as Envoy Extraordinary and Minister Plenipotentiary. He held this position until September 16, 1913. Dr. Furniss holds membership in the following organizations: American Medical Association, American Microscopical Society, American Society of International Law, Indiana Medical Society and American Public Health Association.

Furniss, Dr. Sumner Alexander, was born in Jackson, Mississippi, January 30, 1874, the brother of Henry Watson Furniss. His medical training was received in the Indiana Medical College and the University of Indiana Medical School. Unlike other professional men Dr. Furniss did not hesitate to return to the city of his adoption to engage in the practice of his profession. He set up his shingle in Indianapolis, Indiana, in 1894, and has been practicing there ever since. He was one of those who established the Lincoln Hospital in Indianapolis. He is now the head of the hospital. He holds membership in the following societies: Indianapolis Medical Society, National Medical Association, Indiana State Medical Society and American Medical Association. Like his brother Dr. Furniss is a Republican. He was alternate delegate at large to the Republican National Convention held in Chicago, Illinois, in 1912. He is a 33rd degree Mason, Odd Fellow and Knights of Pythias.

Gilbert, John Wesley, was born in Hepsibah, Georgia, July 6, 1865. He received his early literary training in the public schools of Atlanta, and later as a student in the Theological Department of Morehouse College in Atlanta, Georgia. He severed his connection with this institution to enter Brown University. While at Brown he was exceptionally proficient in the study of the classics and won the Brown Athens Scholarship. He accepted the appointment and a year later was found in Greece pursuing his classical studies.

Mr. Gilbert has taken active part in the various excavations conducted in that ancient classical country in recognition of which he was elected a member of the Archaeological Institution and the Philological Association of America.

While abroad Mr. Gilbert visited Africa and with his assistance the mission at Wiambo, Miami, was established by Bishop W. R. Lambuth. Returning to America he served in various capacities as teacher and preacher and is at present the commissioner for and teacher of Greek in Paine College. The degree of Master of Arts was conferred upon him by Brown University while he was in Athens.

Green, John Paterson, was born at Newbern, N. C., April 2, 1845. When he was five years old his father died and his mother, and two other children beside himself, moved to Cleveland, Ohio. Mr. Green attended the public schools of Cleveland, Ohio, graduating from Central High School in 1869. He entered the Ohio Union Law School and received his LL. B. degree in 1870, and that same year was admitted to the Ohio Bar.

1. JOHN WESLEY GILBERT.   3. HON. JOHN P. GREEN.
2. SMITH WENDELL GREENE.   4. WILLIAM HARRISON.
5. J. H. HARMON, Houston, Tex.

Mr. Green went to South Carolina, and began the practice of law but returned to Cleveland in 1872. After ten years of successful practice in Cleveland, he was elected to the Ohio House of Representatives 1882-4, and re-elected in 1888. He served out a two year term and was elected to the Senate of Ohio in 1890, and served until 1892, the only Negro who has ever been elected to that body.

While a member of the Ohio Legislature he introduced the Labor Day bill which was passed by the House. For this Mr. Green is called the "Daddy of Labor Day." Congress subsequently made it a National holiday. While a member of the Senate he presided over that body once. In recognition of his services to the Nation, Wilberforce University conferred upon him the LL. D. degree in 1890, and Kentucky Central College did the same in 1912. Mr. Green was appointed agent of postage stamps for the Postoffice of the United States in 1898, and served until 1907. He was at one time acting superintendent of finance, serving in that capacity eighteen months.

Mr. Green has traveled extensively and during one of his trips abroad he and his family were presented to Pope Pius X and received his benediction. He has four children all of whom are grown. Mr. Green is now engaged in the practice of law in Cleveland, is a Mason, and the author of "Recollections of the Carolinas."

Green, Smith Wendell, is a Louisianian by birth. His early life does not differ in any essential from the life of any Negro youth in this country. However, unlike many he took advantage of every opportunity which came his way and they stood him in good stead when he was called upon to direct the destiny of the Grand Lodge of the K. of P. of the State of Louisiana.

Mr. Green joined the order of K. of P. on July 17, 1883, as a charter member of Pride of Tensos Lodge No. 21, of St. Joseph, La. The interest which he manifested in the organization commended him to the attention of his colleagues and as a reward for his interest he was elected V. C. of the lodge. For some reason or other he did not fill this post but served rather as C. C. until June 30, 1886. He was sent to the Grand Lodge as a Grand Representative of his lodge and the same zeal and qualities which commended him to the local lodge won for him the admiration of the Grand Lodge. He was elected G. M. of F. in May 1884, to restore the financial stability of the organization. This position he filled for a year. From that time on Mr. Green's rise in the organization was rapid. He was elected G. K. of R. and S. in 1886, G. C. in 1892 and served five years. He was re-elected to that position in 1899 to find the treasury of the organization depleted and a deficit of over $3,000 overhanging it. Under his direction the order took on new life; the membership increased to 9,000; a new temple was erected in New Orleans, La., at a cost of approximately $200,000 and the finances of the organization increased to $100,-000. His capacity and ability to do big things were recognized by the Supreme Lodge and in 1905 he was elected Vice Chancellor, and ex-officio Supreme Worthy Chancellor. He was re-elected in 1907 and the following year was elected Supreme Chancellor.

Greener, Richard Theodore, was born at Philadelphia, Penn., January 30, 1844. His preparatory education was received at Andover Academy and Oberlin College, Ohio. He entered Harvard and graduated in 1870, the first Negro to graduate from that institution. He was professor of Mathematics and Logic in the University of South Carolina from 1873-1877. He was

admitted to the South Carolina Bar in 1876 and that of
the District of Columbia in 1877. For five years 1877-82
he was dean of the Law School of Howard University
and law clerk to the first comptroller of United States
Treasury. In 1882 a precedent was established thru his
effort in a case in which West Point was involved by
obtaining a court martial trial of a cadet. He was admitted to the Supreme Court in 1907 and subsequently
moved to Chicago, Illinois.

Mr. Greener has had a remarkable political career.
From 1885-90 he was a member of the Board of Exam-
iners in the New York Municipal Civil Service; was
American Consul to Bombay, India, in 1898 and in Vladi-
vostok, Siberia, Russia, until 1906. For his service to the
Chinese during the Boxer War and for material assistance given the sufferers during the Shansi famine the
Chinese Imperial government in 1902 decorated him with
the order of Double Dragon. During the Russo-Japanese
war he was in charge of Japanese and British interests in
Russia. In recognition of his achievements the following
institutions of learning have conferred upon him these
honors: Monrovia College, Liberia, the LL. D. degree
in 1882 and the same degree by Howard University,
Washington, D. C., in 1898.

Dr. Greener belongs to the following organizations:
The Society for the Exploration of the Amoor, Narra-
gansett Riverside, Reform and Commonwealth Clubs,
the Anthropological Society and the Iroquois Club.

Grimke, Archibald Henry, was born August 17, 1849,
near Charleston, S. C. Mr. Grimke received his preliminary training at Lincoln University, Penn., where the
A. B. degree was conferred upon him in the spring of
1870 and M. A. degree two years later. He entered the
Harvard Law School subsequently and received the
LL. B. in 1874.

After his graduation Mr. Grimke entered the field of journalism in Boston and edited a weekly paper called the "Hub." He was engaged as a special writer for the Boston Traveler and the Boston Herald. For the next ten years (1884-94) he was secretary of the board of trustees of the Westboro Insane Hospital. He resigned this position to accept the appointment as U. S. Consul to Santo Domingo, Dominican Republic. He served in that capacity from 1894-8. Mr. Grimke has written numerous pamphlets and books all of which have received favorable comment from literary critics. Among these works are: "Life of William Lloyd Garrison," which appeared in 1891, "Life of Charles Sumner," which appeared a year later, "Rights on the Scaffold or the Martyrs of 1822," "The Negro and Elective Franchise Symposium," and other articles of an anti-slavery nature contributed to magazines.

Mr. Grimke is president of the National Association for the Advancement of Colored People and also holds membership in the Authors' Club of London, England, the Authors' League of America, American Social Science Association, Frederick Douglass Memorial and Historical Association. In this last he has been president for a number of years.

Hare, Maude Cuney, was born at Galveston, Texas, February 6, 1879. She attended the public schools of Galveston and at the completion of the High School course entered the New England Conservatory of Music, Boston, Mass. She supplemented her literary training by pursuing courses at Lowell Institute. She placed herself under the private instruction of Liszt, Edmund Ludwig, of the Imperial Russian Institute for Noble Ladies and Edwin Klahre.

Mrs. Hare began her career as teacher of music in the

Texas Deaf, Dumb and Blind Institute for Colored Youths at Austin, Texas. A year later she was piano teacher at Institution Church, Chicago, Ill., and in 1903-4 music teacher in the State Normal and Industrial College, Prairie View, Texas. Since 1904 she has devoted herself to the private teaching of music and as a concert soloist.

Mrs. Hare is the author of the biography of "Norris Wright Cuney," her father, which appeared in 1913, and editor of the Music and Art Column for the "Crisis."

Harris, George Westly, was born at Topeka, Kansas, August 1, 1884. He received his public school training at Topeka and later entered the preparatory department of Tufts College, Medford, Mass. From Tufts he matriculated at Harvard and graduated with the A. B. degree in 1907. He spent the year 1907-8 in the Law School pursuing courses in law. He abandoned the legal training to enter journalism, first as a newspaper correspondent and later as associate editor of the New York Age, a Negro weekly.

Mr. Harris' next move in the field of journalism was to become the editor of the Amsterdam News, of New York City, another Negro weekly. Severing his connection with this weekly he began the publication of a weekly paper called the New York "News" of which he is editor. The "News" maintains a Charity Bureau which helps materially to alleviate the suffering of the poor of that city.

In politics Mr. Harris is a Republican and in the election of 1919 was elected to the State Assembly.

Harrison, William, was born on a farm in Clay county, Mississippi, in 1874. His first step was to seek to prepare himself for the life which he had mapped out for himself; and so, when things were quiet on the farm he went to the city and enrolled in the public school. He soon recognized the inadequacy of such a program and after some deliberation he decided to abandon his farm activities altogether and devote himself to his preparation for the study of law.

He entered Roger Williams University, Nashville, Tennessee, where he pursued the preparatory course, and later the University of Chicago where he pursued his college course. He returned to Nashville, after leaving Chicago, and entered Walden University Law School. At the completion of his law course he went to Oklahoma, took the state bar examination, and was admitted to practice before the bar in 1902. From that day Mr. Harrison's course has been steadily upward. He gained admittance to practice first in Federal Court and then in the United States Supreme Court.

At one time he presided as a special judge of the Superior court in a case in which white lawyers were involved. He holds membership in the Chamber of Commerce, of Oklahoma City, in the Knights of Pythias (Past Grand Chancellor), president People's Protective Circle and president of the Negro Civic League.

Hathaway, Isaac Scott, was born in Lexington, Kentucky, April 4, 1874. He received his literary training in the Chandler Normal School, Lexington, Kentucky, from which institution he graduated in 1891. Having mapped out for himself a sculptor's career he began the study of the Arts in the New England Conservatory of Music, Boston, Mass., in 1894. He subsequently entered the Cincinnati Art Academy and studied there for a year (1898-9).

Mr. Hathaway spent some time as a school teacher but since 1898 he has devoted himself to sculpturing and as a dealer in art. He has made a number of models and busts among them the miniature of Transylvania University of Lexington, Kentucky, which was exhibited at the Louisiana Purchase Exposition, St. Louis, Mo., in 1904, and the busts, life and death masks of such men as W. E. B. DuBois, C. M. Clay, Paul Lawrence Dunbar, Kelly Miller, Booker T. Washington, Frederick Douglass, Bishop Richard Allen, etc. He assisted Dr. Allen to arrange the government exhibit at the U. S. National Museum at the Panama Pacific Exposition in 1915. Some of his works have been purchased by the Smithsonian Institute, Washington, D. C., Wards Museum in Rochester, N. Y., and the Field Museum of National History, Chicago, Illinois.

Hawkins, Mason Albert, was born at Charlotteville, Virginia, October 21, 1874. He received his preparatory schooling in Morgan College, Baltimore, Md., and his literary course at Harvard where he received his A. B. degree in 1901, matriculating in the Post Graduate School of Columbia University, New York City. He received his Master of Arts degree in 1901.

Mr. Hawkins began life as a teacher of German and Latin in the Colored High School in Baltimore, Md., in 1901. Five years later he was promoted to the head of the modern language department and in 1909, vice-principal and principal respectively.

Principal Hawkins takes a live interest in the civic life of Baltimore. He is president of the Maryland Colored Public Health Association; treasurer of the Maryland Colored Blind Association; a member of the Board of Provident Hospital, member of the commission on Preparedness and Defense for the Colored People of Maryland. He holds membership in the following societies: The American Academy of Political and Social Sciences, Fellow of the American Geographical Society. He is also a contributor to a number of magazines among them: "Education," "Vocational Education," "Crisis."

Hawkins, Walter Everette, was born at Warrenton, North Carolina, November 17, 1883, the son of Ossian and Christiana Hawkins. He attended the public schools of Warrenton and entered Kittrell College in North Carolina, graduating from this institution in 1901.

Mr. Hawkins is a verse writer whose works have been published in this country as well as in London, England. His "Chords and Discords," was published by Murry Brothers, Washington, D. C., in 1909, and other of his works, viz, "Too Much Religion," "The Black Soldiers," "Where Air of Freedom Is," "Love's Unchangeableness," etc., have appeared in the African Times and Oriental Review of London.

Since 1912 Mr. Hawkins has been connected with the railway mail service. He is a member of the Negro Society for Historical Research.

Hawkins, William Ashlie, was born at Lynchburg, Virginia, August 2, 1862. He received his literary training at Morgan College, Baltimore, Maryland, and graduated in 1881. He entered the Law School of Howard University, Washington, D. C., and graduated in 1892. He was admitted to the Maryland Bar in 1892 and entered into the practice of law. As a lawyer he has successfully represented the cause of the Negro before the courts of justice of Maryland.

In church connection he is Methodist Episcopal and has been twice elected a delegate to the General Conference. He holds membership in the following organizations: Sigma Pi Phi; the N. A. A. C. P., National Independent Political League, Gamma Boule, 33rd degree Mason, Knights of Pythias. He is the author of a number of pamphlets among them, "The Negro in Court."

Hayes, Lemuel, theologian, born July 18, 1753. He
25

received his honorary degree of Master of Arts from Middleberry College in 1804. His sermons which were published and which passed through nine or ten editions, were taken from Genesis Three and Four. Mr. Hayes was the most popular preacher in the state of Vermont during that period.

Hayes, Dr. George Edmund, was born at Pine Bluff, Arkansas, May 11, 1880. His preparatory training was received in the Agricultural and Mechanical College, Normal, Alabama. He matriculated at Fisk University, Nashville, Tennessee, and received his A. B. in 1903. He attended the summer sessions of Chicago University and Columbia University, New York, receiving the Ph. D. degree from the latter in 1912. He finished the course offered by the New York School of Philanthropy in 1910 and received an appointment to the chair of social science at Fisk University, Nashville, Tenn.

Before his appointment on the faculty of Fisk he was for three years the traveling secretary of the International Y. M. C. A. Dr. Hayes is associated with the National League on Urban Conditions Among Negroes in an executive capacity. During the World War the Department of Labor of our National Government borrowed Dr. Hayes from Fisk and gave him charge of a specially created department known as the Department of Negro Economics. As the director of this department he had to husband the resources of the people of color and to make them more conscious of the consequences of economic wastefulness and to formulate definite plans for their economic betterments.

Dr. Hayes holds membership in the following organizations: National Geographical Society, American Academy of Political and Social Science, American Economic Association. He is the author of "The Negro at Work in New York City," and a number of articles contributed to periodicals of a more or less scientific nature.

Hope, John, was born in Augusta, Georgia, June 16, 1868. He received his early education in the public schools and in Worcester Academy. He occupied prominent positions in the student activities of the Academy, serving as editor-in-chief of the Academy Monthly and the commencement speaker and historian of his class. He received his B. A. degree in 1894. He was the orator of his class, a distinction which was conferred upon him by his white colleagues.

In the fall of 1894 Mr. Hope became connected with Roger Williams University of Nashville, Tennessee, as teacher and four years later was sent to Atlanta Baptist College, and was elected to the presidency of that institution upon the resignation of the president. The degree of Master of Arts was conferred upon him by Brown University in 1907. He is a member of the Board of Managers of the Y. M. C. A. of Atlanta; member of the Advisory Board of the N. A. A. C. P.; member of the Executive Committee of the Urban League of New York; was president of the National Association of Teachers in Colored Schools; member of the Anti-Tuberculosis Association of Atlanta; member of the Committee of the Spingarn Medal and has served in an advisory capacity on boards of the State Baptist Convention.

President Hope was appointed special secretary by the Y. M. C. A. to do active work among Negro soldiers in France during the war. His relation with that organization continued even after the war was brought to a successful termination. He resumed his duties as the head of Morehouse College in the fall of 1919.

Howard, Perry W., was born in Obenezer, Holmes

1. Henry Claude Hudson.   3. John Hope.
2. William H. Lewis.   4. Mason Albert Hawkins.

county, Mississippi, June 14, 1878. In 1891 he entered Alcorn A. & M. College. Two years later he matriculated at Rust University, Holly Springs, Mississippi, and in 1899 graduated with the degree of Bachelor of Arts. In the fall of 1899 Mr. Howard was appointed president of Campbell College, Jackson, Miss. He served for a year after which he was called by Alcorn A. & M. College to fill the chair of mathematics. During his incumbency at Alcorn he studied law and pursued summer courses in the Illinois College of Law, Chicago, Illinois. In 1905 he was awarded the LL. B. degree by this institution and he entered immediately into practice of law.

The honorary degree of Master of Arts was conferred upon him by the faculty of Campbell College.

Hudson, Dr. Henry Claude, was born in Morksville, Avoyles Parish, Louisiana, on April 19, 1886. His early school preparation was received in the Eighth District Academy of Alexandria, La., where his parents had moved. From there he went to Wiley University, Marshall, Texas, and while there directed the building of the Carnegie Library and Coe Hall, the young men's dormitory. It may be mentioned here that Dr. Hudson acquired skill as a brickmason in Alexandria, La.

After completing his preparation at Wiley Dr. Hudson entered Howard University Dental School and graduated in the spring of 1913. He returned to Louisiana upon his graduation and began to practice his profession in Shreveport. Dr. Hudson has succeeded remarkably in his profession and is regarded as one of the leading men of his profession.

Jackson, Major Robert R., was born in Malta, Illinois, September 1, 1870. He attended the public schools of Chicago graduating from the high school in 1885.

Major Jackson began as a clerk in the Chicago postoffice, continuing until he was promoted to the position of assistant superintendent of the Armour Station. He resigned this position in 1909 to enter in the publishing and printing business. He became identified with a number of business projects, among them the African Union, of which he was director and auditor; Fraternal Globe Bonding Company; secretary of the Chicago Giants Baseball Club; Mt. Glenwood Cemetery Association. He joined the Illinois National Guard and was promoted to the rank of major. He served in the Spanish-American War and on the Mexican border with distinction. He helped to train a number of men for the American Expeditionary Forces during the World War.

In politics Major Jackson is a Republican. He has been elected to the Illinois General Assembly for three consecutive terms. He was sponsor for the bill which stopped the production of the "Birth of a Nation" in Illinois and the appropriation bill to commemorate the Half Century Anniversary Exposition held in Chicago in 1915.

Major Jackson is a member of the following organizations: National Association of Postoffice Clerks, Mason, Odd Fellow, United Brotherhood of Friendship, Knights of Pythias, Musicians Union of the World and Appomattox Club.

Johnson, Fenton, was born in Chicago, Illinois, May 7, 1888. He attended the public schools of Chicago and Northwestern and Chicago Universities.

Mr. Johnson began life as a teacher of English in the State University of Louisville, Ky. He abandoned the class room to enter the field of journalism. He is a contributor to a number of periodicals, and the author of "Vision of the Dusk," "A Little Dream," poems which appeared in 1913 and "Mrs. Josephine Turck Baker." He is the editor of the "Correct English" Magazine.

JAMES WELDON JOHNSON, FIELD SECRETARY, NATIONAL ASSOCIATION
FOR THE ADVANCEMENT OF COLORED PEOPLE, NEW YORK CITY.

Johnson, Henry Lincoln, was born in Augusta, Georgia, the son of Peter and Martha Johnson. He graduated from Atlanta University with the A. B. degree and entered the law department of the University of Michigan, graduating three years later.

Mr. Johnson was admitted to the bar of Georgia and began the practice of law in Jackson, Ga. In 1909 he was appointed recorder of deeds, Washington, D. C. Since retirement from the Washington office he has been practicing law in Atlanta, Georgia.

Johnson, J. Rosamond, was born in Jacksonville, Florida, in 1873, and studied at the New England Conservatory of Music, subsequently becoming one of the leading musicians of his country. He developed a new style of Negro music which became very popular. Among some of his most popular numbers are:

"I Sold My Love to the Roses," "The Congo Love Song," "Morning Noon and Night," "Under the Bamboo Tree." He has also written light operas for Klaw and Erlanger, theatrical manager, as well as May Erwin, Lillian Russell, Anna Held and several others. He is the composer of the selection entitled "Come Over Here." This was written while he was director of music at a London opera house, England. Mr. Johnson was commissioned during the World-War as first lieutenant in the American National Army; and was the director of the Ninety-second Division band.

Johnson, Jas. Weldon, was born in Jacksonville, Florida, June 17, 1871. He received his A. B. degree at Atlanta University in 1894; and his A. M. in 1904. In 1894 he was appointed the principal of the Colored High School in Jacksonville and served in that capacity for seven years. He was subsequently admitted to the Florida Bar; and in the spring of 1901 he moved to New

York. He formed an association with his brother, producing a number of light operas for the New York stage. He is the author of "In Newport," "Humpty-Dumpty" and has also written the words for a number of classical and popular songs. He is the contributing editor to the New York Age; and in 1916 won the second prize in an editorial contest held by the "Philadelphia Public Ledger." President Roosevelt appointed him United States Consul to Puerto-Cabello, Venezuela. He served there until 1909, when he was transferred to Corinto, Nicaragua.

From 1912 to 1913 he served as United States Consul to the Azores and at the assumption of authority by President Wilson in 1913, he resigned. Mr. Johnson is the national organizer for the National Association for the Advancement of Colored People and in his spare time he contributes poems to the Independent, Century, The American Magazine and other periodicals.

Jones, Eugene Kinckle, was born in Richmond, Va., July 30, 1885. He attended Wayland Academy, of Virginia Union University and at the completion of the course matriculated in Virginia Union University, where he received his A. B. degree in 1906. He enrolled in the graduate school of Cornell University, New York, and received his M. A. degree in 1908.

Since 1911 he has been identified with the National League of Urban Conditions among Negroes, first as assistant director and now its National Executive Secretary. Under his supervision the organization has so developed that it has branches in practically all large industrial centers of the North and Middle West. He has contributed a number of articles of a social nature to magazines.

Mr. Jones belongs to the following societies: Alpha Phi

Alpha, Southern Beneficial League, and is a member of the managing committee of the Sojourner Truth House for Delinquent Colored Girls.

Jones, Dr. Robert Elijah, was born at Greensboro, N. C., on February 19, 1872, the son of Sydney Dallas and Mary Jane Jones. Unlike most men, Dr. Jones received his literary preparation in the city of his birth. He not only attended the public schools but matriculated and received his A. B. degree from Bennet College, in Greensboro, N. C. Three years later, 1898, that institution conferred on him the M. A. degree.

After the completion of his course at Bennet College, Dr. Jones entered Gammon Theological Seminary, Atlanta, Ga., and received the degree of Bachelor of Divinity. He began his career as a local preacher at Leaksburgh, N. C., in 1891, was ordained in the M. E. ministry in 1892, and appointed pastor at Reidsville, N. C., and in 1896 he was made Elder.

Dr. Jones' connection with the Southwestern Christian Advocate began in 1897, when he was appointed assistant manager. He served in that capacity until 1901, when he was appointed field secretary of the Board of Sunday Schools of the M. E. church. He held his position until 1904 and was again returned to the Southwestern Christian Advocate but this time as its editor and has held this position up to the date of writing. In addition to his literary activities he finds time to devote to other phases of society, for example, he is vice-president of the Board of Trustees of Bennet College; trustee of Gammon Theological Seminary; president of the Y. M. C. A. of New Orleans; president of the Travelers' Protective Association; first vice-president of the National Negro Press Association; chairman of the executive committee of the National Negro Business League. In recognition of his distinguished service in his chosen field, Howard University, Washington, D. C., saw fit to confer upon him the degree of LL. D. Dr. Jones is a forceful speaker and is constantly in demand to address audiences in his state as well as elsewhere. Extract from a commencement address delivered to Tuskegee Institute, Ala., was published by Mrs. Alice Dunbar Nelson in her book entitled, "Masterpieces of Negro Eloquence."

Jones, Judge Scipio A., is an Arkansan by birth. He went to school in Arkansas and subsequently took up the study of law. On June 15, 1889, he was admitted to the Pulaski Circuit Bar, and immediately took up the practice of law. Six years after he was called to the bar he was appointed National Attorney General for the Mosaic Templars by J. E. Bush, president and founder of the organization. On November 26, 1900, Judge Jones was admitted to the Supreme Court of Arkansas, to the District Court for the Western Division of the Eastern District of Arkansas, and on October 30, 1901, to the U. S. Circuit Court of Arkansas. Four years later he was admitted to practice before the U. S. Supreme Court. Because of his ability as a lawyer he was elected to the office of Special Judge in the Municipal Court of the City of Little Rock, April 8, 1915. Judge Jones is one of the strongest organization men in his state. In addition to his connection with the Mosaic Templars, he is identified with a number of fraternal organizations.

Just, Ernest Everett, was born in Charleston, S. C., in 1884. He received his A. B. degree at Dartmouth. He was elected member of the Phi Beta Kappa Fraternity, an honor organization for distinctive scholarship.

On leaving school Dr. Just entered vigorously into the field of research in biology and physiology. In 1909 he was called to fill a chair in the department of science of

Howard University, Washington, D. C. His research won for him national recognition as an eminent scientist. Dr. Just is both a student and teacher. The moments which he does not spend in the actual work of the class room he spends in research.

In recognition of his achievements he was awarded a Ph. D. degree and the Spingarn medal, the presentation having been made by Governor Charles S. Whitman of New York City. Dr. Just contributed a number of articles to our best periodicals, every one of which have received flattering comments.

Kemp, William Paul, was born at Plattsmouth, Nebraska, March 13, 1891. He entered the school of music of the University of Nebraska where he pursued courses in music and harmony.

Mr. Kemp entered the field of journalism while yet in his teens as the assistant capital correspondent of the Omaha Bee, a daily paper. In 1899, he established the "Lincoln Leader," but gave it up to become the assistant Washington correspondent of the Nebraska State Journal. He returned to Lincoln in 1900 and resumed the publication of the "Lincoln Leader." He was literary manager of the Nebraska Republican State Central Committee in 1904. On October 8, 1907, he moved to Detroit, Michigan, and two months later established the Detroit Leader. In this journalistic venture he was not successful and had to abandon the project two months later. He secured a position as clerk in the mayor's office and began anew the publication of the Detroit Leader which he has operated successfully ever since. He purchased the Owl Printing Co. and consolidated it with the Howitt Printing Co., all of which is operated in connection with the "Leader."

Mr. Kemp is identified with a number of organizations,

1. WILLIAM PAUL KEMP.
2. W. C. JASON, President State
    College, Dover, Del.
3. JOHN A. KENNEY, M.D.
3. GEORGE L. KNOX, Editor "The
    Freeman."
4. MAJOR ROBERT R. JACKSON.

political as well as social. He is a member of the Detroit Urban League, the N. A. A. C. P., president of the Soldier's Welfare League as well as the District Business League; Republican League Club and Abraham Lincoln Political Club; Publishers' Protective Association; and Detroit Association of Allied Printers. He is a Mason, Knights of Pythias, Elk and True Reformer.

Kenney, Dr. John Andrew, was born in Albemarle county, Va., on June 11, 1874. He entered Hampton Institute, Va. From Hampton he went to Shaw University, North Carolina, where he received his preparation for medicine. At the completion of his preparatory studies he entered Leonard Medical College and received his M. D. degree in 1901.

Dr. Kenney received an Internship at the Freedmen's Hospital, Washington, D. C., (1901-1902) at the end of which he was appointed resident physician at Tuskegee Normal and Industrial Institute, Ala. He organized the nurse training course in that institution and during his regime the John A. Andrew Memorial Hospital has been built, an institution of which he is director. Dr. Kenney was personal physician to the late Booker T. Washington, has served eight years as secretary of the National Medical Association, and in 1912 was unanimously elected its president.

Laney, Miss Lucy C., is one of the remarkable women of the Negro race. Graduating from Atlanta University she immediately entered into the teaching profession and taught school in the state of Georgia for a number of years.

She resigned her position as teacher in 1886 and embarked on a plan for the establishment of a school for the training of young men and women of her race in the useful and cultural arts.

In time Miss Laney saw her dreams materialize. Buildings made their appearance here and there on the campus and a capacity student body pursuing courses of study to fit them for the political, economic and social activities of life. The history of Hines Normal School is the history of Miss Laney's unselfish life and as principal of the institution, she has conducted the school so efficiently that she has received favorable compliments from such men as Ex-President William H. Taft.

Lankford, John Anderson, was born at Potosi, Missouri, December 4, 1874. He attended the public schools of Potosi and later entered Lincoln Institute, Jefferson, Mo. He left Lincoln Institute and matriculated at Tuskegee Normal and Industrial Institute, Normal, Alabama, and subsequently the Architectural College at Scranton, Penn. Since the completion of his course in architecture Mr. Lankford has had numerous engagements throughout the country. He was the director of construction at the Jamestown Exposition for the District of Columbia, supervising architect for the National Negro Fair Association of Mobile, Alabama. He has to his credit the direction and construction of the Masonic Temple at Jacksonville, Florida, at a cost of $125,000; Palmer Hall, A. and M. College, Normal, Alabama, $70,000; a flat iron building for Dr. W. Taylor of Richmond, Virginia, at a cost of $60,000, and he is now the supervising architect for the A. M. E. Church throughout the country. Mr. Lankford is president of the board of trustees of the Army of Rescue and Religion; secretary-treasurer of the sinking fund committee of the Masons in Florida, director of the Y. M. C. A. in Jacksonville, Florida, and a 33rd degree Mason.

Latimer, Lewis Howard, was born at Chelsea, Massachusetts, September 4, 1848.

Mr. Latimer was a draughtsman and secretary for Hiram L. Maxim, the inventor of the Maxim gun. He manufactured the Maxim patent incandescent lamps in London, England, from 1880-2. From 1882-3 he was engaged as an electrical engineer in the Olmstead Electric Light & Power Company, now the General Electric Company. He served there first as draughtsman and later as an investigator of patents in the legal department of the organization. Since 1912 Mr. Latimer has been engaged in private practice as an electrical engineer and solicitor of patents. He has invented several electrical devices, some of which are in use in connection with electrical apparatus.

Mr. Latimer is a member of Post No. 60, G. A. R., of New York; member of New York Electrical Society and the Negro Society for Historical Research. He is the author of "Incandescent Electrical Lighting."

Lee, J. R. E., is a native of Texas. He attended Bishop's College, Marshall, Texas, and received his B. A. He was called to Tuskegee to occupy the chair of mathematics and spent several years in that institution. Leaving Tuskegee Institute he secured connection with Benedict College in South Carolina and subsequently with Corona, Alabama. Just about this time a vacancy occurred in the academic department of Tuskegee Institute and Mr. Lee was called to fill it as head of that department. Under his direction this department took on new life and became the most popular in the institution. An opportunity was presented in the form of a principalship of the Lincoln High School, Kansas City, Mo., and Mr. Lee accepted it. Here he has been able to develop some of the plans which he had conceived at Tuskegee and elsewhere. Mr. Lee combines with teaching an organizing power which has found expression in the organization of national as well as state teachers' associations. He was one of the powers behind the National Negro Business League and has organized a number of clubs in Kansas City, among them the Mother's Club, Saving Clubs, Hospital Clubs, etc. Mr. Lee is the father of seven children, five boys and two girls. The eldest son, Edwin, was an honor man at Columbia University, New York; a physician and captain in the U. S. Army during the war.

Lewis, Dr. Julian, was born in Springfield, Illinois. He attended the public schools of his native city and later matriculated in the University of Illinois, Urbana, Ill. While at Illinois he made his Phi Beta Kappa Key, the most coveted honor in a college or university. He specialized in the sciences preparatory to entering, the field of medicine. At the conclusion of his course he entered the School of Medicine of Chicago University and graduated with honors. He was elected to the two honorary scientific societies and won the Second Annual Howard Taylor Rickett Prize of $250. He was appointed research as sistant in pathology in the Medical School. Dr. Lewis also earned his Master of Arts degree as well as Doctor of Philosophy degree from Chicago University.

Lewis, Perry Rufus, was born in Brooklyn, New York, May 26, 1872. He entered the Law School of New York University and graduated with the LL. B. degree in 1892. He was admitted to the New York Bar the same year and began the practice of law in the City of New York, going later to Brooklyn, his native home.

Mr. Lewis is a proctor in admiralty cases, a director of the Hannibald Realty and Improvement Company and the Foster Coal, Land and Timber Company. He is a French scholar and has published several literary productions in that language: "L'Homme d'après la Science et le Talmur," appeared in 1912; "La Situation Actuele en

26

Haiti," appeared in 1913; "Subrogation," appeared in 1910 and "Positive Anthropology," appeared in 1914.

Mr. Lewis is a member of the following organizations: Brooklyn Bar Association, American Geographical Society, Metropolitan Museum of Fine Arts, American Society of National Science.

Lewis, William Henry, was born in Berkeley, Virginia, November 28, 1868. His early school training was received in Virginia Normal and Collegiate Institute, Petersburg, Va. He entered Amherst College and graduated in 1892. His oratorical skill was recognized by his class which elected him the class orator. In the fall of that year he matriculated at Harvard Law Department and three years later (1895) received his LL. B. degree. While at Harvard he became a member of the football squad and played on the first team for two years. At the conclusion of his course he was made one of the football coaches and served ten years in that capacity.

Mr. Lewis was admitted to the Boston Bar the year of his graduation and entered immediately into the practice of law. As a citizen and lawyer he has had the privilege to serve both the state of his adoption and the nation. He was elected a member of the Cambridge City Council three consecutive occasions and served until 1903 and as assistant U. S. Attorney General for Massachusetts 1903-06, and subsequently was appointed by Mr. Taft to the office of assistant United States Attorney General in 1911.

Mr. Lewis is a member of the American Bar Association, American Academy of Political and Social Science. Wilberforce University conferred upon him the LL. D. degree in 1918 in recognition of his achievements.

Locke, Alain Leroy, was born in Philadelphia, Pennsylvania, September 13, 1886.

Locke matriculated at Harvard and received his A. B. in 1907. Mr. Locke is without a doubt one of the most brilliant men of the race and of the nation. At Harvard he won his Phi Beta Kappa Key, a coveted honor among students. He won the Rhodes Scholarship from Pennsylvania and entered Oxford University, England, and in 1910 received the degree of Bachelor of Literature from this classic institution of learning. Leaving Oxford, he went to Germany and there enrolled in the graduate department of the Emperor Wilhelm University in Berlin. In 1911 he returned to the United States and was appointed assistant professor of English at Howard University, Washington, D. C.

Mr. Locke belongs to the following learned societies: American Academy of Political and Social Science, Negro Society for Historical Research, African Union Society of London, Negro Historical Society of Philadelphia, also the Harvard Club and the United Arts Club of London. He is a contributor to the North American Review, The Independent, The Oxford Cosmopolitan, etc.

Lyons, Ernest, was born in Belize, Honduras, October 22, 1860. He received his early schooling in his native home and his college training in New Orleans University where he received his A. B. degree in 1888. He began his pastorage at La Teche, La., in 1883 and pastored subsequently in a number of communities in Louisiana.

Dr. Lyons was appointed Sunday School Agent for the Louisiana Conference in 1894 and special agent Freedman's Aid and Southern Educational Society a year later In 1896 he was appointed pastor of St. Mark's Church in New York City. He remained there until he was called to the pastorate of John Wesley Church and professor of church history in Morgan College, Baltimore, Md. While in Maryland he established the Maryland Industrial and Agricultural Institute for Colored Youths. Two years later (1903) he was appointed resident minister and consul general of U. S., Monrovia, Liberia. He held this office until 1910 and returning to the United States was appointed Liberian representative to the United States.

Dr. Lyons has represented his race on a number of notable occasions. He was one of the ten lecturers appointed by the department of education of Baltimore to represent the genius, characteristics and contributions of the several races of civilization.

McCoo, Dr. F. A., born Montgomery, Ala., June 17, 1872, educated public schools, State Normal and Moody Bible Institute of Chicago, D. D. at Guadalupe College, entered the ministry in 1899. Organized Berean Baptist Church, Chicago, Second Baptist Church, Wheaton, Ill., and the St. John Baptist Church, of which he is now pastor. The present membership of his church is 5,300, with property valued at $71,000.00. He plans to erect a $200,000 church in the near future.

Mason, James Edward, was born at Wilkesbarre, Penn., March 30, 1859. He received his public school training at Wilkesbarre and subsequently private tuition in theology under Dr. Russell, Professor Brown and Dr. Curtis of Syracuse University. From 1885 to 1886 he was a student of Cornell University. In 1898 the degree of Doctor of Divinity was conferred upon him by Livingston College. He was licensed to preach in the A. M. E. Zion Church in 1876, while he was still in his teens and became known as the "boy preacher and orator." He joined the Genesee Conference in 1877 and became a deacon in 1879 and a Presiding Elder in 1880. He was the leading evangelist in the conference and served on many occasions in white churches. He was elected for two years delegate to the General Conference of the A. M. E. Zion Church; and the M. E. General Conference which met in Chicago, Ill., in 1900. He was also elected to the Ecumenical Conference of Methodism, Toronto, Canada, and was the guest of the Empire Club. Since 1897 he has served as Professor of Political Economy and Financial Secretary of Livingston College at Sallsberry, N. C. Rev. Mason was twice called by the Senate in general prayer at Albany, New York, during the administration of Theodore Roosevelt as governor. He occupied the same carriage with Mr. Roosevelt and spoke on the same platform at the fairgrounds, Elmira, New York. He is a member of the American Academy of Political Economy and Social Science and the author of numerous lectures among which are "Lincoln and the Negro," "The First Century Hero," "The Brother in Black."

Miller, George Frazier, was born November 28, 1864, at Aiken, South Carolina. His public school education was received in his native state and his academic degree (A. B.) from Howard University, Washington, D. C., in 1888. At his graduation he entered the General Theological Seminary, New York City, N. Y., graduating in 1891. In 1893, Howard University conferred upon him the M. A. degree. During the year 1901-2 he pursued courses in philosophy in New York University. In 1896 he was appointed Rector of St. Augustine's Protestant Episcopal Church, Brooklyn, New York.

Dr. Miller is one of the most influential Negroes in the Socialist Party. He is well known in New York and the other Eastern states. He has been among the foremost agitators for an open union, that is, the abolition of the color line in the labor unions. He takes his case to the conventions and meetings of the unions and points out to them the fallacy of their policy. His utterances are freely quoted by publicists in the East. He is the author of "Seventh Day Adventists Answered," and "Socialism and its Ethical Basis" (pamphlet). In 1912 his Alma Mater conferred upon him the degree of Doctor of Divinity.

Miller, Kelly, was born in Winnsboro, South Carolina, July 23, 1863. He received his early training in the public schools of his native town and at Fairfield Institute. He entered Howard University after leaving Fairfield and graduated from the College department in 1886. At the completion of his college course he entered the graduate school of Johns Hopkins University, Baltimore, Md., and spent two years (1897-9) pursuing graduate courses.

Professor Kelly Miller was appointed teacher of mathematics in the Washington, D. C., High School in 1889 and a year later was called by Howard to a chair of mathematics on her faculty in 1907. At the recent reorganization of Howard, Dean Miller was made dean of the Junior College of the University.

Perhaps it is as a sociologist rather than a mathematician that Professor Miller is known. As an authority on the race problem of the United States he has no superior. His research is extensive and his conclusions are based on facts which cannot be questioned by any one who has read his "Race Adjustment," and his "Open Letter to Woodrow Wilson, President of the United States." He is also the author of "Out of the House of Bondage," "Negro Soldier in Our War," and numerous articles contributed to national periodicals. From his pen came the article on "The Education of the Negro," in the report of the United States Bureau of Education of

1. HENRY M. MINTON.   3. IRVINE GARLAND PENN.
2. ELIAS CAMP MORRIS.   4. HERMAN E. PERRY.

1901. His Alma Mater, Howard University, conferred upon him the A. M. degree in 1901, and the LL. D. degree in 1903, for meritorious achievement.

Minton, Dr. Henry McKee, was born in Columbia, South Carolina, December 25, 1871. His early education was had in the Phillips Exeter Academy, New Hampshire, from which he graduated in 1891. He was orator of his class at graduation and assistant managing editor of the Exonian, the semi-weekly paper of the Academy as well as the managing editor of the literary monthly of the school.

Graduating from Phillips Exeter, Dr. Minton entered the Philadelphia College of Pharmacy and graduated in 1895 with the degree of Ph. G. Soon after he graduated he opened a drug store in Philadelphia and operated it until 1903 when he gave it up to pursue a course in medicine. He matriculated in the Jefferson Medical College of Philadelphia and graduated in 1906. In college he specialized in the diseases of the lungs and at his graduation entered vigorously into the practice of medicine, concentrating his attention on tubercular patients. He secured connection with Mercy Hospital, Philadelphia, and became one of its directors.

Dr. Minton is also identified with the following activities: He is a member of the board of directors of Whittier Center; treasurer of the Downington Industrial School; a member of the Sigma Pi Phi; G. U. O. O. F. and a Mason. He is the author of "Causes and Prevention of Tuberculosis," and "Early History of Negroes in Business in Philadelphia."

Montgomery, Isaiah, was born in 1847, a slave of Joseph E. Davis, the brother of Jefferson Davis. His father who had not only learned to read and write, but also attained a fair degree of proficiency in mechanical

DEAN LOUIS B. MOORE, DEAN OF THE TEACHERS' COLLEGE IN HOWARD
UNIVERSITY.

(C) C. M. Battey.

engineering and architecture saw to it that his son Isaiah, as well as his brother and sister received the benefit of his intellectual training. It is said that at the age of eleven Isaiah was handling his master's mail and doing the work about the office.

Young Montgomery took active part in some of the naval expeditions in the Civil War among them the Battle of Grand Gulf, being one of Admiral Porter's cabin boys.

The war over, young Montgomery and his brother William returned home and purchased the Davis plantation which comprised 4,000 acres of land for $300,000, a piece of property considered to be third in size among the largest plantations of its kind.

Mr. Montgomery is the founder of Mound Bayou, a Negro colony, situated in the great Yazoo Mississippi Delta, in Boliva county. He moved to the colony in the spring of 1888 and became one of the leading figures there. He has interests in the leading economic enterprises of the colony, among which are, the Mound Bayou State Bank, of which he is a director, Farmer's Co-operative Mercantile Company (president), and owns a gin and saw mill. He is one of the founders of the National Negro Business League.

Moore, Dr. Louis Baxter, was born in Huntsville, Alabama, September 1, 1866. He received his education at Fisk University from which he graduated in 1889 with the degree of A. B. Four years later the degree of A. M. was conferred upon him. He entered the graduate department of the University of Pennsylvania and received the Ph. D. degree in 1896.

Dr. Moore is among the few American Negroes who have had the opportunity to study abroad. After his graduation from Fisk (1889), Dr. Moore accepted a position as secretary of the S. E. Branch Y. M. C. A. in

Philadelphia, Penn. Leaving this position six years later he was appointed instructor in Howard University, Washington, D. C., 1895-7; assistant professor of Latin and pedagogy, 1898-9; professor of philosophy and education and dean of Teacher's College in 1898. He was ordained a minister of the Congregational Church and pastored the People's Church in Washington, D. C., for seven years, 1903-10.

Moorland, Jesse Edward, was born at Coldwater, Ohio, September 10, 1863. He received his literary training at the Northwestern Normal University. At the completion of his college course he was ordained in the ministry and became the secretary of the Colored Branch of the Y. M. C. A., in Washington, D. C. He remained in this capacity for a year, 1892-1893, when he resigned to resume his work as a pastor. For five years 1893-8 he pastored in Cleveland, Ohio, and in Nashville, Tenn. He resigned his charge once more to engage in the Y. M. C. A. service, this time as the international secretary of the organization.

In 1905 Howard University, Washington, D. C., conferred upon him the degree of Doctor of Divinity in recognition of his service to Christianity.

Dr. Moreland has been singularly successful as an organizer of the Y. M. C. A's. To his effort is due the construction of a number of Y. M. C. A buildings, which are to be found in several communities.

During the war Dr. Moreland was assigned the task of finding competent men to take charge of the Y. M. C. A.'s in the various cantonments in the country and for foreign service. So well did he acquit himself that his assistance was sought in the selection of teachers for the University of the U. S. Expeditionary Army in France.

Dr. Moreland is a trustee of Howard University and

Douglass Home Association, a member of the American Negro Academy. He is the author of a number of monographs which deal with Y. M. C. A. activities.

Morgan, G. A., was born at Paris, Kentucky, but migrated to Cleveland, Ohio, June 1, 1895. Mr. Morgan arrived in Cleveland with an unlined pocket book. One of the first things which he did after finishing his trade was to invent a woman's hat fastener and a belt fastener. He has subsequently made other inventions, the most important of which is a safety hood which is used as a protection against fumes and smoke.

For this invention Mr. Morgan was awarded a gold medal which was the First Grand Prize at the Second International Exposition of Safety and Sanitation, in New York in 1914. Other inventions which bear Mr. Morgan's name are a friction device and a hair straightener.

Mr. Morgan is also engaged in other phases of industry. He is president of the G. A. Morgan Hair Refinery Co., of Cleveland, Ohio. He was at one time engaged in the manufacture of skirts.

He holds membership in the following organizations: Committee for Home of Aged People, Phillis Wheatley Association, N. A. A. C. P., and treasurer of the Cleveland Association of Colored Men.

Morris, Elias Camp, was born near Spring Place, Murray county, Georgia, May 7, 1855. He received his early education at Nashville Institute, now Roger Williams University, Tennessee. Dr. Morris joined the Baptist Church and was ordained in 1879. At his ordination he was appointed pastor of the Centennial Baptist Church in Helena, Ark., a charge which he has held up to this day. Under his supervision the church has been rejuvenated both as to the matter of membership and finance. From a membership of twenty-two, when he took charge of the church, the number has been increased to 700 and a new church building erected valued at $40,000.

He organized the Baptist Home Mission Board in 1899; helped in the organization of the General Convention of America, 1903; the Baptist World Alliance, 1905; the Baptist "Vanguard" weekly paper and is trustee of the Arkansas Baptist College. Dr. Morris was also a member of the Peace Conference of English Speaking People of the World, the director of the Arkansas State Negro Business League. From a political standpoint Dr. Morris is a Republican and was a delegate to the Republican National Convention in 1884, 1888, 1904 and alternate delegate at large in 1908. Since 1895 he has been president of the Regular National Baptist Convention, the largest and wealthiest of the Race.

Mossell, Nathan F., was born at Hamilton, Ontario, Canada, July 27, 1856. When he was nine years old his family moved to Rockport, New York. He matriculated in the medical department of the University of Pennsylvania and graduated in 1882 with the degree of M. D. He pursued post graduate work in the Polyclinic Hospital, Philadelphia, and Guy's Queen College and St. Thomas Hospital, London, England.

He began the practice of medicine in Philadelphia in 1882 and was associated with the Out-Patient Surgical Department of the University of Pennsylvania for a year 1881-2. In 1895 he organized the Frederick Douglass Memorial Hospital and Training School, Philadelphia, and erected a plant valued at $100,000. He is medical, director of the institution. He was appointed a member of the Board of Visitation for the city of Philadelphia.

Dr. Mossell holds membership in the following societies: National Medical Association, American Hospital Association, Philadelphia County Medical Society, Philadelphia Academy of Medicine, and Allied Sciences. He is the author of "Hospital Construction Organization and Management."

Mrs. Mossell is equally as prominent in the civic life of Philadelphia as Dr. Mossell. She began life as a teacher in Camden, New Jersey, and Philadelphia, Pa. Since her marriage she is devoting her time to public life. She is president of the Social Service of the Frederick Douglass Hospital. She is one of the founders of the Bustill Family Association; an organizer of the National Afro-American Council; Member of the Board of Managers of Y. W. C. A., of Philadelphia, member of the Philadelphia Civic Club, Northwestern Federation of Women's Clubs, member of the Harriet Tubman Association, Sojourner Truth Suffrage League. She was a delegate to the National Civic Movement Convention which met in Kansas City, Mo., in 1914. Her appointment came from Governor Tanner of Philadelphia. Mrs. Mossell is also a contributor to the Philadelphia Times and Inquirer. She is the author of "Little Dansie's One Day at Sabbath School" and the "Work of Afro-American Women."

Moton, Robert Russia, was born August 26, 1864, on a plantation in Virginia.

He came into contact with a negro schoolmaster who advised him to go to Hampton where he graduated in 1890 and later became one of its teachers. He was placed in charge of six companies of Negro and Indian students with the rank of Major.

Major Moton belongs to the conservative element of his race. He, like his predecessor at Tuskegee, Dr. Washington, recognized the necessity for a harmonious

ALICE MOORE DUNBAR NELSON, WHO SO SUCCESSFULLY MOBILIZED
THE COLORED WOMEN FOR WAR WORK.

relationship between his race and its next door neighbor and toward that end he is directing all attention, energy and his resourceful mind.

Nelson, Alice Dunbar, was born in New Orleans, La., on July 19, 1875. She received her early training in the public schools of Louisiana and Straight University, New Orleans. She graduated from the latter institution and entered the teaching profession. She taught in the public schools of Louisiana for three years after which she left the South and went North to pursue courses in manual training. She has served on the teaching staff of Hampton Institute, State College, Dover, Delaware, National Religious Training School, Durham, N. C., Howard High School, Wilmington, Delaware. She and others organized the Douglass Publishing Co., of Harrisburgh, Pa., and was vice president. She edited and published the "Masterpieces of Negro Eloquence," "Violets and Other Tales," "Goodness of St. Rocque," "The Negro of Louisiana," "A Biography of Dunbar and His Poems," "The New Negro Speaker," and has contributed to a number of periodicals, among them: Ladies' Home Journal, Lippincott's, McClure's, Smart Set, The Crisis, Education, and a number of daily papers. Mrs. Nelson met and married Paul Lawrence Dunbar, the Negro poet, on March 6, 1893. Since the death of her husband, which occurred in 1906, she has devoted her time to teaching and in literary pursuits. Her second marriage occurred recently. During the war she was active as one of the organizers of the Negro women for war duties under the auspices of the Council of National Defense. Mrs. Nelson is identified with the following organizations: Teachers Beneficial Association, Negro Society for Historical Research and Suffrage Study Club.

Nutter, Isaac Henry, was born in Princess Anne,

Maryland, August 20, 1878. The preparation for his legal course was received in his native state. He matriculated at Howard University Law School, Washington, D. C., and graduated with the degree of LL. B. He was admitted to the bar of New Jersey in 1905. He began the practice of law in Atlantic City, N. J., and later became the law associate of ex-Judge John J. Crandall. He is solicitor of the Atlantic County Republican League; General Advisor of the New Jersey State Republican League and president of Nutter's Real Estate Company. In 1913 Wilberforce conferred upon him the LL. D. degree for his achievement in the legal field.

Penn, Dr. Irvine Garland, was born at New Glascow, Va., October 7, 1867. He graduated from the high school of Lynchburg. He was appointed principal and later he was appointed National Commissioner of Negro Exhibits at the Cotton States and International Exposition. Resigning that position at the end of a year, he became identified with the M. E. Church and has served first as general secretary of the Epworth League of the M. E. Church for Colored People, and is now one of the corresponding secretaries of the Freedmen's Aid Society. Rust College conferred the degree of Master of Arts upon him and Wiley University, Marshall, Texas, the degree of Doctor of Letters in recognition of his distinguished service.

Dr. Penn has been a member of the M. E. Church General Conference for 28 consecutive years and is the author of the "Afro-American Press."

Perry, Herman E., was born in Houston, Texas, March 5, 1873. He attended public school and left before he reached the eighth grade. After leaving school he helped his father, first in his grocery store and then on the farm. For twelve years he sold insurance policies

27

and after he had gained considerable information in regard to the inner working of an insurance company he left New York and returned to Atlanta, Georgia, for the purpose of organizing an insurance company.

His first attempt was unsuccessful and his failure served as a greater stimulus rather than discouragement. Almost the very day after his first attempt had failed he launched out the new campaign which culminated in the organization of the Standard Life Insurance Company of Atlanta, Georgia, the only old line Negro life insurance company. In 1918 the insurance in force amounted to $8,208,720, and the premium income to $339,327.77. The total death claims paid in 1918 was $79,733.47.

Mr. Perry has organized a number of other successful enterprises since. For example, he organized the Service Company with a capital stock of $100,000 and the Citizen Trust Company with a capital stock of $250,000 and a surplus of $250,000.

Pickens, Dr. William, was born in Anderson county, South Carolina, on January 15, 1881. His father and mother migrated to Arkansas in 1888 where young Pickens had his early training for the singular career which he was destined to carve out for himself.

Young Pickens graduated from the high school as valedictorian in 1899 and in the fall of the same year entered Talladega College, Alabama, as a sophomore. While a student at Talladega he won the oratorical and literary prizes and led in all the studies. He received his A. B. degree from Talladega in the spring of 1902 and in the fall of the same year he entered Yale University.

Dr. Pickens' success at Yale was not less phenomenal than his success in Talladega. In 1903 he won the Henry James Ten Eycks oratorical prize, with first honor over a class of over three hundred. He graduated from Yale

in 1904 after having been elected to the honor college-
fraternity of Phi Beta Kappa, and the ranking student of
his class.

His services as teacher of languages were retained by
Talladega from 1904 to 1914. In 1913 he toured Europe
and in 1914 was called to the chair of Greek and sociology
by Wiley University, Marshall, Texas, where he remained but one year. In the fall of 1919 he was appointed dean of Morgan College, Baltimore, Maryland.
He held this position for three years, at the end of which
he was elected vice president of the institution. He
held the degree of LL. D. from Wiley University in
recognition of distinguished services to the school.

When the United States declared war against the
Central Powers in 1917, and the question of the establishment of Negro Officers' Training Camps was under consideration, Dr. Pickens with Mr. J. E. Spingern were the
moving spirits behind the plan. Indeed, it may safely be
said that they originated the movement. Through their
efforts the school was established in Fort Des Moines,
Iowa, the only camp of its kind known in the history of
America.

Dr. Pickens is the author of "The New Negro,"
"The Heir of Slaves," and many pamphlets and published
addresses. He is also a contributing editor to a number
of Negro weeklies. At present he is a member of the
Colored Section of the Maryland Council of Defense and
member of the Executive Committee of the Roosevelt
Memorial Association of Maryland.

Pickens typifies what he himself calls the New Negro.
He is one of the most convincing platform orators of the
race. Recently he has addressed several legislative bodies
and mixed audiences in relation to the attitude of the
two races to one another. In spite of the radical program

to which he has committed himself he commands the respect of the white men both in the North and in the South.

Powell, A. Clayton, was born in Franklin county, Virginia, May 5, 1865. He entered the Virginia Union University and graduated in 1892. He spent a year in the Yale Divinity School in New Haven, Conn.

Rev. Powell was ordained in the Baptist ministry in 1892 and that same year he was elected pastor of a charge in Philadelphia, Penn. He served subsequently as pastor in New Haven, Conn., 1893-1908, resigning to become pastor of the Abyssinian Church, New York City. He has successfully ministered unto the people of this charge since 1908. This church is considered the wealthiest Negro Baptist church in the country. Its property holdings amount to $350,000 and its membership 3,300.

There are other activities in which Reverend Powell is interested. For example he is a member of the National Urban League, the National Association for the Advancement of Colored People, the White Rose Industrial Home, the Y. M. C. A. and other organizations of a social nature. He is a trustee of the following institutions: Virginia Seminary and College, National Training School for Women and Girls, Downington Industrial and Agricultural School. In addition to that he has published a number of pamphlets, some of which are: "The Valley of Dry Bones," "Some Rights Not Denied the Negro Race," "Power of the Spirit," "The Need of the Hour," etc.

Powell, William Frank, was born at Troy, New York, June 26, 1845. He attended Lincoln University, New York School of Pharmacy and the New Jersey Collegiate Institute. From the last school he graduated in 1865.

1. HENRY HUGH PROCTOR.   3. REV. A. CLAYTON POWELL.
2. EUGENE P. ROBERTS.   4. MACK MATTHEW RODGERS.

Dr. Powell began life as a teacher, appointed by the Presbyterian Board of Home Missions to the Freedman School at Leesburg, Va. He was responsible for the opening of the first Freedmen's School in Alexandria, Va. In 1875 he was called to the principalship of Bordertown School, New Jersey. He served until 1881 and resigned to become a bookkeeper in the U. S. Treasury. His next business appointment was as district superintendent of schools, Camden, N. J. He introduced manual training in his district. In 1897 he was appointed Envoy Extraordinary and Minister Plenipotentiary to the Republic of Haiti and charge d' affaires to Santo Domingo. He held this position until 1905. Returning to the United States he became identified with the Philadelphia Tribune as an editorial writer. In recognition of his distinguished service Lincoln University conferred upon him the LL. D. degree in 1907.

Proctor, Henry Hugh, was born in Fayetteville, Tennessee, December 8, 1868, the son of Richard and Hannah Proctor. He entered Fisk University, Nashville, Tennessee, and graduated in 1891. He entered Yale Divinity School, in New Haven, Connecticut, and graduated with the degree of Bachelor of Divinity in 1894.

After his graduation Dr. Proctor was appointed pastor of the Congregational Church, Atlanta, Georgia, a charge he has held since. Under his pastorage, there is a free public library with 3,000 volumes; Avery Congregational House for Girls; A gymnasium which is kept open afternoons and evenings; the prison mission; the trouble department; the Conally water fountain; the Georgia Music Association and auditorium with a seating capacity of 1,000, with modern equipment and sanitary conveniences. But his activities do not stop there. He is the vice-president of the American Missionary Association, of New York; President of the Carrie Steel Orphanage, of Atlanta; Secretary of the Congregational Workers among Colored People; Moderator of the National Council of the Congregational Church. He is chairman of the Arkansas State Mission Board since 1900. He is also an executive member of the American Executive Committee of the Baptist World Alliance, and the General Convention of America.

Randolph, Florence, was born in Charleston, South Carolina. She received her early education in Avery Normal Institute and in the public schools of Charleston, S. C.

Mrs. Randolph left the South and went to the North and settled in New Jersey. There she became identified with the A. M. E. Church and in 1897 was licensed to preach in New Jersey. Bishop Alexander Walters recommended that she be admitted to the Conference and in 1901 she was ordained a Deaconess and two years later an Elder. She was elected a delegate to the Ecumenical Conference which met in London in 1901.

Rev. Randolph has served as pastor of several churches in New Jersey and New York. While in Europe she preached in the Primitive Methodist Church of Mattison Road, London, England. She spends a great deal of her time ministering to the prisoners of New York and New Jersey. She is an ardent supporter of the temperance movement relative to which she lectures in New Jersey and in other communities. She holds membership in the New Jersey State Federation of Women's Clubs, Executive Board of the New Jersey State Suffrage Association and its chaplain, chaplain of the Northeastern Federation of Colored Women's Clubs, President of the Women's Home and Foreign Missionary Society of the A. M. E. Zion Curch.

Ransom, Reverdy Cassins, was born at Flushing, Ohio, January 4, 1861. He entered the Theological School of Wilberforce University, Ohio, and graduated with the B. D. degree in 1886.

Dr. Ransom was licensed to preach in the A. M. E. church in 1883 and ordained Elder in 1888. He has served as pastor of charges in Pennsylvania, Ohio, Massachusetts and New York. He held the charge in New York City from 1907-1912. In 1912 he was elected editor of the A. M. E. Church Review at Kansas City, Mo. His literary works number among them the addresses of John Brown, William Lloyd Garrison, Wendell Phillips, Robert G. Ingersoll and Charles Sumners' "School Days at Wilberforce."

The degree of Doctor of Divinity was conferred upon him in 1897 by Wilberforce University, Ohio, an institution of which he is a trustee.

Raphael, The Very Reverend Father, was born at Chapelton, Clarendon, Jamaica, B. W. I. His elementary education was received in his native land. From an early age he left home and going first to Colon, Republic of Panama, then to the United States and Europe. He came under the influence of the Protestant Episcopal Church and was made a lay reader. His more advanced literary training was received in Freetown, Sierra Leone, West Africa. He took private studies preparatory to entering the ministry and later entered St. Aidon's Theological College, Brookshead, England, and King's College, University of London. Was ordained in America in the Protestant Episcopal Church, and became honorary curate in St. Matthew's Wilmington, Delaware. He taught in the public schools of Delaware for a short time, returning to Europe subsequently.

Father Raphael became dissatisfied with the Anglican

Church and became interested in the Greek Church, and returning to the United States was ordained in the Greek Orthodox Catholic Church of Philadelphia, Penn., the only Negro to be identified with this religion. He founded and became Superior of the Order of the Cross of Golgotha, a religious fraternity.

Roberts, Eugene P., was born in Louisburg, North Carolina, October 5, 1868. He received his elementary training in his native home and entered Lincoln University, Chester, Pennsylvania, in 1887, from which he graduated with the degree of A. B. in 1891. He entered Flower Hospital and the New York Homeopathic Medical Association and graduated in 1894. The degree of M. A. was conferred upon him by Lincoln in recognition of his merit in his chosen field.

Dr. Robert is a specialist in diseases of children, a lecturer on care of babies, and an inspector of the department of health. Recognizing his merits in this field he has been asked several times by the National Medical Association to address them on the subject of children's diseases. He holds membership in the following organizations: Medical Club, New York County Medical Association, National Medical Association, New York Materia Medica Society, Academy of Pathological Science, Medico-Chirurgical Society, chairman of the Colored Branch, Y. M. C. A., National League for the Protection of Colored Women, and a member of the Executive Board of the National Urban League.

Rodgers, Mack Matthew, was born in Wharton county, Texas, July 13, 1859. He entered Prairie View State Normal School, Prairie View, Texas, from which institution he graduated with honors in 1881.

Mr. Rodgers moved to LaGrange, Texas, in 1887, and was elected to the principalship of the city school. He became interested in politics and as a reward for his activity was for three successive terms elected alderman of the city of LaGrange. He has been elected delegate to the National Republican Convention five times, 1888, 1892, 1900, 1904, 1912. In 1897, he was appointed deputy Collector of Internal Revenue for the third district of Texas, the first Negro to have received this appointment.

He has served as secretary of the LaGrange Baptist Association; Secretary of the Baptist Missionary and Educational Convention of Texas. Under his influence the convention was incorporated and thereby removing some of the pressure of personal responsibility. He is auditor of the National Baptist Convention of the United States, and Grand Keeper of the Records, Seals and Secretary of the Knights of Pythias. He was one of the commissioners who supervised the construction of the Pythian Temple of Dallas.

Roman, Dr. Charles Victor, was born at Williamsport, Pa., on July 4, 1864. He attended the Hamilton Collegiate Institution, Hamilton, Ontario, and completed the course of studies. Returning to the U. S., Dr. Roman taught for a while in the public schools of Kentucky and Tennessee, and later matriculated in the Medical College of Meharry. He received his M. D. degree from that institution in 1890. Not content with merely getting the fundamentals of his profession he took post graduate courses in Chicago, Ill., and in the Royal London Ophthalmic Hospital and Central London Nose, Throat and Ear Hospital, England.

Dr. Roman first settled in Dallas, Texas, and engaged in the practice of medicine until 1904 when he moved to Nashville, Tenn. He was appointed professor of ear, eye, nose and throat diseases in Meharry College of Medicine. He is identified with many other activities among them, director of the One Cent Saving Bank; he holds membership in the National Medical Association, American Academy of Political and Social Sciences, Southern Sociological Congress, Odd Fellows, Knights of Pythias, and editor of the National Medical Journal.

He is the author of a number of books and pamphlets, among them, "Eye, Ear, Nose and Throat Formulary," (1909); "Racial Solidarity," (1911); "Science and Christian Ethics," (1913); "Dethronement of a King," (1913); and "American Civilization and the Negro."

Scarbrough, Dr. William Sanders, was born at Macon, Georgia, February 16, 1854, the son of Jeremiah and Frances Scarbrough. He received his preparation for his course at Atlanta University, Atlanta, Ga. He entered Oberlin College, Ohio, and graduated in 1875 and received his M. A. degree in 1878.

Dr. Scarbrough began life as a teacher of Greek at Wilberforce University in 1877, and continued until 1891, when he resigned to become professor of Hellenic Greek at Payne Theological Seminary. In 1895 he was called back to Wilberforce and appointed professor of Greek and head of the classical department. He subsequently became vice-president and from 1908 he has been president.

Dr. Scarbrough holds membership in a number of societies. Among them are: Archaeological Institute of America; American Philological Association; American Academy of Political and Social Science; American Social Science Association; American Dialectic Society; National Geographical Society; American Negro Academy; American Folk-Lore Society. He is a trustee of the Lincoln Memorial Association of Ohio; was delegate to the Ecumenical Conference of Methodism at London, England, in 1901, and delegate to the Universal

HON. EMMETT J. SCOTT, SECRETARY-TREASURER, HOWARD UNIVERSITY, WASHINGTON, D. C.
Formerly Special Assistant to the Secretary of War.

Race Congress. Dr. Scarbrough is the author of "Our Political Status," "Theory and Function of the Thematic Vowel of the Greek Verb," "First Lessons in Greek," and "Birds of Aristophanes, a Theory of Interpretation."

In recognition of his achievements in the literary world State University, Louisville, Ky., conferred upon him the degree of Ph. D. and Morris Brown College the degree of A. M.

Scott, Emmett J., Dr., was born in Houston, Texas, 44 years ago. He received his intellectual training from the Wiley University, Marshall, Texas, from which institution he received his A. B. degree.

Dr. Booker T. Washington was attracted by Mr. Scott's work as newspaper correspondent of the Houston Post and was further impressed by the executive ability which he demonstrated in arranging a monster and well planned mass meeting of white and colored citizens of Texas. As a result, Scott was tendered the position of confidential secretary to Dr. Washington in which capacity he served efficiently for 18 years and was later elected secretary of Tuskegee Institute.

In addition to his duties as secretary of Tuskegee he was editor of "The Tuskegee Student," the organ of the institution. Dr. Scott has acted as secretary of the National Negro Business League, ever since its organization in Boston, Massachusetts, eighteen years ago. This organization is perhaps the most influential Negro organization in America and exercises a most potent effect on racial and civic affairs, through its more than five hundred local business leagues and branches of the parent organization which are operating in various communities throughout the country.

During the administration of Hon. William H. Taft, President of the United States, Mr. Scott was appointed

Special Commissioner to Liberia to help investigate and adjust financial and other important matters relating to that Negro republic.

Our entrance in the European conflict and its attendant problems both social and economic made it necessary for the Secretary of War, Hon. Newton D. Baker, to mobilize not only the fighting forces of the nation but also its social forces. In order effectively to accomplish this all grounds for discontent had to be cleared and national harmony for once at least established. The Negro as an individual and as a race was the greatest sufferer. The injustices which he was suffering at the hands of the nation were exploited by German agents to such an extent that the government became alarmed and its conscience suffered a righteous awakening. Another Booker T. Washington had to be found and the choice fell on Scott. He was borrowed from Tuskegee and appointed Special Assistant Secretary of War in charge of Negro Problems, both military and civil.

Mr. Scott, though new to official Washington, approached his big job with the coolness of a veteran. No bombast attended his accession to his office. He had no preconceived "policies" to put over—no personal axes to grind. He had no friends to reward and no enemies to punish. He did not "attitudinize" for the purpose of magnifying the importance of his mission or himself. Modestly he took hold of his work with half a desk as his quarters and there he mapped out his program with the one intent uppermost in his mind—to serve to the limit of his powers the people whom he was chosen to represent.

Mr. Scott was called upon to settle numerous vexing problems arising from the relation between the two races as they labored together for the defeat of the enemy.

Some of the changes he was instrumental in having brought about are:

1. The enrollment of Colored Red Cross Nurses.

2. The extension to young colored men of the opportunity for special training.

3. The establishment of a woman's branch under the Council of National Defense.

4. Opening of every branch of the military services to colored men.

Mr. Scott is now the secretary and treasurer of Howard University, Washington, D. C., a position which is equally as important as that previously held by him.

Smith, Rev. C. H., was born a slave September 8, 1864, in Edgecombe county, North Carolina.

Rev. Smith is in every sense of the word a self made man who found it necessary to push for himself at a very early age.

He founded the Vienna Oak Missionary Baptist Sunday School Convention in 1888, and acted as its president for fourteen years. Roanoke Institute of Wilmington, North Carolina, numbers Rev. Smith among its founders. He organized more Sunday Schools than any other man in the state and has been prominently associated with many national orders and religious societies.

At present Rev. Smith is pastor of the Mt. Piszah Baptist Church in Washington, which he founded in May, 1906.

Smith, Ezekiel Ezra, was born at Mt. Olive, North Carolina, May 23, 1852. He entered Shaw University and graduated in 1878 with the A. B. degree.

He began life as a journalist but later became principal of the State Colored Normal School. He resigned in 1888 to accept a federal appointment as Minister Resident and Consul-General of Liberia. He remained in diplomatic service for three years and returned to the United States to enter into business. He is president of the Farmer's and Mechanic's Building and Loan Association and the Cape Fear Investment Company.

During the Spanish-American War he was regimental adjutant, having been commissioned in 1881 Major of the Fourth Battalion, N. C. State Guard. He has been secretary of the Baptist State Convention for 30 years. Shaw University conferred upon him the A. M. degree in 1881 and the Ph. D. degree in 1892.

Smith, Robert L. was born in Charleston, South Carolina, January 8, 1861. His early education was received in Avery Normal Institute and South Carolina University and Atlanta University, Atlanta, Georgia.

Leaving school Mr. Smith went to Texas and entered the teaching profession. He became interested in the public life of his adopted community and without his knowledge was nominated for a seat in the Texas Legislature. He ran for the office and not only won but was re-elected the following term.

While teaching in Oakland the condition of the farmers was brought to his notice. Most of the land which they owned was heavily mortgaged and all badly in debt. In order to assist these farmers, Mr. Smith organized a Farmers' Improvement Society which undertook to buy and distribute farm commodities to the farmers at cost. In addition to the society Mr. Smith has also established a bank and a school for the benefit of the farmers. The bank does business under the name of Farmers' Improvement Bank and the school, the F. I. S. Agricultural College, located at Landonia, North Texas. He also established an overall factory. Under his influence the farmers of the community have purchased lands to the amount of 80,000 acres with live stock, estimated at $1,500,000.

Talbert, Mary Burnett, born at Oberlin, Ohio, September 17, 1863, educated at Oberlin College, a teacher, lecturer, and prominent club woman. (See writeup on page 181.) She is president of Empire State Federation and a member of the Household of Ruth and of the Eastern Star.

Tanner, Henry Ossawa, one of the most distinguished of present day American artists, was born at Pittsburgh, Pa., June 21, 1859; son of Rt. Rev. Benjamin T. and Sarah Elizabeth (Miller) Tanner. He was married in London, England, to Jessie Macauley, of San Francisco, California, December 14, 1899. He studied in the Pennsylvania Academy of Fine Arts under Thomas Eakins; was a pupil in Paris of Jean Paul Laurens and Benjamin Constant.

He is chiefly a painter of religious subjects; honorable mention in Salon, Paris, 1896; awards, third class medal, 1897; second class medal, 1897; won Walter Lippincott prize at Philadelphia, Pennsylvania, and Harris prize, Chicago, Illinois, 1900; second medal at Paris Exposition, 1900; second medal, Pan-American Exposition, Buffalo, N. Y., 1901; second medal, Louisiana Purchase Exposition, St. Louis, Missouri, 1904. Represented with paintings in the Luxembourg, the Wilstach Collection, Carnegie Institute at Pittsburgh, Pennsylvania Academy of Fine Arts, and Art Institute of Chicago; sold the famous painting, "Raising of Lazarus," to Luxembourg Galleries. He is a member of many National and International Art Societies.

Terrell, Mary Church, born Memphis, Tennessee, A. B. and A. M. degrees at Oberlin College, teacher of foreign languages in the colored High School in Washington. Mrs. Terrell was president of the National

28

Association of Woman's Clubs for three consecutive terms, and of the Bethel Literary Association of Washington. She is a member of the Board of Education of the District of Columbia. (See Chapter X.)

Terrell, Robert Herbertson, was born in Orange county, Va., November 25, 1857. He entered Harvard University and graduated with the degree of A. B. in 1884.

Judge Terrell began life as a teacher in the public schools of Washington, D. C., in 1884, and five years later was appointed principal of the high school. While engaged in the teaching profession he studied law at Howard Law School and received his LL. B. degree in 1889. For four years subsequent to his graduation from the law school he held an official position in the Treasury Department. In 1893 he was admitted to the bar of the District of Columbia and entered immediately into the practice of law with John M. Lynch as a partner. He was appointed a Civil Magistrate in 1902 and seven years later Judge of the Municipal Court of the District of Columbia. The appointment was made by President Roosevelt and subsequently by Taft and Wilson. He is a member of the Sigma Pi Phi and a past grand master of the Masons.

Tobias, Channing Higgie, was born at Augusta, Georgia, February, 1882. He received his A. B. degree from Paine College, Augusta, Ga., in 1902, and matriculated subsequently in Drew Theological Seminary, Madison, N. J., in 1905, and later pursued summer courses at the University of Pennsylvania. He was called back to his Alma Mater to teach Biblical literature. He served in that capacity for six years. From 1911 he has devoted his time and energy in developing the Colored Branch of the International Y. M. C. A. He has served on the most important committees of the organization. He was appointed secretary in 1911; delegate to the International Convention in 1907, in Cincinnati, Ohio, in 1913, World's Students' Christian Federation Conference; Executive Secretary Negro Christian Student Convention in 1914; member of the Executive Committee Federal Council of Churches in America.

Mr. Tobias is one of the national organizers of the organization and devotes his time to the school associations. Mr. Tobias has served as teacher of colored secretaries in Chesapeake Summer School and was one of the conductors of the Negro Student Conference at Kings Mountain in 1912 and 1913.

Tompkins, George Ricks, was born in Rochester, New York, October 23, 1881. He attended the public schools of Buffalo, graduating from the high school in 1900. He matriculated in the Engineering School of Cornell University, Ithaca, N. Y., and graduated with the degree of Engineer in 1907.

He began in the plant of George N. Pierce & Co., manufacturers of the Pierce-Arrow Automobiles and became assistant foreman. He became connected with the Erie Railroad in the Buffalo Division as machinist in 1903. In 1907 he was Engineer of Road Tests for that company. In 1908 he resigned his position with the Erie Railroad Company to become director of the mechanical department of the Agricultural and Mechanical College, Greensboro, N. C. He held this position for two years and resigned to accept a position as instructor of Mechanical Engineering at Wilberforce University, Ohio.

Trotter, William Monroe, was born in Springfield township, Ohio, April 7, 1872. He received his A. B. degree at Harvard in 1895, and his M. A. degree in 1896.

Mr. Trotter is one of the most brilliant Negro students

who graduated from this classic institution. As an undergraduate he was elected to the Phi Beta Kappa fraternity, the honor organization of the leading white institutions of learning. Mr. Trotter, unlike the average Negro graduate, selected a field after his graduation in which he could express the sentiments of his oppressed race. Having felt keenly the vicious thrust of race prejudice he turned to journalism as the most effective means to combat the evil. In 1901 he established The Boston Guardian, a weekly paper to enlighten the public on the evil of race prejudice and the suffering of his people. He possesses the qualities of true leadership in that he is sacrificing everything in order to serve his people. Mr. Trotter's ability could easily win for him an easy berth by compromising the cause of his race. But he has steadfastly refused to be bought either in cold cash or through appointment to a political berth.

Mr. Trotter may be classified as a radical reformer. He is identified with all radical movements and organizations which have for their purpose the absolute emancipation of his people. He is the president of the New England Suffrage League, a member of the National Independent Equal Rights League and was spokesman for the latter organization when its delegates waited on Woodrow Wilson November 6, 1913, to present its grievance. He was again spokesman for that organization the following year, November 12, 1914. His reply to the President was so pointed that he notified the delegation that no audience will be granted it in the future if Mr. Trotter continued as its spokesman. The affair became a national event, at least for a day, and the press of the country was divided on the issue.

During the World War Mr. Trotter made several attempts to secure a passport to go to France but the State

1. WILLIAM ROBERT VALENTINE.
2. VICTOR HUGO TULANE.
3. CHARLES VICTOR ROMAN.
4. HON. ROBERT L. SMITH.

Department refused him one. Trotter-like he secured
passage on a tramp ship as a kitchen hand and eventually
landed in France. He tried to secure an interview with
Mr. Wilson but it was denied him. Returning to the
United States Mr. Trotter disclosed the gross irregular-
ities in the Negro Units and the concerted action of the
white officers to discredit the achievements of the Negro
officers as well as soldiers.

Mr. Trotter occupies a unique place in the race for
Negro leadership. In the first place he is not a white
man's appointed leader; in the second place he has no ax
of his own to grind, and in the third place, he is actuated
by a motive which is pure, unselfish, altruistic and
humanitarian.

Tulane, Victor H., was born in Wetumpka, Alabama,
in 1873, on a farm. At the age of sixteen, he and his
mother moved to Montgomery where by dint of
perseverance of both mother and son they managed to
save a small sum of money which they invested in a small
grocery concern. The same tenacity which characterized
the efforts of Mr. Tulane to save his first $100.00, kept
him at the business even when failure seemed inevitable,
and, as it often happens, his efforts have been crowned
with success. The two-story modern brick building which
stands at the corner of South Ripley and High streets is
the unequivocal testimony of the man's success. From a
shanty with hardly $100.00 worth of stock has grown
this modern grocery store with several thousand dollars
worth of groceries.

Mr. Tulane is also interested in other activities. He
owns real property in the city of Montgomery, and at one
time was prominently connected with the Montgomery
Penny Savings Bank. Other activities with which he is
identified are: Honorary Member of the Montgomery

Chamber of Commerce, a member of the Board of Trustees of Tuskegee Institute, member of the Executive Committee of the National Negro Business League and member of the Swayne School Board.

Turner, Dr. Charles Henry, was born in Cincinnati, Ohio, February 3, 1867. He received his academic degree (B. S.) from the University of Cincinnati in 1891 and the the degree of M. A. from that same institution in 1892.

Dr. Turner entered the teaching profession at the age of twenty-one as public school teacher at Evansville, Indiana. In 1899 he was substituting in the public schools of Cincinnati. He served on the faculty in the University of Cincinnati and in Clark University, Atlanta, Georgia.

Dr. Turner's fame as a biologist is nation-wide. In 1907 he received the degree of Doctor of Philosophy from the University of Chicago. He has made a number of original contributions in the field of biology. Among a few of them are: "Ecological Notes on the Cladocera and Copepoda of Augusta, Ga.," "Morphology of the Nervous System of the Genus Cypris," "The Mushroom Bodies of the Crawfish," "Experiments on the Color Vision of the Honey Bee," "Behavior of the Common Roach," etc. He holds membership in the following societies: Academy of Science of St. Louis, Sigma Chi, Sema Pi Phi, Academy of Science of Illinois, Entomological Society of America.

Tyler, Ralph W., was born at Columbus, Ohio, and received his preparatory and literary training in the public schools of Columbus. After the completion of his high school course he received an appointment on the reporting staff of the Columbus Evening Despatch, and served on that daily for seventeen years, rising from a reporter to the position of assistant to the manager and confidential secretary of the publisher. Mr. Tyler severed his business relation with the Columbus Evening Despatch to join the Ohio State Journal, another white daily, on the staff of which he served three years.

Mr. Tyler's work on these papers did not go unnoticed, for President Roosevelt, in looking for a capable man to fill the vacancy which occurred in the Auditor's Department for the U. S. Navy, selected him to fill that position. That was in 1905, but Mr. Roosevelt's term ended in 1908; however, Mr. Taft, his successor, reappointed him to that position in recognition of his ability. He held the position of auditor of the U. S. Navy until 1913.

Mr. Tyler became publicity agent for Mr. Emmet J. Scott, when the latter was filling the place of assistant to the Secretary of War, and was subsequently sent to France as the official reporter of the government. He was assigned to the sector where the 92nd Division was operating and the stories of this Negro division in action coming from his pen are a veritable literary treat. Returning from France Mr. Taylor took to the platform which a propaganda of the Bourbon white officers was seeking to tarnish. So far, Mr. Tyler has been the only Negro journalist who has been regularly employed on a white daily in his state.

Valentine, William Robert, was born in Loudon county, Virginia, October 7, 1879. He entered Harvard at his graduation from high school and received the A. B. degree in 1904.

Mr. Valentine began life as a teacher and principal in the public schools of Indianapolis, Indiana, becoming later the supervising principal of Public School No. 26. While serving in that capacity he made a number of innovations to the school which elicited favorable comment from John Dewey, of Columbia University, in his

"Schools of Tomorrow." In 1915 he was called to fill the position of principal of Bordentown Industrial School, New Jersey, and is still holding that position.

Vernon, William Tecumseh, was born at Lebanon, Mo., July 11, 1871. He attended the public schools of Missouri and Lincoln Institute, Jefferson City, Mo. From the latter institution he received the degree of Bachelor of Didactics.

He began life as a public school teacher in Missouri and was called to Western University, Quinndaro, Kansas, in 1896 as the head of the institution. Under his regime the school was renovated and its status raised and the equipment and student body were materially increased. In 1906 he was appointed Registrar of the Treasury by Mr. Roosevelt. He continued in the position until 1910 when he resigned to take up educational work in the South. He was elected to the presidency of Campbell College, Jackson, Mississippi.

In recognition of his service to the race and the nation, Lincoln Institute conferred upon him the M. A. degree and Wilberforce University the D. D. and LL. D. degrees. He was ordained a minister in the A. M. E. Church.

Vodery, Will Henry Bennett, was born in Philadelphia, Penn., Oct. 8, 1885. He graduated from the Central High School in 1902, and entered the Hugh A. Clark University, in Pennsylvania, where he studied music under Louis Koemmenick, Grand Director of the University of Leipsic.

Mr. Vodery may be called with safety a musical genius for at the age of nine he was the pianist of his Sunday School and four years later we find him holding the position of church organist. His accomplishment at this tender age marked him out as a prospective musician of high caliber.

Mr. Vodery has written many successful song hits and musical comedies among the most popular being "After The Ball Was Over," "The Time, Place, and Girl," "Me Hun and I," "'Oyster Man," and "Saucy Maid." He has traveled extensively in this country and in Europe, and at one time was custodian for the famous Theodore Thomas Orchestra in Chicago.

Walker, Charles T., born Hephzibah, Louisiana, February 5, 1858, LL. D., Augusta Institute, (Moorehouse College) 1877, D. D. State University, Louisville, Ky., pastored Franklin Covenant Baptist Church, LaGrange Baptist Church, Tabernacle Church, Augusta, Mount Olivet Baptist Church, New York City, founded La-Grange Academy, the Old People's Home, Augusta, and Colored Y. M. C. A. in New York City.

Dr. Walker was a chaplain in the United States Army in Cuba in 1898. His eloquence has won for him the title of the "Black Spurgeon."

He married Miss Violet Franklin in 1879, and has three living children.

Walker, Madam C. J., was born at Delta, La., December 23, 1867. At the age of six her parents died and she was sent to Vicksburg, Miss., to live with her sister. It is said that the inhospitality of her sister's husband forced her into an early marriage at the age of fourteen years. Six years after her marriage her husband died and she and her daughter, Leila, went to St. Louis, Mo., to live. Even in those days Madam Walker found that the problem of caring for a home and a daughter was a vexing one, but by dint of perseverance she was able, not only to keep her home together, but to send her daughter to Fisk University, Nashville, Tenn. It was while she was over her wash tub engaged in the grim business of making a living, that an inspiration came to her, one which she was not slow in capitalizing. It is said that she dreamt of a formula whereby human hair could be made to grow and become straight. The formula was prepared and she experimented on herself and daughter. The result was satisfactory, so far as she was concerned, and she undertook to convince the world of the efficacy of her preparation. Her first attempt was made in Denver, Colorado, and after many unpleasant experiences finally convinced her people of the virtue of her preparation. She decided to broaden her sphere of activity and started out to introduce her preparation. She traveled for two years touching practically every city in this country and overcoming the natural prejudices of the people. She finally settled down in Pittsburgh, Penn., in 1908. Eventually she established a successful mail order business and moved to Indianapolis, Ind., in 1910. Success did not shut her eyes to greater possibilities for her ware. She took advantage of every opportunity which presented itself and had the satisfaction to see her business and her preparation become an international affair. In New York she found a lucrative field for her product and she established a branch of her business there. She built a home and an office in West 136th street, which drew the attention of the daily papers of that metropolis and the New York Times found it necessary to depart from its Anti-Negro tradition to give her and her business a space in its Sunday Magazine section. Two years ago Madam Walker purchased a property at Irvington on the Hudson, and erected for herself a veritable mansion. The company of which she was president was incorporated for $10,000, and her weekly income before her death, which occurred Sunday, May 25,

1919, amounted to $1000. Madam Walker was not only an enterprising woman but she was also a philanthropist. She was giving liberally to every worthy Negro endeavor, especially to the Y. M. C. A. and Y. W. C. A. She contributed $1000 to the building fund of the Y. M. C. A. of Indianapolis, Ind., and contributed annually to the national organization. She maintained an industrial school in Africa before her death. Her fortune, at her death, was estimated at $1,000,000.

Warfield, Dr. William A., was born at Hyattstown, Montgomery county, Maryland, Nov. 17, 1866. He received his early training in Baltimore, Md., from which institution he graduated in 1890. He entered Howard University Medical School and graduated with the degree of M. D. in 1894.

He received an appointment as interne in the Freedman's Hospital in 1894-5. He was then appointed second assistant surgeon and a year later first assistant surgeon. He held this position until 1901 when he was appointed Surgeon in Chief of the Hospital and Professor of Abdominal Surgery at Howard University.

Dr. Warfield has made a number of valuable contributions to the field of surgery. Although not so famous as his former chief, Dr. Dan Williams of Chicago, his experiences in this field have helped considerably to ameliorate human suffering.

Dr. Warfield is a member of a few select scientific societies among which are: The American Hospital Association; National Medical Association; Medico-Chirurgical Society of the District of Columbia. He is also a member of the Board of Children's Guardians in the District of Columbia.

Washington, Dr. Booker T., was undoubtedly one of the most remarkable figures which the nineteenth century produced. Born a slave, he lived to become the confidential adviser of two Republican presidents (Mr. Roosevelt and Mr. Taft), on matters appertaining to his race. A great deal of publicity was given to an incident in the latter part of his life in which Mr. Roosevelt, then president, entertained him at luncheon at the White House.

As an authority on industrial education for Negroes, perhaps he had no equal. Himself a product of that type of education, he had great faith in it as the best measure to insure the economic, political and social emancipation of his people.

Dr. Washington had a genius for organizing and among the many organizations which took shape under his hand is the Negro Business League, one of the strongest Negro organizations in this country.

In addition to his numerous responsibilities Dr. Washington found time to devote to the pursuit of literature. He is the author of several volumes on contemporaneous Negro life, two of which are devoted to the exposition of incidents of his wonderful life. Among his literary works are "Up from Slavery," "My Larger Education," "The Story of My Life and Work," and numerous articles which he contributed to national periodicals.

Dr. Washington was a born leader. Nowhere was this peculiar talent of his brought out more clearly than in his relationship with the white men of the South. Perhaps one-third of the men of his own race who followed him did not believe in his policies, yet he was able to hold them together and whenever it was necessary, he secured their support to his program. His influence among the whites of the South was not less far-reaching. White men and women from far and near laid aside their business of the day to listen to Washington, as he discussed topics familiar to them because of constant repetition.

Washington, Mrs. Margaret J. Murray, was born at Macon, Ga., March 9, 1865. She received her preparatory school training in Macon, and later went to Fisk University for her more advanced work. She received her A. B. degree in 1889. At the completion of her college course at Fisk University, Mrs. Washington was called to the English department of Tuskegee and later became the dean of women, and director of girls' industries at Tuskegee. In 1892, she married Booker T. Washington, the organizer and principal of Tuskegee Institute. Her marriage to the principal of the institution did not curtail her activities. On the contrary she has used her position to broaden her sphere of influence both in the institution and in the community.

Mrs. Washington was appointed chairman of the advisory board of the Boys' Reformatory at Meigs, Alabama, by Governor Emmet Oneal. Her activities at Tuskegee have not kept her from taking part in other phases of worthy endeavors. She has been president of the Alabama State Federation of Colored Women's Clubs, the president of the National Federation of Colored Women's Clubs. She has established Mothers' Clubs, Open Air Sunday Schools, in fact, she is a distinct social asset to the community. The death of her illustrous husband has left her to carry on the good work single-handed. Three children were born to the Washingtons. They are Portia, Ernest D. and Booker T., Jr.

Wheatley, Phillis, born in Africa, brought to the United States in 1761. She was bought from the slave market by John Wheatley of Boston 16 months after her arrival in America. She was able to read English fluently. She became a poetess, visited England where she was received by the nobility. In America she was the guest of George Washington for a short time at the Revolutionary Headquarters.

Wheaton, Frank J., was born at Hagerstown, Maryland, May 8, 1866. He studied law at Howard University, Washington, D. C., and left to enter the University of Minnesota. From the latter institution he received his Bachelor of Law degree in 1894, with the honor of being the orator of his class.

Mr. Wheaton began his practice of law in Hagerstown, his place of nativity, but moved to Minneapolis, Minn., to become clerk of the Municipal Court. He was a member of the House of Representatives of Minnesota in 1898-1900. He subsequently moved to New York and was admitted to the bar.

He is a member of the Bar Association of New York City and was the Grand Exalted Ruler of Elks of the World for two years. Mr. Wheaton is undoubtedly one of the most successful lawyers of his race. In politics he is a Republican. He has been a delegate to the National Convention three times.

White, Clarence Cameron, was born at Clarksville, Tennessee, August 10, 1879. He attended Howard University where he received his literary training and Oberlin Conservatory of Music, Ohio. He received private instruction from such masters as S. Coleridge Taylor, London, England, and M. Zacharewitsch.

Before going to England, Mr. White was engaged for a year as teacher of music in the public schools of Washington, D. C. From 1908-10 he was first violinist in the String Players Club, London, England. Since 1912 he has been engaged as violin soloist and teacher of the instrument in Boston, Mass. In 1913 he became the director of the Victorian Concert Orchestra.

Mr. White has a number of musical compositions to his credit, among them are, "A Comic Opera," and "Improvisation."

Williams, Dr. A. Wilberforce, was born in Monroe, Louisiana, January 31, 1864. At the age of twelve his family moved to Springfield, Missouri, and there for the first time he had an opportunity to attend school. That was in 1876. In 1881 he obtained a license and was teaching in Vernon county, Mo. He matriculated in the Normal Department of Lincoln Institute, Jefferson, Missouri, and at his graduation entered seriously into the business of teaching.

Having decided to study medicine he matriculated at Northwestern University Medical School, Chicago, Illinois, and graduated in the spring of 1884. He soon became identified with Provident Hospital, Chicago, as a member of its staff as a physician and later as attending physician to Provident Hospital Dispensary and the Municipal Tuberculosis Dispensary. Dr. Williams is a specialist in the internal treatment of heart disease and tuberculosis and as a professor in the Post Graduate Department of Provident Hospital he devotes his time solely to this subject. He has contributed a number of articles on the care and treatment of tubercular patients. An article on "Tuberculosis and the Negro," prepared for the Mississippi Conference on Tuberculosis appeared in the "Journal of Outdoor Life" for February, 1915.

Dr. Williams is the Health contributing editor of the Chicago Defender and in addition he is connected with numerous organizations, among them are: National Medical Association, American Medical Association, Illinois State Medical Association, the Chicago Medical Society, Robert Koch Society for the Study and Prevention of Tuberculosis, Frederick Douglass Center, Social Service and Appomattox Clubs.

During the war Dr. Williams rendered singular service to the government. He was a member of the Advisory

Board of the Chicago Local Exemption Board, Chairman of the Second Ward Committee of the Fourth Liberty Loan and Chairman of the Committee of Physicians of the Red Cross Home Service Medical Section.

Williams, Bert, was born in New Providence, Nassau, British Bahama Islands. His parents came to the United States when he was two years old and settled in New York. He graduated from the Riverside High School in due time and set out for San Francisco, California, where he intended to pursue a course in civil engineering. Before matriculating in any school he met and joined a company of young men who were going to try their hands in the local theatrical business. They toured the lumber and mining camps of the California frontier. It was while he was engaged in this venture that it dawned upon him that he might successfully pursue a theatrical career.

He came into contact with George Walker, a clever comedian, and formed a partnership with him under the name of Williams and Walker Co. The cleverness and the high class quality of their performances won for them national recognition. The death of his partner left him alone to face the world. Being confident that his individual work was a drawing card he refrained from forming another alliance. At first theatrical managers were reluctant in billing him, but the high class quality of his work soon removed all barriers and Bert Williams became one of the idols of the stage. For many years Bert Williams and the Follies were synonymous terms to theatre-goers. He sang for the Victor and other talking machine companies. He died suddenly in New York, March 4, 1922, of pneumonia, leaving a widow and no children.

Williams, Dr. Dan Hale, was born in Hollidaysburg, Penn., January 18, 1858. He matriculated in the medical school of Northwestern University and graduated in

29

1883. At his graduation he was appointed a demonstrator in anatomy at Northwestern, a position which he held for four years.

Dr. Williams has served in the capacity of a surgeon on the staff of the following institutions: South Side Dispensary, Protestant Orphan Asylum, Chicago, Illinois; Surgeon in Chief Freedman's Hospital, Washington, D. C. (1893-98), Professor of Clinical Surgery at Meharry Medical School, Nashville, Tennessee.

To Dr. Williams is due the credit of establishing a nurses training school and intern system in The Freedmen's Hospital. He established Provident Hospital, Chicago, and became the attending surgeon. He was the first surgeon successfully to perform an operation on the human heart.

He received the LL. D. degree from Wilberforce University in 1909. He served as a member of the Illinois State Board of Health for four years (1887-91). He has been a fellow of the American College of Surgeons since 1913. His success has been heralded by the entire medical world.

Williams, L. K., born Eufaula, Ala., A. B., Bishop College, and Arkansas Baptist College, D. D., Selma University. In 1894 started to teach and preach in a circuit of Texas churches. He has organized fourteen churches and taken 14,748 people into the Baptist Church. He has been a member of the Illinois Race Commission, S. S. Publishing Board, Vice President National Baptist Convention of America, President State Baptist Convention.

Dr. Williams is now pastor of the Olivet Baptist Church in Chicago, the largest protestant church in America, with eight paid workers, 10,012 members and property valued at $250,000.00.

1. Monroe N. Work.   3. Charles Winter Wood.
2. Richard Arnett Williams.   4. William Taylor Williams.
5. A. Wilberforce Williams.

LIBRARY - Allegheny Campus

Williams, Dr. Richard Arnett, was born in Forest City, Arkansas, September 13, 1879. He received his training in Arkansas Baptist College in Little Rock, Arkansas, and graduated in 1896. He entered Meharry Medical College and graduated from that institution with the M. D. degree.

Dr. Williams settled in Knoxville, Tennessee, after his graduation and began the practice of medicine. In 1905, however, he moved to Helena, Arkansas, and again took up the practice of medicine. Moved by the desire to assist the needy sick and the widows and their dependents, Dr. Williams organized and chartered an organization called the Royal Circle of Friends of the World in 1909, which is fraternal and benevolent. In addition to that he has published a newspaper known as the "Royal Messenger," the organ of the organization. The success of the society is assured since it has filled a long felt need of the poorer class of people. Because of the tremendous amount of business which the organization is doing Dr. Williams was forced to give up part of his practice as a physician to devote himself to it.

Williams, William Taylor Burwell, was born in Stoneridge, Clarke county, Virginia, fifty years ago. His early education was received at Hampton, Virginia, and at Andover, Mass. He matriculated at Harvard and graduated in 1897.

Five years later Hampton Institute appointed him field agent of the institution and the Southern Education Board. His familiarity with Negro education recommended him to the General Education Board; the John E. Stater Fund and the Jeanes Fund, organizations which are interested in Negro education, and he was made their field agent, with headquarters at Hampton Institute. His headquarters are now at Tuskegee Institute, Alabama.

It is safe to say that there is not a phase of Negro education with which Mr. Williams is not familiar. However, he devotes more of his time in promoting industrial education in private schools and colleges of the South. He is identified with all educational movements especially those that vitally interest Negroes. He holds membership in the National Association of Teachers in Colored Schools, of which he was president for two terms; Virginia State Teachers' Association; Negro Organization Society of Virginia, and the National Educational Association. During the war he served in a supervisory capacity of the Committee of Education and Special Training of the War Department in connection with Negro schools. Mr. Williams is also an associate editor of the Cyclopedia of the Colored Race, the first volume of which appeared in 1919.

Wood, Charles Winter, was born in Tennessee, December 17, 1870. He received a part of his public school training in Tennessee, and while still young, moved to Chicago and drifted into the boot-blacking business for a living. At this early age he had learned and cultivated a taste for Shakespeare, which during his spare moments he recited for the entertainment of a few. He was accustomed to recite Shakespeare for the entertainment of his clients and it was in this manner that the attention of the great Gaumsarlens was attracted to him. He became interested in the lad and assisted him to go to school.

From the public school he went to Beloit College where he received his A. B. degree. He matriculated in the Divinity School of Chicago University and received his B. D. degree. Desiring to equip himself more thoroughly, he entered the graduate school of Columbia University and from that institution received his M. A. degree. His graduation from the Saper School of Oratory may be mentioned here.

Mr. Wood's career is a peculiar one. Beginning as a stage actor he ended by becoming a minister of the church, a teacher and the publicity manager of Tuskegee Institute. He was engaged by Booker T. Washington to teach English and Public Speaking but this great organizer soon found that his services could be utilized to better advantage in the field to win sympathizers for Tuskegee. He was commandeered by the government during the war to help to disseminate proper information among the people.

Woodson, Carter Goodwin, was born in New Canton, Virginia, December 19, 1875. He matriculated in Berea College, Kentucky, and received his L. B. degree in 1903. He spent some time traveling in England and Asia, and pursued courses of study in the University of Paris, France. Returning to America Doctor Woodson entered the University of Chicago where he earned the A. B. and A. M. degrees. He subsequently entered the graduate school of Harvard and in 1912 received the Ph. D. degree. Dr. Woodson began his teaching career as the principal of the Douglass High School in West Virginia, serving afterwards as supervisor of schools in the Philippines from 1903-6.

At the reorganization of Howard University, Washington, D. C., Doctor Woodson was called to the deanship of the college department. He is editor of the Journal of Negro History and the Director of Research, The Association for the Study of Negro Life and History, etc.

Doctor Woodson holds membership in the following organizations: American Historical Association, American Negro Academy, and the Mu-so-hit Club. He is the author of "The Education of the Negro Prior to 1861," "Disruption of Virginia and a Century of Negro Migration."

Work, Monroe Nathan, was born in Iredell county, North Carolina, August 15, 1866. In 1895 he entered the Chicago Theological Seminary and graduated in 1898. At the completion of his theological course he matriculated in the college department of the University of Chicago and in 1902 received the degree of Bachelor of Philosophy and a year later the degree of Master of Arts in Sociology.

Mr. Work entered the teaching profession after his graduation first as professor of history and education in the Georgia State Industrial College. In 1908 he was called to Tuskegee Institute to take over the department of statistics and research. He is due the credit for the recording and publication of the yearly lynching statistics. The Negro Year Book which is published at Tuskegee is edited by Mr. Work. This book chronicles the events which affect the life of the Negro from all angles. He contributes articles of a sociological as well as historical nature to the "Southern Workman," "The Survey," and the "Annals of American Academy of Political and Social Science."

Mr. Work is identified with the following societies: The American Sociological Society, The American Economic Association, The National Economic League, The American Negro Academy, The National Geographical Society, The Southern Sociological Congress and The Association for the Study of Negro Life and History.

Wright, Herbert Richard, is an Iowan by birth. He was educated in the public and secondary schools of Iowa. He entered the law department of the State University and graduated with the degree of LL. B. in 1901.

He began the practice of law in Des Moines, Iowa, and continued until January 13, 1909, after which he was appointed United States Consul at Puerto Cabello, Venezuela.

Mr. Wright resigned in 1913, returning home and established a real estate business in Des Moines, Iowa. During the war he was appointed director of the Negro Army Club in Des Moines.

Wright, Richard Robert, Jr., was born at Cuthbert, Ga., April 1, 1878. He received his B. A. degree from the Georgia State Industrial College in 1898, and the M. A. degree in 1901. He also completed the Normal course of that institution with high honors. At the completion of his course of study at the Georgia State College he matriculated in the University of Chicago, received his B. A. degree in 1901, A. M. in 1904 and the Ph. D. degree from the University of Pennsylvania in 1911. Dr. Wright enjoys the rare distinction of being one of the very few Negro intellectuals to have pursued courses of. study in the Universities of Germany. He was a student in the University of Berlin in 1903, and of Leipsic in 1904. A number of academic honors have been thrust upon him.

Returning from Germany he was awarded a Research Fellowship in Sociology in the University of Pennsylvania, 1905-06, and a Special University Fellowship in that same institution, 1906-08.

Dr. Wright is a minister of the A. M. E. Church, having been licensed to preach in 1899, and ordained deacon September, 1900, and a year later he was ordained an elder of the church. He has pastored in a number of communities, among them Chicago, Elgin, Illinois, and the University of Pennsylvania, Pennsylvania. He has held several positions of honor in his church. He was editor of the Christian Recorder; a member of the General Conference and delegate to the Ecumenical Conference, Toronto, Canada, in 1911.

If there were no other proof of Dr. Wright's intellectual capacity the number of literary societies in which he

DR. R. R. WRIGHT, PRESIDENT, GEORGIA COLLEGE, SAVANNAH, GA.
(C) C. M. Battey.

holds membership would attest this fact. He holds membership in the following organizations: American Academy of Political and Social Sciences; American Negro Historical Society; American Negro Academy; National Association of Teachers in Negro Schools; Sigma Pi Phi.

Dr. Wright numbers among his literary productions the following: "The Negro in Pennsylvania," "The Negro Problem," "Teaching of Jesus." His articles and studies have appeared in the leading periodicals of the country and in the reports of the United States Bureau of Labor Other activities with which he has been identified and is still identified are: Clerk, Paymaster's Department, U. S. Army 1898, Secretary People's Saving Banks, 1908-1911, President Eighth Ward Settlement Building and Loan Association, Philadelphia, Penn., Trustee Wilberforce University and Payne Theological Seminary; Spring Street Social Settlement; The Association for the Protection of Colored Women; National Association for the Advancement of Colored People; Director of Exhibits for the Emancipation Proclamation Exposition of Pennsylvania, 1913; Professor of Hebrew and of Greek, Wilberforce University.

Yerby, William James, was born in Arkansas, September 22, 1869. His preparatory training was received in his native state and his Bachelor of Arts degree from Roger Williams University, Nashville, Tenn. He entered Meharry Medical College, Nashville, and received his M. D. degree.

Dr. Yerby began the practice of medicine in Memphis, Tennessee, immediately after his graduation. His name was suggested to President Roosevelt when he was looking for a man to represent the United States in Sierra Leone, West Africa, and he appointed him United States Consul in 1906, and he has been in that position since.

COL. CHARLES YOUNG, U. S. A., RETIRED.
The highest ranking Negro officer in the United States Army.
Colonel Young was recently appointed Military
Attache at Liberia.

Young, Colonel Charles, was born in the state of Kentucky a little over forty years ago. Colonel Young has the distinction of being one of the three Negro graduates from West Point, the United States Military Academy. Colonel Young graduated from West Point in the spring of 1889, and was commissioned to the Tenth Cavalry, a Negro unit. The Colonel's daring and efficiency exhibited both on the battle field in time of war, and in time of peace, won for him coveted military promotions. He served with distinction in the Spanish-American War, where his regiment rescued Colonel Theodore Roosevelt's "Rough Riders" from complete annihilation, as well as in the campaign against Villa, the Mexican revolutionist. When the United States was forced into the World War, the military authorities forced him into retirement under pretense of physical disability—a weak heart. Subsequent expert examination, however, revealed the fact that Colonel Young was in excellent condition and fit for active service. The situation was brought to the attention of the public and the pressure of public opinion was brought to bear upon the administration and the Colonel was called to active duty during the latter part of the war, and assigned to Camp Grant, Illinois.

Colonel Young has served as instructor of military science and tactics at Wilberforce University, Ohio, and also in the Republic of Liberia. He was appointed Military Attache to Liberia. In the Philippines he acquitted himself with honor and credit to his country. Colonel Young was the highest ranking Negro officer in the United States Army.

Colonel Young died in Lagos, Southern Nigeria, January 10, 1922, of Blackwater fever, the result of his participation in a very dangerous reconnaissance. He left a widow and two children.

CHAPTER XVI.

PLANTATION MELODIES.

Hampton and Its Students.—For many years the Hampton school has been making an effort to preserve and collect the spiritual songs of the Negroes in America, and to give to its students so great a love for these beautiful utterances of the emotions of an enslaved and deeply religious race that they would strive as they went out to gather up and preserve a form of emotional expression only too likely to pass away in the transition period through which the colored people are now passing. So impossible is it to reproduce this music under changed conditions that there is danger lest even where both words and music are preserved, the spirit which gives it its peculiar charm may be lost forever. The educated Negro cannot sing the old songs as his father sang them. He may yet evolve a higher and nobler music of his own, but the old spirituals, squeezed as it were out of the human heart by the pressure of slavery, are a part of his history that he cannot afford to lose—a breaking forth from bondage of that thing which could never be enslaved, the genius of a race.

.Hampton and its students have done more to preserve Negro melodies than any other agency.

The following are a few of the many songs that might be given. Most of them are taken from the Hampton collection.

461

THE ANGELS DONE CHANGED MY NAME.

" I went to the hillside, I went to pray;
   I know the angels done changed my name—
Done changed my name for the coming day;
   I knew the angels done changed my name.

" I looked at my hands, my hands was new,
   I knew the angels done changed my name;
I looked at my feet, and my feet was, too—
   Thank God the angels done changed my name."

While the Negro brought out from bondage no literature and no theology, yet he did bring with him the plantation songs which show in Christian song that the doctrines of Christianity were held by these people in the days of slavery. We cannot expect to find the same modes of expression now that prevailed among them while in slavery, but that they held to the fundamental truths of religion must be recognized by all who study these songs. That they believed in Christ as a Savior from sin and in the Atonement is beautifully illustrated in the refrain—

" I've been redeemed! I've been redeemed!
Been washed in de blood ob de lamb."

The Divinity of Christ is shown in—

" Jus' stan' right still and steady yo'self:
   I know that my Redeemer lives.
Oh, jus' let me tell yo' about God hisself:
   I know that my Redeemer lives."

At Tougaloo, Mississippi, they sing a hymn which especially emphasizes the personality of Satan, which, it seems, they never doubted—

" Ole Satan he wears de hypocrite shoe;
If yo' don' min' he slip it on yo'."

Frederick Douglass says that—

" Run to Jesus, shun the danger,
I don't expect to stay much longer here."

sung on the plantation where he was a slave, first suggested to him the thought of escaping from slavery, or, as he put it, " Praying with his feet."

While their lives were full of misery on account of the oppressions of their masters, their songs do not show anywhere a revengeful spirit. They looked forward with confidence, expecting to be relieved in the land of the redeemed

" Shine, shine, I'll meet you in that morning.
Oh, my soul's goin' to shine, to shine:
I'm goin' to sit down to a welcome table—
Shine, shine, my soul's goin' to shine."

SWING LOW, SWEET CHARIOT.

Oh, de good ole chariot swing so low,
Good ole chariot swing so low,
Oh, de good ole chariot swing so low,
I don't want to leave me behind.
Chorus.—Oh, swing low, sweet chariot.
        Swing low, sweet chariot,
        Swing low, sweet chariot,
        I don't want to leave me behind.

Oh, de good ole chariot will take us all home.
I don't want to leave me behind.
Cho.—Oh, swing low, sweet, etc.

THE DANVILLE CHARIOT.

Chorus.—Oh, swing low, sweet chariot;
        Pray let me enter in,
        I don't want to stay here no longer.

I done been to heaven, an' I done been tired,
I been to the water, an' I been baptized—
    I don't want to stay no longer.
O, down to the water I was led,
My soul got fed with heav'nly bread—
    I don't want to stay here no longer.
Cho.—Oh, swing low, sweet chariot, etc.

RUST UNIVERSITY, HOLLY SPRINGS, MISS.

I had a little book, an' I read it through,
I got my Jesus as well as you;
    Oh, I got a mother in the promised land.
I hope my mother will feed dem lambs—
    I don't want to stay here no longer.
Cho.—Oh, swing low, sweet chariot, etc.

Oh, some go to church for to holler an' shout,
Before six months they're all turned out—
    I don't want to stay here no longer.
Oh, some go to church for to laugh an' talk,
But dey knows nothin' 'bout dat Christian walk—
    I don't want to stay here no longer.
Cho.—Oh, swing low, sweet chariot, etc.

Oh, shout, shout, de deb'l is about;
Oh, shut your do' an' keep him out—
    I don't want to stay here no longer.
For he is so much-a like-a snaky in de grass,
Ef you don' mind he will get you at las'—
    I don't want to stay here no longer
Cho.—Oh, swing low, sweet chariot, etc

VIEW DE LAND.

I'm born of God, I know I am—View de land, view de land!
And you deny it if you can—Go view de heav'nly land.
I want to go to heaven when I die—View de land, view de land!
To shout salvation as I fly—Go view de heav'nly land.

Chorus.—
    Oh, 'way over Jordan—View de land, view de land!
    'Way over Jordan—Go view de heavenly land.

What kind of shoes is dem-a you wear?   View de land, etc.
Dat you can walk upon the air?   Go view, etc.
Dem shoes I wear are de Gospel shoes—View the land, etc.
An' you can wear dem ef-a you choose—Go view, etc.—Cho.

Der' is a tree in paradise—View the land, etc.
De Christian he call it de tree ob life—Go view, etc.
I spects to eat de fruit right off o' dat tree—View de land, etc.
Ef busy old Satan will let-a me be—Go view, etc.—Cho.

You say yer Jesus set-a you free—View de land, etc.
Why don't you let-a your neighbor be?   Go view, etc.
30

You say you're aiming for de skies—View de land, etc.
Why don't you stop-a your telling lies? Go view, etc.—Cho.

OH, YES.

Ef eber I land on de oder sho'—Oh, yes!
I'll neber come here for to sing no more—Oh, yes!
A golden band all round my waist,
An' de palms of victory in my hand,
An' de golden slippers on to my feet—
Gwine to walk up an' down o' dem golden street.

> Chorus.—Oh, wait till I put on my robe—
>   Wait till I put on my robe. Oh, yes! Oh, yes:

An', my lobely bretherin, dat ain't all—Oh, yes
I'm not done a-talkin' about my Lord.
An' a golden crown a-placed on-a my head,
An' my long white robe a-come a-dazzlin' down;
Now wait till I get on my Gospel shoes,
Gwine to walk about de heaven an' a-carry de news.—Cho.

I'm anchored in Christ, Christ anchored in me—Oh, yes!
All de debils in hell can't a-pluck me out;
An' I wonder what Satan's grumbling about.
He's bound into hell, an' he can't git out,
But he shall be loose and hab his sway—
Yea, at de great resurrection day.—Cho.

I went down de hillside to make a-one prayer—Oh, yes!
An' when I got dere Ole Satan was dere—Oh, yes!
An' what do you t'ink he said to me? Oh, yes!
Said, "Off from here you'd better be." Oh, yes!
And what for to do I did not know—Oh, yes!
But I fell on my knees and I cried 'Oh, Lord!'—Oh, yes!
Now, my Jesus bein' so good an' kind,
Yea, to the with-er-ed, halt, and blind—
My Jesus lowered His mercy down,
An' snatch-a me from a-dem doors ob hell.
He a-snatch-a me from dem doors ob hell,
An' took-a me in a-wid him to dwell.—Cho.

I was in de church an' prayin' loud,
An' on my knees to Jesus bowed;
Ole Satan tole me to my face

" I'll git you when-a you leave dis place."
Oh, brother, dat scare me to my heart,
I was 'fraid to walk-a when it was dark.—Cho.

I started home, but I did pray,
An' I met ole Satan on de way;
Ole Satan made a-one grab at me,
But he missed my soul an' I went free.
My sins went a-lumberin' down to hell,
An' my soul went a-leaping up Zion's hill.
I tell ye what, bretherin, you'd better not laugh,
Ole Satan'll run you down his path;
If he runs you as he run me
You'll be glad to fall upon your knee.

> Chorus.—Oh, wait till I put on my robe.
> Wait till I put on my robe—Oh, yes! Oh, yes!

MY LORD DELIVERED DANIEL.

I met a pilgrim on de way,
An' I ask him whar he's a gwine.
I'm bound for Canaan's happy land,
An' dis is de shouting band.   Go on!

Chorus.—My Lord delibered Daniel,
My Lord delibered Daniel,
My Lord delibered Daniel—
Why can't he deliber me?

Some say dat John de Baptist
Was nothing but a Jew;
But de Bible doth inform us
Dat he was a preacher, too.—Yes, he was!

Chorus.—My Lord delibered Daniel, etc.

Oh, Daniel cast in the lions' den,
He pray both night and day;
De angel came from Galilee,
And lock de lions' jaw. Dat's so.

Chorus.—My Lord delibered Daniel, etc.

He delibered Daniel from de lions' den,
Jonah from de belly ob de whale,
An' de Hebrew children from de fiery furnace—
An' why not ebery man? Oh, yes!

Chorus.—My Lord delibered Daniel, etc.

De richest man dat eber I saw
Was de one dat beg de most;
His soul was filled wid Jesus,
An' wid de Holy Ghost.   Yes, it was.
Chorus.—My Lord delibered Daniel, etc.

NOBODY KNOWS THE TROUBLE I'VE SEEN.

Sometimes I'm up, sometimes I'm down—Oh, yes, Lord.
Sometimes I'm almost to de groun'—Oh, yes, Lord.
Although you see me goin' long so—Oh, yes, Lord.
I have my trials here below.—Oh, yes, Lord.
Chorus.—Oh, nobody knows de trouble I've seen,
Nobody knows but Jesus;
Nobody knows de trouble I've seen—
Glory Hallelujah!

One day when I was walkin' along—Oh, yes, Lord.
De element opened, an' de love came down—Oh, yes, Lord.
I never shall forget dat day—Oh, yes, Lord.
When Jesus washed my sins away.—Oh, yes, Lord.
Chorus.—Oh, nobody knows the trouble, etc.

HAIL! HAIL! HAIL!

Oh, look up yander, what I see—
I'm on my journey home;
Bright angels comin' arter me—
I'm on my journey home.
Chorus.—Children, hail! hail! hail!
I'm gwine jine saints above,
Hail! hail! hail!
I'm on my journey home.

If you git dere before I do—
I'm on my journey home;
Look out for me, I'm comin' too—
I'm on my journey home.
Chorus.—Children, hail! etc.

Oh, hallelujah to de Lamb!
I'm on my journey home;
King Jesus died for ebery man—
I'm on my journey home.
Chorus.—Children, hail! etc.

SCRIPTURAL REMINISCENCES.

Aunt Patty: "Bress me, Uncle Abum, ef yer doesn't call to mind Baalam gwine down ter J'rusalem."

Uncle Abram (with a weakness for Aunt Patty): "Yaas, and does yer 'member dar stood an angel in de way?"

WISE SAYINGS—"MULTUM IN PARVO."

·"Long ha'r don't hide de brand on de horse."

"Muddy roads call de mile-post a liar."

"'Tis hard to make clo'es fit a miserbul man."

"De stopper gits de longes' res' in de empty jug."

"De church bells sometimes do better wuk dan de sermon."

"Some o' de wus lookin' animals at de county fa'r got to pay to get in."

"De price ob your hat ain't de medjer ob your brain."

"Ef your coat-tail cotch a-fire, don't wait till you kin see de blaze 'fo' you put it out."

"De graveyard is de cheapes' boardin'-house."

"Dar's a fam'ly coolness 'twix' de mule an' de single-tree."

"It pesters a man dreadful when he git mad an' don' know who to cuss."

"Buyin' on credit is robbin' next 'ear's crop."

"Chris'mas without holiday is like a candle without a wick."

" De crawfish in a hurry look like he tryin' to git dar yistiddy."

" Lean houn' lead de pack when de rabbit in sight."

" Little flakes make de deepes' snow."

" Knot in de plank will show froo de whitewash."

" A short yardstick is a po' thing to fight de debbul wid."

" Dirt show de quickes' on de cleanes' cotton."

" De candy-pullin' kin call louder dan de log-rollin'."

" De bes' apple float on de top o' de peck medjer."

" De right sort o' 'ligion heaps de half-bushel."

" De steel hoe dat laughs at de iron one is like de man dat is shamed o' his grand-daddy."

" A mule kin tote so much goodness in his face dat he don't hab none lef' for his hind legs."

" Some grabble walks may lead to de jail."

" De cow-bell can't keep a secret."

" Ripe apples make de tree look taller."

" De red rose don't brag in de dark."

" Blind horse knows when de trough empty."

" De noise of de wheels don't medjer de load in de wagon."

" Las' 'ear's hot spell cools off mighty fast."

" Little hole in your pocket is wusser'n a big one at de knee."

" Appetite don't reggerlate de time o' day."

" De quagmire don't hang out no sign."

" One pusson kin th'ead a needle better than two."

" De pint o' de pin is de easiest en' to find."

" De green top don't medjer de price o' de turnup."

" Muzzle on de yard dog unlocks de smokehouse."

" 'Tis hard for de bes' an' smartes' folks in de wul' to git 'long widout a little tech o' good luck."

" De billy-goat gits in his hardes' licks when he looks like he gwine to back out o' de fight."

Miss Anita Hemming, tall, brunette, and graceful, was one of the graduates at Vassar in 1897, and, although the world did not know it, there was then enacted a great scene, showing the advance of woman into the life-giving but long-forgotten precept that all men are born free and equal. This young woman, who stood side by side with her classmates, keeping pace with them in studies and accomplishments, for four years

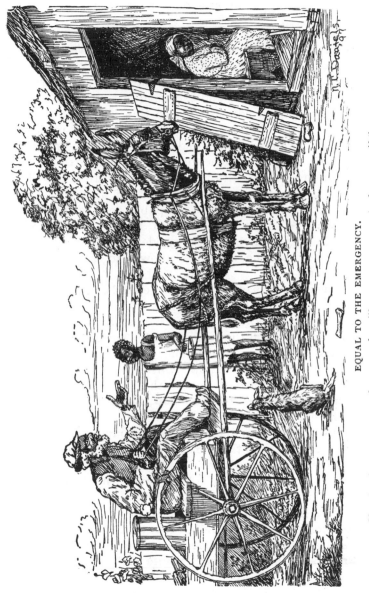

EQUAL TO THE EMERGENCY.

Hebe: "Unc Isrul, mammy says, huccome de milk so watery on top in de mornin'?"
Patriarch: "Tell you' mammy dat's de bes' sort o' milk, dat's de dew on it—de cows been layin' in de dew."
Hebe: "An' she tell me to ax you what meck it so blue."
Patriarch: "You ax your mammy what meck she so black!"

kept the secret of her birth from her associates—the secret that blood that marks a race of slaves flowed through her veins. It was just before examination when the faculty, to their utter astonishment, learned that into that stately and exclusive institution an alien race had gained admission. To this school for young ladies of the highest circle of society this modest, studious, refined young lady had gained admission without making known the secret of her birth. The question for the faculty to decide was a hard one. The girl, in deportment, scholarship, and in every way, was worthy, but yet would the public receive the innovation. After due consideration the young woman, whose only fault lay in the accident of her birth, was informed that she would be allowed to graduate with her class.

Then the girls of the finishing class heard the story. Some of them were from the proudest old families of the South, but they took her hands with right good comradeship, and the real ordeal for her had passed.

Miss Hemming stood among her associates at commencement in her simple white gown, a mark for many eyes. Her dark hair, with its burnished waves, was brushed back from her low, broad brow; a deep flush burned in her cheeks, and she was fairer than many of the blue-blooded girls around her. Then she went out into the world. But the attitude taken by Vassar's august faculty could not be ignored, and the young alumnus of 1897 gained the position of assistant in the Boston public library.

Fred Douglass.—In the course of an address made to a colored school in Talbot county, Maryland, where he was born a slave, Frederick Douglass said: "I once knew a little colored boy, whose father and mother

died when he was six years old.   He was a slave, and
had no one to care for him.   He slept on a dirt floor
in a hovel, and in cold weather would crawl into a
meal bag, headforemost, and leave his feet in the
ashes to keep them warm.   Often he would roast an
ear of corn and eat it to satisfy his hunger, and many
times has he crawled under the barn or stable and
secured eggs, which he would roast in the fire and eat.

This boy did not wear pants, like you do, but a
tow linen shirt.   Schools were unknown to him, and
he learned to spell from an old Webster's spelling
book, and to read and write from posters on cellars
and barn doors, while boys and men would help him.
He would then preach and speak, and soon became
well known.   He became presidential elector, United
states marshal, United States recorder, United States
diplomat, and accumulated some wealth.   He wore
broadcloth, and didn't have to divide crumbs with the
dogs under the table.   That boy was Frederick
Douglass.

What was possible for me is possible for you.
Don't think because you are colored you can't accomplish anything.   Strive earnestly to add to your
knowledge.   So long as you remain in ignorance, so
long will you fail to command the respect of your fellow men.''

Fred Douglass.—Fred Douglass has said that President Lincoln was the only white man with whom he
ever associated in this country who did not make him
feel that he was colored and a supposed inferior, and
that only in England and on the continent among the
Caucasians had he been permitted to realize that he
was a man and an equal.

Everything Must Go.—In a lecture by Rev. William

Johnson, illustrating the law that "everything must go," he gives the following: "A minister told me that he fell in love with his wife at first sight, and married after six months' acquaintance. 'But,' said he, 'during that whole time I went to see her every day. At four o'clock I was always there.' Some young men do not choose that delightful hour to visit, but go later. One young man lingered at the gate after a long visit, and the girl began to cry. He said, 'Dear, don't cry; I will come to see you again.' But she cried on. 'O, darling, don't cry so; I will be sure to come again.' Still she cried. At last he said: 'Love, did I not tell you that I would soon come again to see you?' And through her tears she replied: 'Yes, but I am afraid you never will go; that is what is the matter with me.' We must all go.'"

In the same lecture on the subject of practical philosophy, he gives the following:

"Uncle Jim was once asked a great question. It was: 'If you had to be blown up which would you choose, to be blown up on the railroad or the steamboat?' 'Well,' said Uncle Jim, 'I don't want to be blowed up no way; but if I had to be blowed up I would rather be blowed up on de railroad, because, you see, if you is blowed up on de railroad, dar you is, but if you is blowed up on de steamboat, whar is you?' He was practical in his philosophy."

INDEX

475

W. B. C.